Everything You Ever Wanted
About Sout
and Then Some

Rand-McNally omitted South Dakota from an atlas a few years back and some South Dakotans got mad. Now they can get even.

You are holding the best argument ever to put South Dakota back on the map!

In *The Bet On It! Book of South Dakota Trivia* Stephen C. Bakken has put together a fascinating collection of little-known facts about every aspect of the state:

- **its famous and would-be-famous people,**

- **its history,**

- **its scenic geography,**

- **its quirky weather,**

- **its renowned tourist attractions,**

- **its vital agriculture, farming and business.**

The Bet On It! Book of South Dakota Trivia offers a luscious state in bite-sized nuggets, easy to digest, and is **absolutely guaranteed to contain no cholesterol.** It is the perfect book for the bedside, for the glove compartment, for the long trip by bus or plane.

Welcome to the ultimate book of South Dakota trivia, spanning the ages from the pleistocene to the giddy 90s and including the buzz on everyone and everything from Wild Bill Hickok to Kevin Costner and *Dances With Wolves,* with clever cartoons by world-class artist Carl Grupp chronicling *Bet On It! Trivia Myths.*

Buy it, read it, give it to friends — or to someone from Iowa you want to tick off!

The
Bet On It!
Book of
SOUTH DAKOTA
TRIVIA

**A jackpot of amazing facts
about the state
that Rand McNally forgot!**

BY STEPHEN C. BAKKEN

With Cartoons by Carl Grupp

Ex Machina Publishing Co.
Sioux Falls, S.D.

The Bet On It! Book of South Dakota Trivia © 1992 by Stephen C. Bakken.

Published by EX MACHINA PUBLISHING CO., Box 448, Sioux Falls, SD 57101.

First Edition, First Printing, December, 1992.

Editors: Margaret Robinson, Ron Robinson.

Cartoons by Carl Grupp.

Library of Congress Cataloging-in-Publication Data

Bakken, Stephen C. (Stephen Clifford), 1952-

    The bet on it! : book of South Dakota trivia : a jackpot of amazing facts about the state that Rand McNally forgot! / by Stephen C. Bakken : with cartoons by Carl Grupp. — 1st ed.
    p.   cm.
    Includes bibliographical references.
    ISBN 0-944287-09-3 : $12.95
    1. South Dakota–Miscellanea. 2. Curiosities and wonders–South Dakota. I. Title.
F651.5.B34 1992
978.3 – dc20

                    90-40905
                    CIP

ISBN 0-944287-09-3

DEDICATION

To my Aberdeen mom,
Alice Stoecker Bakken

INTRODUCTION

Greetings:

South Dakota's front yard is the Great Plains, where the buffalo still roam. Just ask the folks who used it to film the Oscar-laden *Dances With Wolves.*

From Crazy Horse and Custer to Calamity Jane and Citibank credit cards, the Coyote State is a panorama of wonderful contrasts.

Against a backdrop of the Black Hills is a heritage as rich as its gold mines, a history as old as the Badlands, and a work ethic as solid as Mount Rushmore. Two examples are Ex Machina publishers Margaret and Ron Robinson, whose support and confidence in this project are deeply appreciated.

Though born in Kentucky, I was raised in South Dakota, where I also taught school in Mobridge. Even after teaching in Minnesota since 1978, my heart still lies in the Sunshine State that remains my vacation home.

Let *The Bet On It! Book of South Dakota Trivia* be your fun, offbeat and informative entry into the land of infinite variety.

Stephen C. Bakken

Aberdeen, South Dakota

February 1992

Stephen C. Bakken was born on an army base in Kentucky in 1952. He was raised in South Dakota, where he also briefly taught. For his annual effort of taking students on a week-long trek around Minnesota, he was named 1989 Minnesota History Teacher of the Year. Bakken and his wife live in Minnesota with their three children.

Carl Grupp is one of the best-known and most respected artists in South Dakota. He did some of his first published cartoons while an undergraduate at Augustana College in Sioux Falls. Now a professor of art at Augustana, his paintings, drawings and lithographs are included in museums and collections around the world, among them the Minneapolis Institute of Art, Walker Art Center, the American Embassy in London, and the Chicago Art Institute. Still, he likes to return to cartooning occasionally, because, as he explains, "Cartoons are fun."

TABLE OF CONTENTS

Carl Grupp's Bet On It! Trivia Myths:
ON LOCATION, AFTER HOURS

TALK ABOUT IDENTIFYING WITH A ROLE!
FINALLY, I HAD TO SAY, "OKAY, KEVIN,
ONE MORE WALTZ, THEN I GOTTA GO!"

THAT'S ENTERTAINMENT!

FIRST SOUTH DAKOTANS ON MAGAZINE COVERS:

- TIME, Fiorella LaGuardia (Ft. Sully), Oct. 23, 1933
- LIFE, Gov. Joe Foss (Sioux Falls), June 7, 1943
- TV GUIDE, Lawrence Welk (Yankton), Jan. 21, 1956
- PLAYBOY, Mamie Van Doren (Rowena), 1963

OPENING LINES:

- "Is this the last one?" — *Dances With Wolves*, filmed in South Dakota, 1991.
- "Even if you accept the beliefs that the high trend index automatically means a rise in sales curve." — *North by Northwest*, filmed at Mount Rushmore, 1959.
- "This land has a name today, and is marked on maps." — *How the West was Won*, filmed in the Black Hills, 1962.
- "Play it loud." — *The One and Only, Genuine, Original Family Band*, about a Rapid City publisher, 1967.
- "Laura was washing the dishes one morning when old Jack, lying in the sunshine on the doorstep, growled to tell her that someone was coming." — *By the Shores of Silver Lake*, by Laura Ingalls Wilder (DeSmet), 1939.
- "Bright, clear sky over a plain so wide that the rim of the heavens cut down on it around the entire horizon." — *Giants in the Earth*, by Ole Rolvaag (Sioux Falls), 1927.
- "Dorothy lived in the midst of the great Kansas prairies, with Uncle Henry, who was a farmer, and Aunt Em, who was the farmer's wife." — *The Wizard of Oz*, by L. Frank Baum (Aberdeen), 1900.

SOUTH DAKOTA MEDIA, 1991:

- 125 newspapers
- 27 FM radio stations
- 25 AM radio stations
- 20 TV stations
- 11 cable systems (with 83 channels)

STATE'S NATIVE AMERICAN STATIONS:

- KILI 88.3 (Rapid City)
- KILI 90.1 (Pine Ridge)
- KILI 90.5 (Cheyenne River)
- KILI 91.7 (Rosebud)
- KINI 96.1 (Rosebud)

DANCES WITH WOLVES

Seventy percent of *Dances With Wolves* was filmed at Triple U Standing Butte Ranch (Ft. Pierre) between July and December 1989. The Triple U is the home of the largest buffalo herd in America.

The script was translated from English into Lakota by college professor Doris Leader Charge (Rosebud) in only three weeks time. Leader Charge agreed to be cast in the movie as Pretty Shield, the wife of Chief Ten Bears, only after actor Kevin Costner was able to get her a leave of absence from her teaching position.

While filming over a six-month period in South Dakota in 1989, the movie required 3,500 buffalo, 175 Native-American extras, 100 horses, 36 tipis and two trained wolves.

The cast began rehearsal of their Lakota dialect outside of Rapid City or practiced privately with a tape made by educator Doris Leader Charge and her cousin.

Doris Leader Charge turned down an offer by Kevin Costner to attend the Hollywood premier of *JFK* because she was too exhausted from tours and speaking engagements in Alaska and the Virgin Islands.

Cathy Smith was Technical Advisor for the costuming and set design. Wardrobes were sewn in Los Angeles for the extras, while Cathy sewed clothes for the principals. Watercolor sketches and notes served as guides.

Michael Lekberg, now working for Sioux Trading Post (Rapid City) did most of the work on the wedding dress of Stands With A Fist.

Thermal underwear, dyed to match buckskin, and panty hose were concealed while being worn by the cast. One hundred pair of pantyhose were worn by the warriors. At the end of each day, most were torn to shreds.

Conditions were difficult in South Dakota. The dressing room was a large tent with a curtain of blankets separating men from the women. Shirts were hemmed with safety pins. Ill-fitting moccasins were stuffed with toilet paper.

Jannel Schumaker (Rapid City) was among the eight local hair stylists whose marathon days with the cast began at 5 a.m. when they were bused out to where the shooting was. Every day Schumaker put full body make-up on 50 actors and extras. Extras were paid $100 to have their heads shaved.

Schumaker got the job when a cast member happened to stop in her Rapid City shop for a haircut.

Severt Young Bear, a Lakota elder and historian (Pine Ridge) was Advisor for Lakota Scalp and Buffalo Dances. Young Bear made certain they put the right songs in the right places. Young Bear had recorded old-time Porcupine Singers in 1962 and had asked the elders to show him the steps.

The final scene was filmed in Spearfish Canyon.

Actor Kevin Costner and his brother Dan opened the Midnight Star gaming hall in Deadwood July 3, 1991. Many *Dances With Wolves* costumes are on display there.

***Dances With Wolves* won seven Oscars in 1991, including Best Picture.**

Thanks to *Dances With Wolves* publicity, tourism in South Dakota rose a whopping 54 percent.

Twenty-two stunt men were used in the film. The movie also had two bison consultants, four wolf trainers and an eight-member crew for the buffalo hunt scene.

Just before the 1990 Los Angeles premier of *Dances With Wolves*, the assistant casting director married the actor who played Wind in His Hair. Assistant director Ka-Mook Nichols (Pine Ridge), the ex-wife of AIM activist Dennis Banks, and her new husband, Rodney A. Grant, had a more traditional Native American wedding the following year.

Rodney A. Grant, Wind in His Hair, was on the verge of being fired from the film because he stumbled over the Lakota dialect. Grant was rescued by casting director Elizabeth Leustig, who gave him daily coaching lessons.

The idea for *Dances With Wolves* came to author Michael Blake when he read an historical account of a Civil War wagoneer who discovered an abandoned frontier fort. Down on his own luck, Blake was living in his 16-year-old Chrysler and working as a dishwasher when actor Kevin Costner phoned and asked him to write a screenplay for his manuscript. Blake's script went through six drafts over the next two and a half years. When filming began in South Dakota in July 1989 Blake and his girlfriend would host Sunday afternoon spaghetti feeds for the cast and crew.

***Dances With Wolves* played a record 46 weeks in Sioux Falls.**

NATIONAL PUBLICATIONS:

- *American Soccer Magazine* (Custer), circulation: 15,000
- *Arts & Leisure* (Custer), circulation: 20,000
- *Buffalo!* (Ft. Pierre), circulation: 1,300
- *Knitters Magazine* (Sioux Falls), circulation: 28,000
- *Lakota Times* (Rapid City), circulation: 10,000
- *Quick 'N Easy Cookin'* (Davis), circulation: 39,000
- *Wool Sack* (Brookings), circulation: 9,000

Sen. James Abourezk (Kennebec) plays the guitar.

The first two books known to have been read in the Black Hills were the Holy Bible, and Milton's Paradise Lost.

The most photographed South Dakotan was Ben Black Elk (Pine Ridge), who posed for over 5,000 photographs every day, in the shadow of Mount Rushmore. Black Elk was in several movies, including *How the West Was Won*.

BOB BARKER AND THE PRICE:

- Despite hosting TV shows for three decades, Bob Barker (Mission) did not receive his first Emmy until The Price is Right, 1982.
- Barker won five Emmys by the time he got to host its first prime-time Emmy ceremony in 1991.
- Barker left his role as a beauty pageant host over a dispute concerning the displaying of furs, 1987.

Corson County, S.D., has America's lowest circulation of *Penthouse* magazine.

Upon arriving in Mitchell and seeing the muddied streets, John Philip Sousa refused to get off the train to dedicate the Corn Palace (Mitchell) in 1904, until he was paid his fee. Bankers waded through the mud to bring out the $7,000 in cash, to the train.

Ears of corn just beginning to lose their milk are chosen to be used in the murals at the Corn Palace.

Gen. George Custer brought the first band to South Dakota. In 1874 Custer's 16-piece band played often throughout the Black Hills, including at funerals. The band stayed behind when Custer went to Little Bighorn two years later.

Bob Clayton (Sioux Falls) hosted NBC's *Concentration*.

Jack Crawford was illiterate as a young man. While recovering from wounds suffered during the Civil War, he learned to read and eventually became the first newspaper reporter in the Black Hills, composing poetry during his spare time. As a scout, Crawford was riding to find Custer when he learned the general had been wiped out. Crawford continued composing poetry, becoming known as the "Poet Scout."

There is no documented evidence, except her word, that Calamity Jane (Deadwood) was an expert shot.

The Coughlin Campanile (Brookings) reaches 170 feet high and was built in 1929.

The Crook City *Tribune* published a single edition for its 3,000 residents, on June 10, 1876. When the railroad bypassed the town, it soon became a ghost town.

Deadwood is the only South Dakota place name featured in cards. In poker, it is the discard pile. In Rummy, it is the unmatched cards in a hand.

In 1991 Deadwood had more gaming halls — 59 — than any other place in South Dakota.

Deadwood Dick was a popular dime novel hero of the 1880s, created by Edward L. Wheeler, of Pennsylvania. The character was inspired by Deadwood prospector Richard W. Clark, who was a Custer scout and Pony Express rider.

Goldiggers Hotel and Gaming (Deadwood) has an 18-ft. colossal slot machine.

Four artists created the miniature First Ladies of the White House exhibit at Enchanted World of Dolls Museum (Mitchell).

The first Disney musical set in South Dakota was their 1968 *The One and Only, Genuine, Original Family Band*, which saw a musical family involved in the 1888 presidential campaign. This was also Goldie Hawn's first movie.

The first newspaper published in South Dakota was *The Dakota Democrat*, published by Sam Albright on July 2, 1859, in Sioux Falls. Three years later angry Native Americans dumped Albright's press into the river, and took his lead type, some of which was later placed inside their peace pipes.

South Dakota has 12 daily papers, 1992.

When a fellow wanted a dance to be held at the Harney Peak Hotel (Hill City) in the 1890s, he told the local barber. The barber turned his calendar, which read "Dance Tonight" around in the window, and chalked the same words on the sidewalk. The dance time spread through an efficient grapevine system.

At one of the dances an Englishman living at the Harney Peak Hotel (Hill City) boasted he could throw a plate farther than anyone else. When challenged, the Briton simply hurled the plate through a window and was similarly thrown out himself.

Five Little House on the Prairie novels are set in DeSmet, S.D.

THE TOM BROKAW FILE

As a high school teenager, Tom Brokaw (Yankton) once rode the dryers in a Deadwood, S.D., laundromat for the most revolutions. When the police arrived, Brokaw escaped through the bathroom window.

Brokaw keeps a large photo of a South Dakota tombstone over his desk in New York.

The three cameras used by NBC to film Brokaw during the news are nicknamed "Larry, Curly and Moe."

During December 1987 Brokaw had an exclusive one-hour interview with Soviet President Mikhail Gorbachev. Seventy-two hours later Brokaw hosted the first televised debate between all presidential candidates (12 of them).

Brokaw married Miss South Dakota on Aug. 17, 1962. Meredith Auld Brokaw, an English teacher, also owns a toy store.

Brokaw accepted a position on the *Today* Show, as long as he didn't have to do commercials.

Brokaw was 15 when he got an announcing job on KYNT (Yankton).

While waiting to interview Mikhail Gorbachev in Moscow in America's first one-on-one interview with the Soviet leader, May 1988, Brokaw made small talk by mentioning that he came from the Great Plains and had operated a combine. Gorbachev replied that he had, too.

So much animosity existed between Brokaw and his station manager at a Marshall, Minn., radio station, that the manager locked Brokaw's sandwich meat up in the refrigerator. In less than a week Brokaw had quit and hitchhiked home.

Brokaw screened 217 applicants before selecting Jane Pauley as his *Today Show* co-host.

During Brokaw's final day as host of *Today*, President Ronald Reagan appeared to say goodbye.

After Tom Brokaw joined Tom Krens in forming a company called 'Tom-Tom Productions' in 1989, they obtained a minority loan to start a country and western radio station in Rapid City, S.D.

NBC's Brokaw has agreed to appear on PBS with Robert MacNeil and Jim Lehrer to cover the 1992 presidential conventions.

> Then Gov. Joe Foss (Sioux Falls) and Boys State Gov. Tom
> Brokaw won $1,225 on a New York T.V. show, *Two for the
> Money*, on August 3, 1957. Host Herb Shriner billed them as
> the "Two Governors from South Dakota." A sample question
> was "Name as many trees as you can that begin with the letter
> B."
>
> Brokaw kayaks, mountain climbs and rides horses on his 5,000-
> acre ranch near Big Timber, Mont.

In the movie *Dakota!* mythical Ma Hastings heads a gang of outlaws
that terrorizes the Badlands.

**Don Fedderson (Beresford) created *My Three Sons*, *Family
Affair* and *Who Do You Trust?* He was also consultant to the
Lawrence Welk Show.**

The first South Dakota State Fair was in Huron in 1885. The site
rotated each year until railroad barons deeded 85 acres for a permanent site 20 years later. The first grandstand was moved to Huron,
from Yankton.

**Joe Floyd (Sioux Falls) pioneered America's original *Dating
Game* during January 1943. Floyd soon sold his G.I. *Blind Date* to
NBC.**

On November 18, 1963, Andy Fischer (Aberdeen) was presented as
"Mr. X" by Garry Moore on *I've Got A Secret*. It took panelist Bill
Cullen just three quick questions to guess him as father of the quints.
Mary Ann Fischer was then introduced to the audience.

**Smoky Joe was the title proposed by Hollywood movie pro-
ducer Hall Bartlett in 1955 for a film he wanted to make about
Gov. Joe Foss (Sioux Falls).**

Gov. Joe Foss plays the saxophone.

**Myron Floren (Roslyn) got his first accordion through a mail-
order catalog at the age of seven.**

As a youth Myron Floren used to practice four hours before school,
during his lunch hour, and then another four hours after farm chores
were done.

**Nuns in Wisconsin guarded Myron Floren's accordion after it
was stolen and later found.**

Gov. Archie Gubbrud once appeared on *Candid Camera*. Allen Funt
secretly filmed the reaction of folks as they passed the governor sitting
peacefully on the grounds of the state Capitol.

**Giants in the Earth was based upon the lives of the six Berdahl
brothers (Canton).**

ABERDEEN'S MUSIC MAN

John Cacavas (Aberdeen) has composed the music for TV shows *Kojak, Eischied, B.J. & the Bear, Matlock, The Equalizer, Hawaii Five-O, Still the Beaver, Magnum P.I., Buck Rogers, Columbo, By Reason of Insanity, Switch, Bionic Woman, Four Seasons* and the *NBC Mystery Movie*.

Popular commercial tunes composed by John Cacavas include jingles for Alberto VO-5, American Motors, Rubbermaid and Sinclair.

Hit records composed by Cacavas include "Gallant Men" recorded by the late Sen. Everett Dirksen, "Black is Beautiful," and the theme from *Airport '75*.

Cacavas has composed over 2,000 published works in the areas of symphonic band, orchestra, choir, piano and ensembles. Cacavas has also written the music for over 400 TV programs, 60 TV movies, 15 feature motion pictures and three mini-series.

Cacavas has composed over 300 pieces of background music for libraries throughout the world.

The first South Dakotan to win a Pulitzer Prize was Hamlin Garland, for *Daughters of the Middle Border*, 1922.

Henry Brockhouse displayed his big game collection in his Sioux Falls hardware store until attorney D.J. Delbridge donated the stuffed animals to the Great Plains Zoo.

Pharmacist Hubert Humphrey (Huron) appeared on NBC's *Meet the Press* more than any other guest.

Hubert Humphrey's father bought radio time in Huron to read poetry because he felt people needed to hear it.

July 4, 1916, tight rope walker Ivy Baldwin crossed the Open Cut — 1,800 feet — at the Homestake Gold Mine (Lead).

The High Plains Cowboy and Indian Museum (Spearfish) features a $3 million *Wounded Bunkie* bronze by Frederic Remington, and a 17-ft. high *Waters Ahead* by Gary Shoop.

Wild Bill Hickok (Deadwood) was an accurate shot. He was able to hit a dime tossed into the air nine times out of ten.

Wild Bill Hickok and Buffalo Bill Cody once performed in a Black Hills play, *Scouts of the Prairies*.

Hal Hackett (Madison) got his first movie role when a Hollywood agent visiting a hospital happened to overhear Hackett singing while in bed with a fractured back.

THERE SHE IS!

Two South Dakotans have been finalists for Miss America: Carol Quinn, 1949, and Mary Hart, 1970.

Twenty-three years after Dorothy Erickson was crowned 1947 Augustana Homecoming Queen, her daughter, Mary Hart, was selected as Miss South Dakota.

Hart (Sioux Falls) can tightrope walk.

Her musical influences were Elvis and the Beatles.

Since 1982 Hart has cohosted *Entertainment Tonight.*

Hart frequently sings the National Anthem at home games for the California Angels and L.A. Dodgers.

Roselyn Anderson (St. Onge) was crowned the first Miss South Dakota in 1947 in Hot Springs, S.D. Her talent was playing the piano.

Miss South Dakota 1950 Mary O'Connor was first-runner-up at the Miss America Pageant. That is as close as the state has ever got to capturing the national crown.

Hot Springs, S.D., has held the Miss America Pageant Franchise longer than any other city in the U.S.

Like her predecessors, Miss South Dakota 1991 Melissa Brown (Rapid City) got to keep her tiara, traveled 25,000 miles while making up to 80 appearances, and got full use of a car and mink coat during her year-long reign.

SONGS SUNG BY MISS SOUTH DAKOTA MARY HART AT 1970 MISS AMERICA PAGEANT:
- "Something"
- "Yesterday"
- "You Make Me So Very Happy"

At age 99, America's oldest former Marine, Arthur Hanson (Rapid City), rode in the 1991 Black Hills' Fourth of July parade.

How the West was Won is a 1963 classic filmed in South Dakota and features South Dakotans Richard Widmark and Ben Black Elk.

***How the West Was Won* was the first movie filmed in South Dakota nominated for Best Picture. The 1963 film garnered eight nominations and three Oscars.**

Hill City, S.D., is home to the 1880 train, featured in several movies and TV shows, like *Gunsmoke, Scandalous John*, several Disney movies, *General Hospital* and *Orphan Train.*

Ron Holgate (Aberdeen) earned a Tony for his role as Richard Henry Lee in the 1,217 Broadway performances of *1776*. Lee was also in the 1972 film version.

Pharmacist Ted Hustead (Wall) once appeared on *To Tell The Truth*.

Gov. Bill Janklow has a collection of over 20,000 rock and roll records.

As presidential candidate Robert Kennedy was touring Pine Ridge in 1968, an excited crowd broke through a fence and ignored Kennedy in their rush to get the autograph of CBS reporter Roger Mudd.

The original tape of the final phone conversation of Robert Kennedy calling Bill Dougherty in Sioux Falls, June 4, 1968, is in the John F. Kennedy Presidential Library in Massachusetts.

In 1922 the state's first radio station, WCAT, broadcast from Rapid City under direction of the South Dakota School of Mines.

When South Dakota Gov. Richard Kneip hosted NBC's *Saturday Night Live*, he presented a Black Hills Gold ring to comic John Belushi.

Cheryl Ladd (Huron) is fitness advisor to ABC's *GoodMorning, America*.

Cheryl Ladd was the fourth Charlie's Angel.

Cheryl Ladd stars as a time traveler in the 1989 motion picture *Millennium*. Ladd portrays Louise Baltimore who boards planes about to crash and beams passengers into the future.

The Lakota Times (Rapid City) is the nation's largest publication serving Native American communities. Tim Giago published the first issue in July 1981.

Eric Henfler directed the Lincoln High School Band (Sioux Falls), which was among the 22 bands marching in the 103rd Tournament of Roses Parade, watched by one million people, Jan. 1, 1992.

Kitty LeRoy (Deadwood) married her first husband because he had let her shoot an apple off his head.

In 1880 culture hit the Black Hills when a distinguished English actor, Jack Langrishe, rented a saloon and began performances of everything from *Uncle Tom's Cabin* to Shakespeare. Amazingly, Langrishe was well-received by the uncultured gold miners.

New York Mayor Fiorella LaGuardia was raised at Ft. Sully, S.D., where his father was army bandmaster. While there Fiorella learned to play the cornet.

THE CAPTAIN AND KELO-LAND

The first Captain 11 was broadcast on KELO-Land TV March 7, 1955, with the time converter made from an old pinball machine.

As Captain 11, Dave Dedrick (Sioux Falls) has gone through 14 uniforms.

Despite being touched, tried on or grabbed by thousands upon thousands of children over the years, the cap of Captain 11, Dave Dedrick, has never been damaged, but was once stolen — not by a child, but by an adult from Minneapolis.

South Dakota's first remote telecast was a basketball game and a football game with Jim Burt as announcer.

When KELO-Land (Sioux Falls) began broadcasting May 19, 1953, it was the first all-film station in America. Early programs were taped, developed, edited and rushed seven miles to a transmitter, where they were aired. Two years later film operation was abandoned, and live telecasting began.

Among the most durable TV journalists are KELO-Land's Dave Dedrick, who's been there since 1953; Steve Hemmingsen, since 1969; and Doug Lund, 1974.

KELO-Land's 2,000-ft. TV tower in Rowena, S.D., has twice toppled. In 1968 it was hit by a plane. Seven years later it fell during a blizzard.

KELO-LAND's Doug Lund (Sioux Falls) is a drummer in the 'Mogan's Heroes' band.

My Melancholy Baby **was written by piano player George Norton (Lead) while working in a brothel. The pianist had TB and wrote the song for the love of his life, Maybelle, a call girl. Norton scribbled the tune on an envelope while awaiting his love at a train station. Ernie Burnett later put lyrics to what became the hit tune of WWI.**

Black Hills Maze (Rapid City) features 1.2 miles of walkways.

In the movie *Mermaids* Louis Landsky plays a Jewish shoe salesman from South Dakota.

The state's smallest newspaper is the Alpena Journal (Wessington Springs), whose circulation is 200.

The state's largest newspaper is the *Argus Leader* (Sioux Falls), whose Sunday circulation in 1992 was 64,842.

Hollywood producer Oscar Micheaux (Gregory), the grandson of a slave, once was a Pullman porter in South Dakota.

SHERWIN LINTON COUNTRY

Johnny Cash called country western singer Sherwin Linton (Watertown) on stage at the South Dakota State Fair where Cash removed his boots and presented them to Linton.

At the age of three Linton was playing the piano. By age six Linton had built his first guitar out of a ruler, cigar box and rubber bands. Linton received a real guitar at ten and was singing on the radio a year later. By the time he was 15 he had his own radio show on KWAT (Watertown).

He played the tuba in high school marching band because it was the only instrument he could rent.

Linton owns 90 guitars.

Linton's band names include The Strummer, The Rocketeer, Cotton Kings and Silver Shadow.

The governors of Arkansas, Kentucky, Minnesota and South Dakota (twice) have each proclaimed a 'Sherwin Linton Day.'

In addition to singing on the Grand Ole Opry, Sherwin Linton has been nominated three times for Country Music Association's Male Vocalist of the Year and Entertainer of the Year.

Sen. George McGovern (Mitchell) plays the piano.

The most star-studded event of McGovern's 1972 presidential campaign occurred June 14, 1972, at a fundraiser that featured Warren Beatty, Jack Nicholson, Shirley MacLaine, Dustin Hoffman, Paul Newman, Simon and Garfunkel and Candice Bergen.

Since his father could not read, it was the responsibility of young Frederick Manfred (Vermillion) to read the Bible to his family. By the time Manfred left for college he had read the Bible through seven times.

Frederick Manfred met his wife while the two of them were hospitalized with TB.

The Associated Press picked as its 1947 Book of the Year a novel by Frederick Manfred called *This is the Year*.

Teddy Roosevelt, Mark Twain and Lillian Russell were each guests in the unusually-shaped home of Corbin Morse (Rapid City).

Native Americans in the Black Hills made flutes to imitate the musical tones which blew through holes in Wind Cave.

No South Dakotan has received an Oscar.

HITCHCOCK VS. RUSHMORE

North by Northwest is a 1959 comedy-thriller featuring a bewildered ad executive chased by spies across country. The finale occurs atop Mount Rushmore, between Cary Grant, Eva Marie Saint, Martin Landau and James Mason.

North by Northwest features Martin Landau falling to his death as he attempts to kill Cary Grant atop Mount Rushmore. Actually, Mouth Rushmore was a combination synthetic rubber and paper mache creation in a Hollywood studio.

Alfred Hitchcock personally designed on a paper dinner napkin the climatic chase atop Mount Rushmore.

When Hitchcock arrived in Rapid City during September 1958 to begin filming on Mount Rushmore, the Department of the Interior met him at the airport and served an injunction halting any filming. Earlier permits were lifted under a little-known law Interior said covered "patent desecration of a monument." Furthermore, Hitchcock was forbidden to even use special effects to show people climbing or standing on the monument.

After a heated standoff between Hitchcock and Parks officials, a minimum compromise was reached and minimal filming was done.

By September 17, 1958, Hitchcock had left the Black Hills and returned to Hollywood where he had artist Robert Boyle create the world's largest replica of Mount Rushmore out of paper mache, wire and wood. The complicated final scene on Mount Rushmore was filmed entirely in MGM studios 1,500 miles from South Dakota.

Only actual background, cafeteria and distance shots of Mount Rushmore were used from Hitchcock's filming in South Dakota.

Because of all the restrictions and headaches caused him, Hitchcock listed neither the U.S. Department of the Interior or the National Park Service in the movie's credits.

Northwest by Northwest received three nominations, but no Oscars, in 1959. Ironically, thanks to the Mount Rushmore replica Robert Boyle was forced to build, he received an Oscar nomination.

DEPARTMENT OF INTERIOR RESTRICTIONS GIVEN ALFRED HITCH-
COCK WHILE FILMING *NORTH BY NORTHWEST:*

- Hitchcock may show the entire Mount Rushmore monument, but
  only from a distance.
- Hitchcock may show close-ups of the four Presidents "on condition that only the shoulder, or below the chin line" was shown.
- Actors may be shown between – but never touching, or on – the
  presidential faces.
- Must show Soviet spies being defeated on Mount Rushmore.

**Gary Owens (Mitchell) is the cartoon voice of Roger Ramjet,
Space Ghost and the Blue Falcon.**

Gary Owens was the first host of the *Gong Show,*1976.

**Elvis Presley performed his final South Dakota concert in
Sioux Falls on June 22, 1977. Six weeks later he died of a drug
overdose.**

While in Sioux Falls in 1977 Elvis got a complimentary suite at the
Holiday Inn. A store donated a king-size brass bed, complete with red
and white linen.

**Twenty-five off-duty officers guarded Elvis during his single
hour on stage. Elvis wore his white, gold-sequinned jumpsuit and
tossed blue scarves to the crowd.**

Elvis Presley gave one of his 200 diamond rings to a Sioux Falls
hospital employee after a 1977 concert when it slipped off into her
hand.

In 1991 the South Dakota Gaming Commission gave casino owners
permission to play poker in their own places, as long as they wear
name tags.

**Poker Alice (Sturgis) drank constantly, was always giving to the
needy, and often paid for her services with her cooking.**

Poker Alice would never play poker on Sundays.

Sen. Larry Pressler (Humboldt) rollerskates and plays tennis.

CBS Sportscaster Pat O'Brien (Sioux Falls) did not letter in any
sport in high school.

**Actor Marlon Brando flew in to help the Native Americans at
the murder trial of Leonard Peltier (Pine Ridge).**

Edgar Allen Poe wrote about a "petrified forest near the head waters
of the Cheyenne River which has its source in the Black Hills."

**The Black Hills Playhouse (Rapid City) was founded by Dr. War-
ren M. Lee in 1946.**

S.O.B. FILE

Allen Neuharth (Eureka) bought his first house with $700 won in a poker game. The silver-and-black trailer house had no toilet and stretched 18 feet.

Neuharth is twice married, twice divorced.

He wears a huge diamond-studded *USA TODAY* ring on his third finger, left hand.

In order to communicate with his girlfriend during WWII, Neuharth devised a unique code of letters and numbers that would tell her where he was in Europe with the Army's 86th Infantry Division.

Neuharth banned his wife's parents from attending his wedding to their daughter, a move for which his mother-in-law never forgave him.

It wasn't until years later that Sen. Lori Neuharth learned that the 16 yellow roses sent her on the 16th of every month by her husband, Al, was part of the job description of his secretary.

When Neuharth bought a girlfriend a white Rolls-Royce, the grateful blonde took out a full-page thank-you ad in *Florida TODAY*.

Neuharth used pennies to teach his daughter, Janet, how to play poker at age eight.

Neuharth is the first male journalist to win the highest award given by the Women in Communications Association.

Neuharth does his writing from a beach house overlooking the launch pads of the Kennedy Space Center.

Neuharth's autobiography, *Confessions of an S.O.B.*, was a best-seller translated into three languages.

Potato Creek Johnny discovered the largest gold nugget ever found in the Black Hills. He kept it tied inside a silk handkerchief and offered to show it to folks for a drink. It took four drinks to get the knots untied.

A quilt made by Dawn Amos (Rapid City) represented South Dakota in the 1986 Statue of Liberty Contest in New York.

Congressman Clint Roberts (Presho) has filmed commercials for Schlitz beer and was a sheriff in the movie *The Duchess and the Dirtwater Fox*. Roberts was beat out as the Marlboro man by a Wyoming cowboy.

THE PASSION PLAY

From 1938 to 1991 Josef Meier and a supporting cast of 250, performed his *Black Hills Passion Play* (Spearfish). The evening, outdoor performance runs 2 hours 15 minutes.

The Passion Play has 22 scenes.

Josef Meier was the seventh of his name to play the Christus. Nephew Heinrich Meier was groomed to replace him.

The Passion Play is based upon the original Passion Play dating from 1272, in Lunen, Germany.

The lighted stage for the Passion Play is three blocks long. The Christus carries an actual 160-pound cross during the play.

Josef Meier was knighted by Pope Paul VI in 1965.

Josef Meier fled Germany during 1932, and toured America with the Passion Play. Meier was impressed with the natural beauty of the Black Hills and made it home to the Passion Play.

Clint Roberts turned down a mountain man part in *Centennial* because he was too busy campaigning for governor of South Dakota.

So eager was Ole Rolvaag (Elk Point) to leave Norway that the 15-year-old went to sea counted as "half a man" in order to come to America and settle in South Dakota.

Ole Rolvaag wrote his masterpiece *Giants in the Earth* while living in Minnesota, Sioux Falls, England and Norway.

The first radio station in South Dakota, KUSD, was started by mining students in Rapid City on May 27, 1922. The state now has 65 radio stations.

The Shrine to Music (Vermillion) houses the world's largest collection of antique musical instruments, over 4,500. Established in 1973, the Shrine is also a National Landmark.

The premiere of the motion picture *Sitting Bull* opened in Rapid City, S.D., August 19, 1954, with a gesture of peace between the chief's son, John, and the grand nephew of Gen. Custer, George Custer III. During that same performance Little Bighorn survivor Chief Dewey Beard, 97, fell asleep during the Little Bighorn scenes.

People Magazine spent nearly a day taking 1,296 photographs of surrogate Grandmother Arlette Schweitzer (Aberdeen), yet used only a single photo in their story.

Ladies Home Journal photographed both Arlette Schweitzer and Barbra Streisand for a 1992 cover story, but the singer aced the grandmother out.

The South Dakota Snow Queen Pageant (Aberdeen) was created in 1946 when the town's Junior Chamber of Commerce accepted an offer to send a Queen of the Snows to the St. Paul Winter Carnival in Minnesota.

The original South Dakota Snow Queen Festival was a small affair, with contestants coming from nearby towns. The pageant was funded with $10 donations from local merchants. By 1992 the festival had grown to involving 1,200 participants from 50 communities.

The first professional entertainer at the South Dakota Snow Queen Festival was big bandleader Billy Bishop.

The first Snow Queen was Dorothy Lockington, 1946; first Frosty, George Bassingwaite, 1949; Junior Snow Queen, Karen Ringsley, 1955; and appearance of the first Princesses, 1989.

Only nine percent of all South Dakota Snow Queens have been from the host city of Aberdeen.

Governors Foss and Boe and Congressman Ben Reifel have been Frosty. Frosty is guarded by six guards, each of whom must be a past Chamber or Snow Queen president.

Red Stangland (Sioux Falls) was a radio deejay who had a knack for telling jokes. He turned that talent into cash by authoring the first Norwegian joke book in 1973. Over half a million copies later Stangland is still telling jokes.

In 1892 — at his wife's suggestion — Ft. Meade commandant Col. Caleb Carlton ordered the post band to play the unknown *Star Spangled Banner* when the flag was taken down each evening. This was the first known official use of the song that Congress adopted in 1931 as our national anthem.

Schmeckfest is a food-tasting fair sponsored each spring by the Mennonites of Freeman.

During the silent movie era the exterior wall of the Farmers' Store (Bushnell) was used as a screen and folks would park their buggies to watch the evening show.

Mark Twain visited Deadwood in June 1877. Twain was amused by the way the prostitutes flagrantly drummed up business, even during breakfast.

Tabor hosts Czech Days each June.

AH-ONE, AH-TWO, AH-WELK!

Lawrence Welk (Yankton) built a violin at age three.

During the year Welk worked as a piano salesman he was unable to sell even one piano.

Welk never asked any musician to sign a contract.

When Welk left home at age 21 he spoke only German, had only a fourth-grade education and carried $3 in his pocket.

Over the years Welk inherited the ABC dressing rooms of Frank Sinatra, Jerry Lewis, Sonny Bono and Julie Andrews.

The instruments that Welk's band took on road tours weighed 27.5 tons.

Welk's road agent, Lon Varnell, also happened to be a Methodist minister.

Welk was originally booked on TV as a summer replacement in July 1955.

Welk's Nielson ratings for his show quadrupled from 7.1 to 32.5 within a single year.

Welk was a self-taught musician who performed in his first band in 1927. He gained instant popularity over WNAX (Yankton).

On a cue given by Lawrence Welk 1,429 contestants, each armed with a gold shovel supplied by KELO-Land TV, entered a gold field near Manchester to dig for $35,000 in cash and prizes. Mrs. Floyd Carlon (Sioux Falls) unearthed a capsule worth $10,000 in the August 27 Gold Rush of 1961. A baton twirling sister team and a quartet won trips to the Ted Mack Amateur Hour.

Lawrence Welk composed his theme song, *Bubbles in the Wine*. His first Champagne music was in 1938.

Welk's band carried 70 pounds of music whenever they toured.

The first time Welk heard Myron Floren play his accordion, he crawled under a piano and waved a white handkerchief.

Welk broke the ground for his California office building by donning bib overalls and using a mule and plow.

Myron Floren received a silver hoe upon the occasion of his 25th year with Lawrence Welk.

Yankton-native Fern Renner agreed to an early-dawn wedding to Lawrence Welk in Iowa so that her new husband could make it to a musical engagement in Nebraska later in the day.

AH-ONE, AH-TWO (CONTINUED)

One time Welk had to hock his diamond ring in order to buy food for his expectant wife and to pay his band.

A replica of radio station WNAX (Yankton) is in the Lawrence Welk museum in Escondido, Calif.

One critic told Welk to throw his accordion in the river. Another critic said Welk's music reminded him of a poor grade of beer.

Welk once played to a crowd of one. Welk tried to give the lady her money back so he wouldn't have to do the show, but it turned out she owned the place and was in on a pass anyway.

Welk lived on the same street as Ronald Reagan in Pacific Palisades, Calif.

Lawrence Welk left his North Dakota farm to form a six-musician dance band called "Biggest Little Band in America." Before long they had built up a wide-following in South Dakota. In 1925 radio station WNAX began to feature their music. A steady job for Welk came the next year.

Welk, whose musicians are known as "Champagne Music Makers," did not drink.

Welk golfed.

Welk's first TV show was a locally-produced one in California in 1952. Three years later the show went national on ABC-TV under sponsorship of Dodge cars. For a brief period in the 1950s Welk's weekly live shows from the Aragon Ballroom in Santa Monica, Calif., were the nation's top box office attraction.

No key musician in Welk's band was eligible for service during WWII because all were heads of families.

During WWII Welk's band devoted every free day to performing at a base, hospital or service club.

Welk changed his format very little over the decades except to enlarge his band.

Myron Floren took a salary cut in order to join Welk's band in 1950.

Lawrence Welk once celebrated a big booking by buying some new underwear and shirts.

AH-ONE, AH-TWO (CONTINUED)

Lawrence Welk's original music stands were designed to look like silver champagne buckets, complete with plastic ice cubes and a champagne bottle sticking out of the top.

ABC originally was going to have the Lawrence Welk show feature a comic and some scantily clad dancing girls, until Welk refused to go along with it. ABC backed down.

ABC's first studio given Lawrence Welk for broadcasting his TV show was a structure originally housing *Phantom of the Opera*. The sagging building had so many holes that the crew was constantly stuffing rags in the roof to keep out the rain, sun and whistling wind.

Lawrence Welk's first record, produced in Yankton, S.D., had *Spiked Beer* on one side and *Shanghai Honeymoon* on the other.

CREDO OF LAWRENCE WELK:
- We learn by doing.
- America needs an apprentice program.
- Repeal the child labor law.
- Business people should have profit-sharing.
- No contracts.
- Allow moonlighting.
- Care for fellow-workers.
- Give and ye shall receive.

Taylor Music (Aberdeen) is the state's largest wholesaler of band, orchestra and marching band music.

President Nixon kept a photo of Mamie Van Doren (Rowena) in the lower left drawer of his desk in the Oval Office.

When Mamie Van Doren went on her first date with George Hamilton, they were chaperoned by his mother.

Mamie Van Doren turned down an offer of LSD from Cary Grant.

Mamie Van Doren's first break came in landing a small part on Broadway in a play starring Jackie Gleason.

Mamie Van Doren was Miss Palm Springs 1948 and Miss Eight Ball 1949.

Boxer Jack Dempsey gave actress Mamie Van Doren $1,000 for an abortion in 1951. Van Doren wasn't pregnant, but she needed the cash.

Karl Mundt (Madison) authored the legislation to create the Voice of America.

Laura Ingalls Wilder (De Smet) did not write any of her Little House stories until encouraged years later by the successful journalism career of her own daughter, Rose Lane. After divorcing and moving back home, Rose taught Laura ways to polish her writing.

Laura Ingalls agreed to let her husband harvest wheat near De Smet, but only for four years. If the experiment proved unsuccessful her husband, Almanzo Wilder, agreed to pursue another career.

Because editors at Harper and Brothers thought teenage readers would refuse to read any book with "hard" in the title, Laura Ingalls Wilder's *The Hard Winter* was changed to *The Long Winter* in 1940.

The Wild West Historical Wax Museum (Wall) has an extensive barbed wire collection.

Western Woodcarvings (Custer) were created by a Disney animator.

Mayor Jack White (Sioux Falls) chaperoned 10 deserving children rewarded vacations to Disneyland.

Comedians Williams and Ree first did Native American and white skits while students at Black Hills State College (Spearfish) in 1968.

Since 1989 South Dakota comedians Williams and Ree have appeared regularly on TV's *Hee Haw*, where all their segments are shot in four days and used throughout the TV season. They are America's most popular Native American/white guy comic duo.

The first motion picture shown in South Dakota was *The San Francisco Earthquake,* in Brookings.

The Master Kimball organ orginally built for the Capitol movie theater in Aberdeen, S.D., is currently housed in the statehouse in Juneau, Alaska.

The 1992 State Fair (Huron) featured for the first time bungee jumping, Senior Citizens' Day events, School Essays and a 500th anniversary celebration of the arrival of Christopher Columbus.

The state fair maintains on its 180-acre spread 164,000 square feet of indoor exhibit space within 83 buildings and 30 acres of outdoor exhibit space.

MACY'S THANKSGIVING DAY PARADE BALLOONS, BY RAVEN/ AEROSTAR (SIOUX FALLS):
- Babar the Elephant
- Betty Boop
- Big Bird

- Bugs Bunny
- Clifford, the Big Red Dog
- Garfield
- Nestle's Quik Bunny
- Pink Panther
- Raggedy Ann
- Shamu
- Snoopy
- Snuggles
- Spider Man
- Woodstock

South Dakotan Kevin Pfeiffer won an Emmy in 1991 for his work on *Dinosaurs.*

Thunderheart, filmed in South Dakota during 1991, starred Val Kilmer, Sam Shepard and Graham Greene.

STATE'S TOP 10 EVENTS, 1980S:

- 1980: Sen. McGovern defeated after three terms
- 1981: Missouri River water sold
- 1982: John Mathias (Mt. Vernon) acquitted in the shooting deaths of his wife and sons
- 1983: Gov. Janklow sues two magazines for rape allegations
- 1984: University of South Dakota (Springfield) campus is converted into prison
- 1985: 6,000 farmers converge on Pierre to protest farm financial crises
- 1986: Democrats elect U.S. senator, congressmen and gain 10 legislative seats
- 1987: New governor, senator and congressman sworn in
- 1988: Worst drought in half century
- 1989: Prison officials caught in 1985 scandal involving drugs-for-blades trade
- 1990: National Guard readies for Gulf War

FEATURES FROM *QUICK 'N EASY COUNTRY COOKIN'* (DAVIS):

- Preserving With a Microwave
- Skits for Church Women
- Porcupine Balls
- Hand-Aids for Arthritic Cooks
- Diabetic Cookbook
- Peanut Butter Muffins
- Zucchini by the Zillions

MOUNT RUSHMORE

FOUR FACES AND WHO DEDICATED THEM:
- George Washington, by J.S. Culligan, in 1930
- Thomas Jefferson, by President Franklin Roosevelt, 1936
- Abe Lincoln, by Sen. Ed Burke, 1937
- Teddy Roosevelt, by Gov. Harlan Bushfield, 1939

WHY?

Seeing a stone sculpture of a lion in Switzerland gave South Dakota historian Doane Robinson the idea of having something carved in the Black Hills.

Mount Rushmore was created with the hope of drawing tourists to the state to see a colossal work of famous frontiersmen and pioneers, carved in rock. Instead, four presidents were selected.

George Washington was picked because he was America's first president. Tom Jefferson wrote the Declaration of Independence. Teddy Roosevelt protected natural resources. Abe Lincoln preserved the Union.

OWNERS OF RUSHMORE'S ORIGINAL DRILLS:
- President Coolidge
- Sculptor Gutzon Borglum
- Historian Doane Robinson
- Gov. Peter Norbeck

BEGINNING:

Gutzon Borglum (Keystone) was working on the world's largest sculpture, Stone Mountain, Georgia, when hired to carve Mount Rushmore.

Borglum had one condition concerning his first visit to scout sites for Mount Rushmore: no publicity.

Work on Mount Rushmore began Aug. 10, 1927, the same day President Coolidge dedicated it as a National Memorial. Bad weather and lack of funds caused delays over a 14-year period before Mount Rushmore was completed. Only 6.5 years were spent in actual construction.

LOCATION:

Borglum followed Native American paths as he scouted possible monument sites in the Black Hills.

The site of Mount Rushmore was suggested by a forest ranger.

Mount Rushmore faces southeast.

Borglum had a studio with enormous windows built at the base of Mount Rushmore.

At the base of Mount Rushmore is the Sphinx Rock.

Mount Rushmore was ironically located in the Black Hills, once home to thousands of Native Americans. All four presidents receive poor marks in their treatment of Native Americans.

Teddy Roosevelt was the only one of the four presidents to ever visit South Dakota. The other three died before statehood.

TIMELINE:

Gutzon Borglum planned to carve Mount Rushmore within five years. It took 14. Only six years were spent in actual carving.

- Dec. 28, 1923: Colossal Black Hills sculpture suggested
- March 3, 1925: Government authorizes sculpture
- Oct. 1, 1925: Mount Rushmore dedicated as national memorial
- Aug. 10, 1927: Coolidge presents Borglum the drills
- Oct. 4, 1927: Drilling begins
- July 4, 1930: Washington dedicated
- Aug. 30, 1936: Jefferson dedicated
- Sept. 17, 1937: Lincoln dedicated
- July 2, 1939: Roosevelt dedicated
- March 6, 1941: Borglum dies
- Oct. 31, 1941: Final drilling

The final seven months were completed by Lincoln Borglum. The last remaining funds were spent on Roosevelt's face, which was never completed.

The only body part visible on Mount Rushmore, other than four heads, is Lincoln's right hand under his chin.

CARVING?

Rushmore was not really carved in the traditional sense. Over 450,000 tons of rock were removed in the process, 90 percent of it with the help of dynamite.

Experienced miners removed granite, cutting within three inches of the final surface of Mount Rushmore. So skilled were the miners, who used jackhammers and dynamite, that even traditional mallets and chisels were unnecessary on the eyes and lips of the four presidents.

Borglum used binoculars from miles away to study each presidential face, as it took form on Mount Rushmore. He would make notes, then return to the mountain with adjustments.

Dynamite blasting removed granite to within three inches of the actual surface. The sculpture was brought to a smooth finish with a small air hammer by a process called "bumping."

Borglum used engineering techniques he had developed during his work on Stone Mountain.

It took workers 90 minutes to climb up Mount Rushmore each day.

Workers were lowered over the sides of Mount Rushmore by swing harnesses developed in Georgia.

Discovery of unexpected cracks in the granite caused nine design changes in Mount Rushmore.

Borglum used white lead and granite dust to seal cracks on Washington's face.

Roosevelt was the favorite face of Lincoln Borglum, son of the sculptor. He was 12 when he first climbed atop Mount Rushmore. Lincoln Borglum once lowered himself and painted Jefferson's pupils red, in order to study its shadow in the morning light.

Two Jeffersons were sculpted. The second Jefferson was sunk 60-feet back, where granite was more solid.

COPY CATS:

The world's largest replica of Mount Rushmore is made of Lego blocks in the country of Denmark.

Borglum's first Mount Rushmore was a small clay model, then a papier mâché model, then the mountain.

The plaster model of Washington's face was five feet high.

If all Mount Rushmore coins are sold it will generate $18.7 million for the monument.

Ten billion Mount Rushmore stamps were printed in 1991.

The first Hollywood motion picture featuring Mount Rushmore was Hitchcock's 1959 spy thriller, *North by Northwest*. (See "Hitchcock vs. Rushmore," in "That's Entertainment," the first section of this book.)

In 1945 journalist Eric Severeid suggested South Dakota make its invitation to be the U.N. headquarters remembered by presenting bronze Mount Rushmore statues to U.N. delegates.

Wall Drug (Wall) has a Mount Rushmore for picture-taking purposes.

DIMENSIONS:

Mount Rushmore is visible from 60 miles away.

Carved to scale, the presidents on Mount Rushmore could stand 465 feet tall.

Borglum's studio model of Washington was 24 feet tall and scaled to 240 feet on the mountain.

Each head measures 60 feet high. Noses are 20 feet long. Each mouth is 18 feet wide. Eyes are 11 feet across and five feet high.

Lincoln's nose is bigger than Egypt's Sphinx.

Borglum used models on a scale of one inch to a foot.

Mount Rushmore is not the world's largest sculpture.

SUPPORTERS:

To honor early Mount Rushmore supporters and contributors Borglum hosted a luncheon for dignitaries 2,000 feet underground at Homestake Gold Mine (Lead) Oct. 21, 1931.

Tours were allowed atop Mount Rushmore until WWII.

George Bush was the only one among the five living U.S. presidents to accept an invitation to the formal dedication of Mount Rushmore in 1991. The first formal dedication of the entire monument of Mount Rushmore occurred a half century after it was completed.

A Los Angeles newspaper in 1969 theorized that Roosevelt is really a self-sculpture of Borglum.

Borglum told President Coolidge he would carve his bust if he would vacation in the Black Hills in 1927.

To herald the arrival of President Coolidge for the dedication of Mount Rushmore in 1927, 21 stumps were blasted for a new road, since no cannon was available.

One time Borglum sketched Mount Rushmore at a White House luncheon, adding President Franklin Roosevelt's image. After that federal funds were easier to obtain.

Gov. Bill Bulow had the first road put in around Mount Rushmore after sculptor Gutzon Borglum complained about all the dust he was getting on his shoes and trousers.

Mount Rushmore was partly financed by penny drives of American school children during the Great Depression.

New York attorney Charles Rushmore was so embarrassed by reporters trying to find out what he had done to have a mountain named after him (he had done nothing) that he hastily contributed $5,000 to Borglum's efforts.

To celebrate the 50th anniversary of the death of sculptor Gutzon Borglum, Radio City Music Hall planned "By the Dawn's Early Light," a memorial program staged at Mount Rushmore in August 1991.

In 1990 Hershey's Chocolate of Hershey, Penn., held a $125,000 sweepstakes in which 10,001 prizes were awarded through July 31,

1991. Hershey donated a dime to Mount Rushmore for every contest entry.

Lincoln's dedication included taps blown by a state trooper suspended from the side of Washington's head.

Since 1976 a National Parks Serviceman has annually dangled from atop the memorial to fill in its cracks. In 1991 Bob Chrisman (Rapid City) began using silicone caulking to fill in the cracks on Mount Rushmore.

Mount Rushmore is one of the seven man-made Wonders of the U.S.

1991 DEDICATION SPEAKERS, WITH PRESIDENT BUSH:
- Barry Boswick honored Washington
- Jimmy Stewart honored Lincoln
- Billy Dee Williams honored Jefferson
- Barbara Eden honored Roosevelt

WHAT MIGHT HAVE BEEN:

Sculptor Lorado Taft was selected by South Dakota historian Doane Robinson to carve in the Black Hills huge statues of western heroes, including Lewis and Clark, Wild Bill Cody, Sacajawea and Chief Red Cloud. Because of ill health, Taft turned the project down. Robinson then asked his second choice, Gutzon Borglum.

Borglum originally wanted to carve Teddy Roosevelt on horseback, on Old Baldy, but settled for his face on Mount Rushmore.

Borglum intended to sculpt the four presidents down to the waist, but died before completing the sculpture.

Originally, explorer Kit Carson was going to be sculpted on a Needle, instead of four Presidents on granite-faced Mount Rushmore.

Until the U.S. Government officially recognized the existence of Mount Rushmore through the U.S. Board of Geographic names in June 1930, the monument was listed on various maps as Cougar Mountain or Slaughterhouse Rock.

Abe Lincoln was sculpted where a large time line tablet was going to be inscribed.

Two Jeffersons were carved on Mount Rushmore. The original Jefferson, on the other side of Washington, was blasted away in 1934 and placed on the other side, 60 feet back.

During the 1930s Democrats in Congress threatened to withhold federal funding unless Woodrow Wilson's image replaced that of Teddy Roosevelt.

Borglum originally wanted to carve full statues of Washington and Lincoln in the Needles and Teddy Roosevelt on Old Baldy.

In 1937 Congress debated adding crusader Susan B. Anthony to Mount Rushmore. In 1947 Sen. Hubert Humphrey introduced a bill calling for Franklin Roosevelt to be added. In 1963 Congress discussed adding John Kennedy, and in 1969, Gen. Eisenhower.

Borglum refused to carve a western hero on Mount Rushmore.

By 1928 the four presidents had been chosen for Mount Rushmore. Borglum also wanted a vast tablet, 80 by 100 feet, upon which would be written the nine great events in American history, each written with dates in three-foot letters.

The most frequently mentioned suggestion for a fifth face on Mount Rushmore is Susan B. Anthony.

In 1949 the U.S. Senate voted against adding President Franklin Roosevelt's bust to Mount Rushmore. The bill's sponsor was Huron druggist Sen. Hubert Humphrey.

In 1977 experts believed a Native American profile had been carved on Mount Rushmore. Lincoln Borglum said it had not.

The original design of Mount Rushmore was Jefferson-Washington-Lincoln. Borglum died before finalizing his plans to carve the entire U.S. Constitution in Latin, Chinese and English on the other side of Mount Rushmore.

Borglum was also going to add an inscription composed by President Coolidge. The words would have stretched 120 feet and have been carved in gilded letters five inches deep. Coolidge, usually known for brevity, wrote a 500-word history of the U.S. that was to have been carved on Mount Rushmore. Coolidge became miffed when Borglum severely edited the prose. At any rate, nothing was ever done with it.

Borglum needed another $600,000 to complete the Hall of Records, but died before raising the funds. The Hall of Records penetrates Mount Rushmore 70 feet and then stops, incomplete.

WORDS BORGLUM PLANNED TO ADD ON FRONT:
- Alaska
- California
- Constitution
- Declaration of Independence
- Florida
- Louisiana Purchase
- Oregon
- Panama Canal
- Texas

OFF THE WALL

WALL HANGINGS:

Since July 1936 Wall Drug (Wall) has been quenching thirsty tourists with free ice water. Dorothy Hustead hatched the idea on a sweltering day during the Great Depression. A teenager was hired to put up four Free Ice Water signs outside Wall. Tourists responded immediately. The following year eight girls were hired to deal with the sudden rush of hot customers. By 1991, 120 college students and 100 Wall residents were employed to assist some two million annual visitors to Wall Drug.

Wall Drug goes through 1.5 tons of ice each day. Originally, the Husteads cut ice from a nearby lake during the winter, and stored it until summer. Now machines make it.

During WWII Leonel Jensen handed out the first Wall Drug signs while serving the American Red Cross in Europe. Later tourists saw the signs, and wrote to Wall Drug for their own.

Wall Drug rents 250 billboards and signs, mostly throughout the Midwest. The thickest cluster of Wall Drug signs are 53 within a 45-mile stretch of I-90.

The Wall Drug sign posted the farthest away from South Dakota, was photographed 10,645 miles away in Antarctica.

The Husteads pay a guy twice a year to wash and clean the Wall Drug sign in Amsterdam, The Netherlands.

Vietnam servicemen posted 127 Wall Drug signs in South Vietnam, during the Vietnam War.

AMONG THE 5,000 PLACES DISPLAYING WALL DRUG SIGNS:
- Railway station in Kenya, Africa
- Mt. Fujiama, Japan
- North Pole
- Taj Mahal, India
- Pyramids of Gisa
- Eiffel Tower, France

ICE WATER DRINKERS AT WALL DRUG:
- Jack Dempsey
- Donna Fargo
- Clark Gable
- Stewart Granger
- Mary Hart
- Ernest Hemingway
- The Ink Spots
- Val Kilmer
- Joe E. Lewis

- Guy Lombardo
- Mrs. Douglas MacArthur
- Anthony Quinn
- Sam Shepard
- Robert Taylor
- Sandra Locke
- Robert Urich

As of January 1992, Wall Drug has appeared in 710 international feature stories, as well as on national TV. Wall Drug has been written up in articles appearing in Ireland, New Zealand, Great Britain, the Netherlands and Norway.

The most popular souvenirs sold at Wall Drug are mugs.

Three generations of Husteads have been pharmacists.

Wall Drug is indeed a drug store, with a pharmacist on duty 24 hours a day. Approximately three dozens prescriptions are filled each day.

Drug-related items displayed at Wall Drug include a Hand Cranked Suppository Machine, medical saddle bag and 1889 dosage book.

Wall Drug features lifesize statues of Annie Oakley, Butch Cassidy and the Sundance Kid, Chief Crazy Horse and Buffalo Bill Cody, carved from a 187-year-old cedar tree.

Six nationwide schools of business have done case studies of business management at Wall Drug.

Wall Drug had outhouses until 1950.

Wall Drug Store features 183 original oil paintings by western artists, 600 cattle brands and nickel coffee.

Wall Drug is near an 80-foot Brontosaurus dinosaur statue.

One-third of Wall residents work for Wall Drug.

To save money, Dorothy and Ted Hustead and son, Bill, slept behind a curtain in back of Wall Drug for six years.

Forty-five percent of all cars westward-bound on I-90 stop at Wall Drug.

Wall Drug serves 6,000 doughnuts and 3,000 eggs each summer day.

Wall Drug's cafe is built around a huge cottonwood tree.

In 1950 Hollywood actor Frederic March had all of his mail forwarded to Wall Drug and then picked it up during his Black Hills vacation.

Wall Drug houses one of the state's largest collection of regional art.

Among the most-photographed art at Wall Drug are the four lifesize Dakota Chiefs: Red Cloud, Gall, Crazy Horse and Spotted Tail, each carved by Harold Skunk (Rapid City).

The automated Cowboy Orchestra, Christmas on the Range, came from a Denver department store in 1952. The Chuckwagon Quartet came from Montana.

Among Wall Drug's tourists each year are 400 pharmacists.

Medicine accounts for only 15 percent of all sales at Wall Drug (Wall).

Wall, S.D., was Ted Hustead's fourth pharmacy job in less than two years. The Sioux Falls druggist had scouted 15 locations before settling on Wall, where he established his drug store in 1931. Free ice water wasn't offered until five years later.

CRAZY HORSE

NO CRAZY IDEA

Since 1948 two generations of a family have been carving on Thunderhead Mountain (Custer) the world's largest sculpture. Immortalized in stone will be Dakota Chief Crazy Horse and his nameless horse.

Carving Crazy Horse was suggested to New England sculptor Korczak Ziolkowski by Chief Henry Standing-Bear.

The five survivors of Little Bighorn dedicated Crazy Horse on Thunderhead Mountain on June 3, 1948.

Ziolkowski began blasting away at the first granite covering Thunderhead Mountain (Crazy Horse) on June 3, 1948. He worked on the monument for the next 35 years, until his death in 1982.

The first carving on Crazy Horse was done under the mane of the horse.

Ziolkowski had $174 to his name when he arrived at Crazy Horse in 1947. Custer banks refused to lend Ziolkowski any money in 1949.

Ziolkowski lived in a tent during the seven months he built his house.

Ziolkowski was so poor during the early stages of carving Crazy Horse that he raised livestock in order to have food, and went for years without roads, electricity and running water.

Ziolkowski once sold all his chickens in order to make a payroll.

Ziolkowski could not read a slide rule.

Ziolkowski twice turned down $10 million in federal funding.

Ziolkowski carried 29 tons of lumber on his back up the mountain in order to build a 741-step staircase.

CHIPPING AWAY

Since there is no known photo of Crazy Horse, the monument is modeled after descriptions by Native Americans who knew him.

The initial tools used by Korczak to begin carving Crazy Horse included a jeep, crowbar and jackhammer. It wasn't until 1966 that Korczak raised enough money to buy a bulldozer.

Using 174 gallons of paint, Ziolkowski painted a six-foot strip outlining Crazy Horse. Ziolkowski's wife, Ruth, stood a mile away and used binoculars and an Army telephone to help the sculptor keep his perspective.

Ziolkowski used a chunk of Thunderhead granite to carve a tombstone for the grave of Sitting Bull (Mobridge). Ziolkowski used his $5,000 fee to buy a bulldozer for Crazy Horse Mountain.

Ziolkowski had to drive over four miles every day to get to the top of Crazy Horse. The sculptor had to wait 17 years for a permit from the railroads to build an entry bridge.

Eight lighting companies donated a $70,000 floodlight system.

DIMENSIONS:
The dimensions of Crazy Horse will make it the largest sculpture in the world. In back of the chief will be a large plaque.

- Nose, 27.5 ft.
- Forehead, 32 ft.
- Hand, 33 ft.
- Feather, 44 ft.
- Mane, 62 ft.
- Head, 87.5 ft.
- Arm hole, 110 ft.
- Horse's head, 219 ft.
- Left arm, 263 ft.
- Height, 563 ft.
- Length, 641 ft.

The left arm of Crazy Horse points to the East, where his dead are buried.

When Crazy Horse is completed, a house could easily fit inside the horse's nostril and 4,000 people could stand on the chief's outstretched arm. Mount Rushmore will be able to fit inside Crazy Horse's head.

STORYTELLER IN STONE
Ziolkowski and Gutzon Borglum once impulsively phoned India to see if it was raining. It was.

Ziolkowski's works, including Paderewski, which won first prize at the 1939 New York World's Fair, were vandalized by a relative.

Ziolkowski literally rode shotgun enroute to Sitting Bull's grave in Mobridge, S.D., to make sure his six-ton bust of the chief wasn't hijacked by North Dakotans,

ONGOING PROGRESS
Since the death of Ziolkowski in 1982, widow Ruth Ziolkowski manages the Crazy Horse project with seven of their 10 children. The

crew works 12 months a year, with Ruth at times manning a jack-hammer or bulldozer to speed things along.

Ziolkowski left his wife three detailed books on how to proceed with the carving.

The outline of Crazy Horse's eyebrows, eyes and nose started to emerge in 1991. In 1990 nine miles of explosive detonation cord were used. In order to blast 5,005 tons off the face of Crazy Horse, 2,421 boreholes had to be hand-drilled into granite.

The eyes of Crazy Horse were opened in 1991. A network of 86 boreholes outline each of Crazy Horse's eyes.

Mild winters helped nudge carving of Crazy Horse Mountain two years ahead of schedule.

A 16-ton, 18.5-ft. plaster model of Crazy Horse rests at the entrance of a thousand-car parking lot at the base of Thunderhead Mountain. The model of Crazy Horse was created in 1965 on a scale of one foot equaling 34 feet on the mountain.

Crazy Horse is not a state or federal project. It is a non-profit mountain carving to and for the Native American people of America.

Son Casimir Ziolkowski once jumped free as a bulldozer's brakes failed and the machine fell 250 feet over the side of Crazy Horse.

During the June 6-7, 1992, Volksmarch tourists were allowed to climb Crazy Horse and earn a medal.

As of February 1992, 8.3 million tons of granite had been removed.

There has never been a completion date set for Crazy Horse.

BODY PARTS

HEIGHTS:
4 feet, 3 inches:
- Prospector Potato Creek Johnny Perrett (Deadwood)

4 feet, 11 inches:
- Lecturer Eleanor McGovern (Woonsocket)

5 feet, 1 inch:
- Free ice water originator Dorothy Hustead (Wall)

5 feet, 2 inches:
- Author Laura Ingalls Wilder (De Smet)
- New York Mayor Fiorella La Guardia (Fort Sully)

5 feet, 3 inches:
- *Dances With Wolves* translator Doris Leader Charge (Parmalee)

5 feet, 4 inches:
- Actress Cheryl Ladd (Huron)
- First Lady Nancy Kneip (Salem)

5 feet, 5 inches:
- Actress Mary Hart (Sioux Falls)
- Sculptor Ruth Ziolkowski (Crazy Horse)

5 feet, 6 inches:
- Quint mother Mary Ann Fischer (Aberdeen)

5 feet, 7 inches:
- Dakota Chief Crazy Horse (Black Hills)
- Boston Red Sox Marv Olson (Gaysville)
- USA Today Publisher Allen Neuharth (Eureka)

5 feet, 8 inches:
- Composer John Cacavas (Aberdeen)
- First Lady Linda Mickelson (Pierre)
- Pharmacist Bill Hustead (Wall)
- Sen. Tom Daschle (Aberdeen)
- Surrogate Grandmother Arlette Schweitzer (Aberdeen)

5 feet, 9 inches:
- Artist Oscar Howe (Vermillion)
- Bandleader Lawrence Welk (Yankton)
- Detroit Tiger Sparky Anderson (Bridgewater)
- Journalist Steve Hemmingsen (Sioux Falls)
- New York Yankee Delmar Paddock (Volga)
- World basketball spinner Bruce Crevier (Elkton)

5 feet, 10 inches:
- Lt. Gov. Bill Dougherty (Sioux Falls)
- Pharmacist Ted Hustead (Wall)
- Rodeo champ Paul Tierney (Piedmont)
- Toronto Blue Jay Dave Collins (Rapid City)

5 feet, 10.5 inches:
- Chicago Cub Biggs Wehde (Sioux Falls)
- Vice President Hubert Humphrey (Huron)

5 feet, 11 inches:
- Brooklyn Dodger Lou Koupal (Tabor)

- Buffalo king Roy Houck (Fort Pierre)
- Carpenter Leonard Peltier (Pine Ridge)
- Cleveland Indian Tito Francona (Aberdeen)
- Congressman Tim Johnson (Canton)
- Detroit Tiger George Disch (Rapid City)
- Gov. Richard Kneip (Salem)
- Journalist Tom Brokaw (Yankton)
- St. Louis Cardinal Kermit Wahl (Columbia)

5 feet, 11.5 inches:
- Brooklyn Dodger Redskin Aitchison (Tyndall)
- Cincinnati Red Bob Ingersoll (Rapid City)

6 feet:
- Captain 11 Dave Dedrick (Sioux Falls)
- Cincinnati Red Len Rice (Lead)
- Cleveland Indian Tony Faeth (Aberdeen)
- Cycle Classic founder Pappy Hoel (Sturgis)
- Dakota Chief Sitting Bull (Grand River)
- Gov. Joe Foss (Sioux Falls)
- Houston Astro Pork Chop Hoffman (Aberdeen)
- Minnesota Twins' Kevin Bruce Stanfield (Huron) & Carroll Hardy (Sturgis)
- Notre Dame coach Frank Leahy (Winner)
- Rodeo Rancher Jim Sutton (Onida)
- Sculptor Korczak Ziolkowski (Crazy Horse)
- U.S.S. South Dakota Captain Tom Gatch
- Washington Senator Jug Thesenga (Jefferson)

6 feet, 1 inch:
- Chicago White Sox Death Valley Jim Scott (Deadwood)
- Chicago Cub Terry Francona (Aberdeen)
- Country western singer Sherwin Linton (Volga)
- Gen. George Custer (Custer)
- Gunslinger Wild Bill Hickok (Deadwood)
- Houston Expo Floyd Bannister (Pierre)
- Journalist Doug Lund (Sioux Falls)
- Mayor Tim Rich (Aberdeen)
- New York Met John Strohmayer (Belle Fourche)
- Sen. George McGovern (Mitchell)
- Sports announcer Pat O'Brien (Sioux Falls)
- St. Louis Cardinal Ole Ward (Herrick)
- Vikings coach Norm Van Brocklin (Parade)
- Washington Senator Bullet Ben Benson (Harley)

6 feet, 1.5 inches:
- Artist Harvey Dunn (Manchester)

6 feet, 2 inches:
- AIM activist Russell Means (Pine Ridge)
- Boston Red Sox Jiggs Parson (Parker)
- Explorer Jedediah Smith (Mobridge)

- Mayor Jackson White (Sioux Falls)
- Minnesota Twin Jerry Crider (Sioux Falls)
- Nebraska Sen. James Exon (Geddes)
- State Attorney General John Pyle (Huron)
- Super 8 CEO Jack Pacak (Aberdeen)

6 feet, 3 inches:
- Cincinnati Red Ramrod Nelson (Viborg)
- Quint physician Dr. James Berbos (Aberdeen)
- Los Angeles Dodger Terry Forester (Sioux Falls)
- Mayor Ed McLaughlin (Rapid City)

6 feet, 4 inches:
- Atlanta Brave Tom Hausman (Mobridge)
- Evan's Plunge originator Fred Evans (Hot Springs)
- Gov. George S. Mickelson (Mobridge)
- New York Met Rube Fischer (Carlock)
- New York Met Bob Rauch (Brookings)

6 feet, 5 inches:
- Skyforce coach Kevin McKenna (Sioux Falls)

6 feet, 6 inches:
- Executed cop killer George Sitts (Sioux Falls)

6 feet 9 inches:
- Author Frederick Manfred (Vermillion)
- Thriller center Jarvis Basnight (Rapid City)

7 feet, 2 inches:
- Skyforce center Petur Gudmundsson (Sioux Falls)

WEIGHTS:
10 ounces:
- Uchytil twins, carried by surrogate grandmother (Aberdeen)

12 pounds, 15.5 ounces:
- Siamese twins Kaci and Keri Archer (Gettysburg)

15 pounds, 10 ounces:
- Fischer Quintuplets (Aberdeen)

93 pounds:
- Speaker Eleanor McGovern (Woonsocket)

130 pounds:
- First Lady Nancy Kneip (Salem)

142 pounds:
- Lt. Gov. Bill Dougherty (Sioux Falls)

150 pounds:
- First Lady Linda Mickelson (Sioux Falls)
- Quint mother Mary Ann Fischer (Aberdeen)
- Sen. Tom Daschle (Aberdeen)

155 pounds:
- Composer John Cacavas (Aberdeen)

160 pounds:
- Boston Red Sox Marv Olson (Gaysville)
- Dakota Chief Crazy Horse (Black Hills)

- World basketball spinner Bruce Crevier (Elkton)

162 pounds:
- Free ice water originator Dorothy Hustead (Wall)
- Journalist Tom Brokaw (Webster)
- Pharmacist Bill Hustead (Wall)

165 pounds:
- Chicago White Sox Delmar Paddock (Volga)

168 pounds:
- Detroit Tiger Sparky Anderson (Bridgewater)

170 pounds:
- *Dances With Wolves* host Roy Houck (Fort Pierre)
- Mayor Jackson White (Sioux Falls)
- Sports announcer Pat O'Brien (Sioux Falls)
- St. Louis Cardinal Kermit Wahl (Columbia)

175 pounds:
- Brooklyn Dodger Redskin Aitchison (Tyndall)
- Cincinnati Red Bob Ingersoll (Rapid City)
- Congressman Tim Johnson (Canton)
- Executed cop killer George Sitts (Sioux Falls)
- Detroit Tiger Dave Collins (Rapid City)
- Pittsburgh Pirate Lou Koupal (Tabor)
- Sen. George McGovern (Mitchell)

180 pounds:
- Boston Red Sox Jiggs Parson (Parker)
- Chicago Cub Biggs Wehde (Sioux Falls)
- Cincinnati Red Sox Ramrod Nelson (Viborg) and Len Rice (Lead)
- Cleveland Indian Tony Faeth (Aberdeen)
- Rodeo champ Paul Tierney (Piedmont)
- Notre Dame coach Frank Leahy (Winner)

181 pounds:
- Montreal Expo John Strohmayer (Belle Fourche)

182 pounds:
- Pharmacist Ted Hustead (Wall)

185 pounds:
- Cycle Classic founder Pappy Hoel (Sturgis)
- Mayor Tim Rich (Aberdeen)
- Minnesota Twin Carroll Hardy (Sturgis)
- Washington Senator Bullet Ben Benson (Harley)
- Vice President Hubert Humphrey (Doland)

190 pounds:
- Atlanta Brave Tom Hausman (Mobridge)
- Baltimore Oriole Tito Francona (Aberdeen)
- Houston Astros Floyd Bannister (Pierre) and Pork Chop Hoffman (Aberdeen)
- Minnesota Twin Kevin Stanfield (Huron)
- Montreal Expo Terry Francona (Aberdeen)
- New York Met Rube Fischer (Carlock)

- Sculptor Korczak Ziolkowski (Crazy Horse)

195 pounds:
- Skyforce coach Kevin McKenna (Sioux Falls)

198 pounds:
- Chicago Cub Ole Ward (Herrick)

199 pounds:
- Vikings coach Norm Van Brocklin (Parade)

200 pounds:
- Carpenter Leonard Peltier (Pine Ridge)
- Country western singer Sherwin Linton (Volga)
- Los Angeles Dodger Terry Forester (Sioux Falls)
- Minnesota Twin Jerry Crider (Sioux Falls)
- New York Met Bob Rauch (Brookings)
- Washington Senator Jug Thesenga (Jefferson)

210 pounds:
- Mayor Ed McLaughlin (Rapid City)
- Quint physician Dr. James Berbos (Aberdeen)

215 pounds:
- Author Frederick Manfred (Vermillion)

220 pounds:
- Journalist Doug Lund (Sioux Falls)
- Rancher Jim Sutton (Onida)
- State Attorney General John Pyle (Huron)

223 pounds:
- Nebraska Sen. James Exon (Geddes)

225 pounds:
- Sen. Peter Norbeck (Vermillion)

235 pounds:
- Chicago White Sox Death Valley Jim Scott (Deadwood)

240 pounds:
- Super 8 CEO Jack Pacak (Aberdeen)

255 pounds:
- Gov. George S. Mickelson (Mobridge)

260 pounds:
- Thriller Wayne Engelstad (Rapid City)

265 pounds:
- Captain 11 Dave Dedrick (Sioux Falls)

TOPS & bottoms:
While doing a story on winter living conditions at Wounded Knee, Geraldo Rivera had the painful and humiliating experience of having his fanny stick—frozen—to a wooden seat in an outhouse on the Pine Ridge Indian Reservation.

The largest collection of artificial breasts in South Dakota are owned by the American Cancer Society, South Dakota Division (Sioux Falls).

Miss South Dakota Mary Hart wore a white swimsuit to accent her 34-24-34 figure in the 1970 Miss America Pageant.

Entry into some unofficial events at the Black Hills Motorcycle Classic held each August in Sturgis, S.D., includes having each man show his genitals or each woman bare her breasts.

Norm Van Brocklin (Parade) rewarded a bronze jockstrap to Vikings who seriously injured opponents during professional football games.

Hollywood censors originally banned *Untamed Youth* because Mamie Van Doren (Rowena) wiggled her hips too much.

Lawrence Welk gave a kiss and certificate of appreciation to each female volunteer appearing at a cancer foundation breakfast in Rapid City. When a gentleman suddenly stepped forward to receive his certificate, Welk paused awkwardly until First Lady Nancy Kneip appeared and kissed the man on his bald head. As the man bowed, the crowd roared with laughter when they saw Nancy's lipstick on top of the man's dome.

A furor arose when a huge mural of a bare-breasted maiden, draped in the American flag, was painted by Charles Holloway on the ceiling of the Capitol's Senate Chamber (Pierre) in 1910. The out-of-state artist claimed the maiden represented the state of Louisiana being welcomed by an angel and a knight.

While riding his horse as he searched for gold in the Black Hills in 1874, Gen. George Armstrong Custer wore a special jockstrap.

Just before he won a Gold in the 1964 Olympics in Japan, runner Billy Mills (Pine Ridge) was given a sex test, but none of the women athletes were.

Super 8 Motel headquarters (Aberdeen) reports that one of their startled female desk clerks had to give a spare key to a naked gentleman who had locked himself out of his room. He had no idea that all Super 8 doors are self-locking.

In her 1987 autobiography actress Mamie Van Doren (Rowena) says she slept with Rock Hudson, Burt Reynolds, Jack Dempsey, Joe Namath, Steve McQueen and Al Capone's cousin.

Skin-colored balloons were glued over the breasts and belly-button of Mamie Van Doren (Rowena) in order for her to portray Eve in *Adam and Eve*, 1960.

The Dahl Fine Arts Center (Rapid City) covered all its nude paintings when a religious group renting the theater, objected.

Calamity Jane (Deadwood) swam naked with men.

L.A. Raider Lyle Alzado (Yankton) had injected so many steroids that a plastic surgeon was able to remove one baseball-sized lump of destroyed tissue from Alzado's buttocks.

MISSING SOMETHING:
South Dakota's first Episcopal Bishop, William Hare, had no right eye.

Award-winning wildlife artist Terry Redlin (Watertown) lost a leg in a cycle crash, at age 15.

Deadwood Dick (Deadwood) was missing the trigger finger of his right hand.

South Dakota state Supreme Court Justice W.W. Brookings lost both legs in a snowstorm.

In the 1800s, on opening day at the Pine Ridge boarding school, the white teachers cut off the braids of each Native American child.

In earlier times unfaithful Native American women in South Dakota had their noses cut off by their husbands.

Samuel Jerome Brown lost both legs as a result of getting caught in a South Dakota snowstorm on April 19, 1866, while riding to warn settlers of a possible Native American attack. There was no attack.

Inventor J.L.W. Zietlow (Aberdeen) had no right arm. As an individual who played a key role in the development of the telephone, Zietlow once tied a replacement wire to a kite in order to get it across a flood and over to a telephone pole.

When Dr. Noe Auther (Rapid City) accidentally sawed off his left hand in 1971, both his hand and he were flown to Kentucky, where the hand was reattached.

Only 25 bones — the body has 207 — were discovered in the North Dakota grave of Sitting Bull, when his remains were relocated at night, Mobridge, S.D.

WINKS AND BLINKS:
Jack McCall (Deadwood) was cross-eyed.

Wild Bill Hickok (Deadwood) had poor and failing eyesight, the result of gonorrhea.

Chief Red Cloud (Pine Ridge) died blind.

Mary Ingalls turned blind just before her family moved to De Smet. Her sister, Laura, had to serve as Mary's eyes and ears while living on the prairie.

The eyes of executed cop killer George Sitts (Sioux Falls) were immediately donated to an eye bank. After the body was wrapped in a rubber sheet, a swift funeral was held by a Baptist preacher before Sitts' body was buried in an unmarked grave in Sioux Falls.

All five Fischer quints (Aberdeen) needed glasses.

LEG TO STAND ON:
Thousands of letters of protest poured in to Entertainment Tonight when a new set, installed in 1986, covered the legs of Mary Hart (Sioux Falls).

A Nashville, Tenn., TV station prepared a special Entertainment Tonight promo tape featuring just clips of nothing but Mary Hart's legs.

Mary Hart wore high heels during the taping of Entertainment Tonight because the elevation made her legs look more feminine.

Mauled by a grizzly bear and left for dead in the Black Hills by his two companions, Hugh Glass crawled over 200 miles back to civilization to Fort Kiowa, S.D., an odyssey that was captured in many 19th century songs and poems. During his three-month ordeal (Sept.-Nov., 1823), Glass survived, alone, by eating dirt, raw gophers, raw mice, roots, rattlesnakes, his buckskin shirt, cactus, plums, rotting buffalo, a dog, leaves and live ants. His water came from rivers, rain and the wet moss on trees.

Crazy Horse (Black Hills) limped as the result of getting an arrow in his right leg, at age 14.

World rodeo champ Paul Tierney (Piedmont) has never broken a bone while riding any wild bulls and feisty horses. He broke his leg when a nearby horse happened to kick him.

Almanzo Wilder (De Smet) walked with a limp, the result of being crippled from diphtheria.

Lightning hit a box of dynamite atop Mount Rushmore Aug. 20, 1936, injuring three workers, including one who had his shoes blown off.

Chief Sitting Bull (Mobridge) limped after being shot in the left foot while raiding enemy Crows for their horses.

BEING HIP, ETC.:
Wind Cave National Park (Black Hills) was discovered by two resting cowboys whose cowboy hats were suddenly blown off their heads.

Twenty percent of South Dakota teens experiment by sniffing glue.

Alica Thiele (Brandon), spelled "MISSISSIPPI" with her belly button on America's Funniest People, 1991.

Gov. George S. Mickelson is taller than Arnold Schwarzenegger. The duo met at a Sioux Falls school in 1991.

The Fischer Quintuplets (Aberdeen) were baptized and confirmed at the age of one day old.

During the 1990 Bike Week Rally in Sturgis, S.D., there were 11 deaths, 44 drug arrests, 57 injuries, 278 ambulance runs and 451 emergency room visits.

Cleveland Hall (Wessington Springs) carried the order that saved Washington from the Confederates during the Civil War. Hall endured seven gunshots and two saber wounds, as well as several horses being shot out from under him, to successfully get a message to the Union that the South would attack shortly.

One time an aerial tram carrying five workers to Mount Rushmore fell 500 feet. One guy jumped, and broke several bones. The other four held tightly onto an emergency brake until they were safely rescued.

When Lyndon Johnson informed Hubert Humphrey (Huron) that LBJ was not running for reelection in 1968, Humphrey gave him a hug.

At age 11 Lawrence Welk (Yankton) developed blood poisoning from a ruptured appendix. For over two months the teen had to sleep on a cot next to a pump organ, with a tube draining poisons from his ribs. When his strength came back the first thing Welk did was learn to play that pump organ!

Lawrence Welk had minor surgery in a Yankton hospital so he could be closer to a nurse named Fern Renner, whom he married.

Author Frederick Manfred (Vermillion) was in a sanatorium recovering from tuberculosis when he met his future wife.

Madam Mustache (Deadwood) was a bewhiskered French lady who was a card shark in 1876.

Black Elk (Black Hills) wore his dark hair in four braids down to his waist. He would mark his progress in school by cutting off pieces of braid.

Gov. Bill Janklow (Pierre) had to have his jaw wired shut after surviving a plane crash.

Arriving in Japan for the 1964 Olympics, America's top hope, Gerry Lindgren, sprained his right ankle. His replacement was Billy Mills (Pine Ridge) who became the first American to win the 10,000-meter run.

Wild Bill Hickok (Deadwood) would get so afraid before a gunfight that his face would turn as white as chalk.

Wild Bill Hickok was known as "Duck Bill" as a child, because his lower lip stuck out, and he had a long nose.

The fatal bullet that killed Wild Bill Hickok went through his head and lodged into the left arm of Captain Frank Massie, who never had it removed.

Wild Bill Hickok wore his blonde hair shoulder length, carefully forming ringlets he kept in place with perfume. He kept his mustache long, drooping, waxed and twirled up at both ends.

Nine out of every 1,000 pregnant South Dakota women get an abortion.

Congress thought that Gov. Peter Norbeck (Redfield) was insane for trying to save the Badlands.

George "Baby Face" Nelson shot police officer Hale Keith while robbing the Security National Bank (Sioux Falls) in 1934.

Deadwood Dick (Deadwood) never sat with his back to the door.

Jack McCall (Deadwood) was nicknamed "Crooked Nose Jack."

The nation's oldest former Marine, Arthur Hanson (Rapid City) rode in a parade on July 4, 1991, in Rapid City. Hanson was wounded June 2, 1918, in France.

Chief Gall (Moreau River) was once charged with a phony murder, arrested and stabbed, yet crawled away and survived.

Gov. Joe Foss (Sioux Falls) became a born-again Christian when he nearly died of arsenic poisoning in 1966.

During WWII, Gov. Joe Foss survived a plane crash and being shot in the head by Japanese.

Arlette Schweitzer (Aberdeen) is the first known American to carry her own grandchildren. Schweitzer, a 42-year-old librarian, was implanted with eggs from her daughter, Christa Uchytil, 22, when it was discovered Christa had no uterus. Eleven eggs were removed from daughter Christa Uchytil, in a 50-minute procedure February 21, 1991. Four eggs were fertilized with sperm from husband, Kevin, and implanted in the uterus of Christa's mother. Twins Chelsea and Chad Uchytil were born premature but healthy in Aberdeen, S.D., on October 12, 1991.

Arlette Schweitzer will publically discuss her uterus but refuses to divulge her weight.

Arlette Schweitzer had to give herself shots for three months preceding the birth of her twin grandchildren, whom she was carrying.

The birth certificate of twins Chelsea and Chad Uchytil, carried by their surrogate grandmother, lists Christa Uchytil as their mother .

The chronic asthma suffered all her life by Arlette Schweitzer ceased while carrying her twin grandchildren.

The New England Journal of Medicine reports one woman TV viewer who gets ill from listening to the voice of Mary Hart (Sioux Falls).

Oscar Howe (Joe Creek) suffered a heart attack while waiting to go on as a guest on "To Tell The Truth" in New York City in 1974.

Siamese twins born to Melissa and Kelly Archer (Gettysburg) in Minneapolis were joined at the liver and successfully separated two weeks after their 1991 birth. Each baby girl was left with her own liver.

While hiking through the Black Hills in 1823, Jedediah Smith temporarily buried a dehydrated friend up to his neck in moist soil while Smith and others searched for water.

Deadwood dance hall girl Kitty LeRoy always kept a dagger tucked into her long curly hair.

After Calamity Jane (Deadwood) got drunk, she would often go into the Black Hills and howl like a wolf.

Once when Calamity Jane got drunk and shot out all the lights in a saloon, it took three deputies to haul her off to jail for the night.

Offended that a play's heroine deserted her family for a lover, Calamity Jane strode up on stage in Deadwood and spit tobacco juice all over the actress' gown.

Joe Floyd (Sioux Falls) grew a mustache, which he said he would keep if his wife gave birth to a son. She did, and he did.

Joe Floyd always had an unlit cigar in his mouth, a habit he picked up from an early movie he once saw.

CBS Sportscaster Pat O'Brien (Sioux Falls) wears his earpiece in his right ear.

Country western singer Sherwin Linton (Watertown) twice tattooed himself with his initials on his hands in high school.

Three-month-old Deeann Hackett (Brookings) received a DPT vaccination February 19, 1965. That evening she became feverish, irritable, went into seizures and was unconsolable. Eventually she became 95 percent disabled. During 1991 Hackett became the first South Dakotan to receive federal compensation from the 1986 National Childhood Vaccine Injury Act, with the judgment estimated at $2 million.

Two hundred fifty-nine kissing couples fell 46 puckers short of breaking the world kissing record, in Vermillion in April 1991.

Mamie Van Doren (Rowena) had an abortion, with the pregnancy conceived with baseball player Lee Meyers.

Gov. George Mickelson was hospitalized for blood clots, in Sioux Falls, during December 1991.

Early Deadwood card dealers would grow one of their fingernails longer than the rest in order to more easily scoop up gold dust bet during the games.

A full half-hour of continuous cannon shots heralded the arrival of Yellow Stone ship at Fort Pierre, S.D., in 1831. This contributed to the deafness of artist George Catlin, a passenger on board.

Dr. Ben Munson (Rapid City) created a furor in 1967 when he openly added abortions to his medical practice. Munson performed 3,000 abortions before being arrested for doing so, in 1969. While awaiting trial, the U.S. Supreme Court legalized abortion, 1973.

In 1992 an Iowa man sued a Sioux Falls hospital for $250,000 for accidentally burning him in the back during brain surgery.

Dave Dedrick (Sioux Falls) has the most-recognized face in South Dakota.

BOOOOOOO:
Sica Hollow (Sisseton) harbors eerie legends.

Country western singer Sherwin Linton (Watertown) is convinced that in 1977 he saw apparitions, dressed in outfits from the 1940s, entering an abandoned church along Highway 81 in South Dakota.

Yellow Doll is a "fallen angel" said to haunt the Bodega Saloon (Deadwood).

The ax of hanged Swedish woodchopper Nils Swenson is still heard in mines near Carbonite.

Kitty LeRoy and Sam Curley have been reported to haunt the Lone Star Saloon (Deadwood)

SOUTH DAKOTA RANKS*

First in animated woodcarvings, arrowhead collections, bison, blue grass, credit cards, crystal caves, farm bankruptcies, geese, gold mining, honey, oats, prehistoric mammoth bones, rose quartz, rye and vertebrate fossils.

Second in farmers, flax, one-room schoolhouses, Republicans, spring wheat and sunflower seeds.

Third in farm land, Lutherans, marriages, nuclear warheads, oats, people who walk to work and teen suicide.

Fourth in Christians, hay, honey, hydroelectric power, lambs, meat packing, sheep and spring wheat.

Fifth in beef cattle, judges and shopping centers.

Sixth in hottest temperatures, nursing homes, senior citizens, spring wheat and winter wheat.

Seventh in barley, calves, campaign spending, parks and sorghum.

Eighth in accidental deaths and winter temperatures.

Ninth in cattle.

Tenth in corn, motorcycles, Presbyterians and wheat.

Eleventh in fire deaths, longevity and pigs.

Twelfth in railroads.

Thirteenth in birth rate, heart disease, Methodists and oats.

Fourteenth in deaths, Independent voters, Mormons, poverty, sales tax, Seventh Day Adventists and welfare fraud.

Sixteenth in land area.

Seventeenth in Democrats.

Twentieth in Catholics, child abuse, nuclear fuels and teenage mothers.

Twenty-first in federal lands and savings accounts.

Twenty-second in malpractice suits and total taxes paid.

Twenty-third in energy costs, lobbyists and turkeys.

Twenty-fourth in gasoline taxes, hospital costs, oil, symphony attendance and well-adjusted children.

Twenty-fifth in farms and healthy citizens.

* Many of these rankings are per capita, not necessarily total numbers.

Twenty-sixth in high school graduates.

Twenty-seventh in college SAT scores.

Twenty-eighth in AIDS budgeting and water.

Twenty-ninth in boats and chickens.

Thirtieth in runaways.

Thirty-first where actors live.

Thirty-second in governmental employees, hospital stays and potatoes.

Thirty-third in Baptists, forests and taxes.

Thirty-fourth in bowling, educational spending and passports issued.

Thirty-fifth in natural gas.

Thirty-sixth in suicides.

Thirty-seventh in cancer, cars, gonorrhea and highway miles.

Thirty-eighth in coal consumption, dentists, Japanese industry, liquor consumption.

Thirty-ninth in alcoholism, fishing, legislative size and rape.

Fortieth in Hispanics and income.

Forty-first in foreigners.

Forty-second in divorces and motorcycle deaths.

Forty-third in classroom size, executions and farmland values.

Forty-fourth in population, psychiatrists and school enrollment.

Forty-fifth in child support collection, defense installations, lawyers, low birth weights, teacher salaries and union members.

Forty-seventh in car insurance, crime, drug arrests and population.

Forty-eighth in carpooling, car theft, college students, population, prisoners, prostitution, stockholders and tennis players.

Forty-ninth in buses, murder, retail sales and UFO sightings.

Fiftieth in abortions, doctors, frisbee players, illiteracy, income, legislative salaries, stress and unemployment.

WHO'S ON FIRST?

The most widely-read South Dakotan is Allen Neuharth (Eureka), whose USA Today "Plain Talk" column reaches 22 million readers each week.

George McGovern (Mitchell) was named the No. 1 high school debater in the Midwest, February 1943.

Gen. George Custer (Custer) ranked 35th out of 35 in his 1861 class at West Point.

The first time Tom Brokaw (Yankton) and Dan Rather finished in a dead-heat for news ratings was in April 1986.

Two of the 10 most popular children's books were authored by Frank Baum (Aberdeen), who penned *The Wizard of Oz*, and Laura Ingalls Wilder (De Smet), who wrote *Little House in the Big Woods*.

In a 1991 poll 30 percent of South Dakotans said they were religious. Seventy percent said they weren't.

Ed McGivern won a world-record shooting match in Lead, S.D., by shooting a .45 five times into an inch-wide target 15 feet away, Aug. 20, 1932.

Red Stangland and Uncle Torvald were named the No.1 comedy act in South Dakota, by the Showtime movie network.

FIRST AND WORST

Corson County, S.D., has America's lowest circulation of *Penthouse* magazine.

Because of a minimum of 160 Missileman missiles originally buried near the Badlands, South Dakota once could have been the third most powerful nation on earth. Rapid City—once the fifth most dangerous area in America—-could have received an estimated 2,000 incoming warheads during the opening minutes of a nuclear attack.

Fall River County, S.D., has the fourth highest circulation for *Reader's Digest* in America.

Huron and Sioux Falls had the state's most polluted water in 1979.

Ellsworth Air Force Base (Rapid City) was the nation's largest operational base in Strategic Air Command. Ellsworth was also the country's largest B-1B base, and the nation's sole four-wing base.

Rapid City, S.D., is among the four best markets for sales of Lawrence Welk records.

Belle Fourche, S.D., was the No. 1 chief shipping point for range cattle in the U.S., during the 1890s.

Carl Grupp's Bet On It! Trivia Myths:
AMERICA'S MOST EXCITING VIDEOS

THE FOOTAGE OF TRIPLE TORNADOS
THAT WON FIRST PRIZE
FOR HARVEY W. SNEET OF RURAL ABERDEEN.
THE AWARD WAS MADE POSTHUMOUSLY.

MINUTE BY MINUTE, SOUTH DAKOTA THROUGH THE-DAY

12:01 a.m., January 1, 1863. Printer Mahlon Gore files the first homestead in U.S. history, claiming land at Elk Point, S.D. Confused, Gore fills out the application incorrectly and is later not granted the land.

12:03 a.m., September 30, 1987. The first lottery ticket is sold in South Dakota. The time draws attention to the first game, Match 3.

12:15 a.m., April 8, 1947. Wearing a football helmet coated on the inside with wet sponges, cop killer George Sitts gets 2878 volts of electricity at the penitentiary in Sioux Falls, in the state's 13th, and most recent, use of capital punishment.

1:00 a.m., October 12, 1991. Arlette Schweitzer (Aberdeen) gives birth to twin grandchildren, Chelsea and Chad Uchytil.

1:58 a.m., September 14, 1963. The first of four girls and one boy quintuplets are born to Mary Ann and Andy Fischer, in Aberdeen, S.D.

2:20 a.m., April 15, 1912. Housewife A. Hewitt (Rapid City) survives, but beer salesman Ole Thorstenson (Aberdeen) drowns when the *Titanic* sinks in the north Atlantic.

2:48 a.m., July 13, 1972. George McGovern (Mitchell) delivers his acceptance speech, as the Democratic presidential nominee, to a scant TV audience.

3 a.m., April 8, 1953. Clarence Grey Eagle (Bullhead) leads a dozen men in secretly exhuming the bones of his uncle, Chief Sitting Bull, from an abandoned North Dakota cemetery, and reburying them atop a hill in Mobridge, S.D., under 20 tons of cement.

4 a.m., June 27, 1975. AIM bombs visitor center at Mount Rushmore.

6:19 a.m., November 8, 1956. A General Mills balloon, launched from Rapid City, reaches a world record height of 14.3 miles over South Dakota.

6:27 a.m., December 15, 1890. Chief Sitting Bull (Grand River) is slain by another Native American.

7:01 a.m., November 11, 1935. The world's largest balloon, Explorer II, is launched from Rapid City and safely ascends to a record 13.7 miles.

7:32 a.m., January 22, 1943. A freakish chinook wind causes the temperature to rise a world-record 49 degrees in two minutes in Spearfish, S.D. Windows crack all over town.

8 a.m., October 14, 1899. Flanked by his Cabinet in front of the Grain Palace (Aberdeen), William McKinley becomes the first U.S. president to visit South Dakota. McKinley welcomes home American troops who fought in the Philippines. Fearing an epileptic fit in public, First Lady Ida McKinley remains aboard the presidential train.

9:50 a.m., March 6, 1934. Gangster George "Baby Face" Nelson kidnaps four women tellers as he robs the Security National Bank (Sioux Falls) of $56,000.

10:10 a.m., August 29, 1945. The *U.S.S. Dakota* drops anchor in Toyko Bay, expecting to host the signing of the surrender by the Japanese, only to learn that President Truman has made a last-minute change, choosing the *U.S.S. Missouri*, for his home state.

10:15 a.m., March 1, 1877. When he is hanged in Yankton, Jack McCall becomes the first of 13 murderers executed by capital punishment in the state,

11:45 a.m., August 17, 1962. Accepting the invitation from a little girl, President John Kennedy, in his final visit to South Dakota, dedicates the Oahe Dam (Pierre).

11:58 a.m., January 20, 1965. Pharmacist Hubert Humphrey (Huron) is sworn in as Lyndon Johnson's vice president in Washington, D.C.

High noon, October 10, 1970. Cincinnati Red Sparky Anderson (Bridgewater) becomes the first South Dakotan to play in a World Series.

12:38 p.m., August 10, 1927. President Calvin Coolidge hands artist Gutzon Borglum drills to begin carving a granite peak known as "Rushmore Mountain."

1:30 p.m., January 16, 1972. The Miami Dolphins, owned by Joe Robbie (Sisseton), begin playing in the first of five Super Bowls.

2:59 p.m., June 3, 1969. With a call for honesty in government officials, President Nixon dedicates the Mundt Library (Madison).

3 p.m., October 15, 1889. The state's first legislature begins making laws. Gov. Andrew Mellette (Watertown) surprises everyone by not making a speech.

3 p.m., August 27, 1961. With salutes from Clint Eastwood and Yogi Bear, and on a cue from Lawrence Welk (Yankton), 1,439 contestants begin digging for $55,000 buried in Manchester in KELO-Land TV's "Gold Rush of 1961."

3:40 p.m., November 2, 1889. At the White House President Benjamin Harrison signs two proclamations creating the 39th and 40th states. A newspaper covers the top halves of the documents, which are signed without the president knowing which is for either North Dakota or South Dakota.

3:59 p.m., May 9, 1900. William Jennings Bryan and Charles Towne are chosen as the Populist party candidates in Sioux Falls in the first national presidential convention held in the state.

4 p.m., March 7, 1955. Using a name borrowed from a Minneapolis TV station, Dave Dedrick (Sioux Falls) stands before a magical Time Converter, built from an old pin ball machine, and begins entertaining children as Captain 11.

4:10 p.m., August 2, 1876. Marshal Wild Bill Hickok (Deadwood), uncharacteristically playing poker with his back to the door, is shot dead by Jack McCall, from whom he had earlier won $110 in poker.

4:25 p.m., March 3, 1979. Heavy snow deflates the teflon roof of the $7.2 million DakotaDome (Vermillion).

4:32 p.m., May 5, 1923. Jockey Earle Sande (Groton), riding Zev, wins the first of three Kentucky Derby races.

5 p.m., December 11, 1943. South Dakota's worst air disaster occurs when a B-17F bomber, on a routine training flight, crashes into a hill in Todd County, killing 10 soldiers.

5:20 p.m., January 20, 1980. A South American plane carrying $18 million worth of illegal drugs lands near Selby, S.D., after flying a thousand miles, undetected through U.S. air space.

5:30 p.m., April 7, 1982. Tom Brokaw (Yankton) begins co-anchoring the NBC Nightly News..

7 p.m., January 22, 1968. Gary Owens (Mitchell) begins as one of the four regulars on *Rowan and Martin's Laugh-In*, NBC-TV.

8 p.m., July 2, 1955. Accordionist Myron Floren (Roslyn) begins performing on *The Lawrence Welk Show*, ABC-TV.

8 p.m., September 7, 1956. Bob Barker (Mission) begins an 18-year odyssey as the third host of *Truth or Consequences*.

8 p.m., March 16, 1969. Ron Holgate (Aberdeen) begins portraying Richard Lee in the first of 1,217 Broadway performances of *1776*.

8 p.m., January 26, 1979. Catherine Bach (Faith) begins portraying Daisy Duke on *The Dukes of Hazzard*, CBS-TV.

8 p.m., November 9, 1989. Skyforce begins their first basketball game, eventually losing 117-99 to the Omaha Racers, in Barnett Center (Aberdeen).

8:11 p.m., April 4, 991. A lottery ticket is issued a customer at Mr. G's (Dallas) The customer refuses the ticket, which is later purchased by employee Ionia Klein.

8:30 p.m., September 23, 1969. Julie Sommars (Aberdeen) begins portraying Jennifer Jo Drinkwater on *The Governor and J.J.*, CBS-TV.

9 p.m., September 29, 1960. *My Three Sons*, produced by Don Fedderson (Beresford), begins a 12-year run on ABC-TV.

9 p.m., February 27, 1973. Two hundred members of the American Indian Movement seize Wounded Knee, S.D. and demand that Senators Ted Kennedy and J.William Fulbright come and hear their grievances.

9 p.m., October 24, 1973. *Kojak*, with music by John Cacavas (Aberdeen), first airs on CBS.

9 p.m., September 1977. Cheryl Ladd (Huron) begins portraying Kris Munroe on *Charlie's Angels*, ABC-TV.

10:07 p.m., October 12, 1981. A Sioux Falls-made balloon named Super Chicken II completes the first non-stop flight across America.

10:30 p.m., June 9, 1972. Canyon Lake Park Dam (Rapid City) collapses and a four-foot wall of water crashes through the Black Hills, killing hundreds of tourists.

10:32 p.m., June 4, 1968. Minutes before he is assassinated in California, presidential candidate Robert Kennedy concludes his final phone conversation, with Bill Dougherty at the Cataract Hotel (Sioux Falls).

BIRTHDAYS OF FOOTNOTE FOLKS!

Birth Date: Name (Birth Place or their S.D. connection)

JANUARY

1, 1838: Gov. William Beadle (Sioux Falls)
1, 1883: Poet laureate Badger Clark (Hot Springs)
4, 1866: Horticulturalist Niels Hansen (Brookings)
6, 1912: Author Frederick Manfred (Vermillion)
7, 1933: Gov. Richard F. Kneip (Salem)
10, 1827: Preacher Henry Weston Smith (Deadwood)
10, 1865: Blind pioneer Mary Ingalls (De Smet)
11, 1888: Gov. Merrell Quentin Sharpe (Kennebec)
12, 1861: Yellowstone Trail originator Joe Parmley (Ipswich)
13, 1864: Gov. William J. Bulow (Beresford)
22, 1904: Gov. Sigurd Anderson (Webster)
23, 1946: Journalist Doug Lund (Volga)
30, 1801: Fr. Peter De Smet, and twin, Coleta (Fort Pierre)
30, 1935: Actor/Congressman Clint Roberts (Presho)
31, 1941: Gov. George S. Mickelson (Mobridge)

FEBRUARY

6, 1933: Actress Mamie Van Doren (Rowena)
6, 1940: Journalist Tom Brokaw (Webster)
7, 1867: Author Laura Ingalls Wilder (De Smet)
7, 1922: Jokester Blondie Stangland (Hetland)
13, 1923: Sen. James Abdnor (Kennebec)
14, 1948: Sportscaster Pat O'Brien (Sioux Falls)
20, 1912: Sen. Muriel Buck Humphrey Brown (Huron)
22, 1934: Tigers manager Sparky Anderson (Bridgewater)
24, 1931: Sen. James Abourezk (Wood)
28, 1905: Buffalo king Roy Houck (Gettysburg)

MARCH

1, 1954: Actress Catherine Bach (Faith)
5, 1929: Rodeo star Casey Tibbs (Mission Ridge)
7, 1906: Cowboy Hall of Famer originator Baxter Berry (Belvidere)
8, 1884: Artist Harvey Dunn (Manchester)
9, 1925: Quint father Andy Fischer (Eagle Butte)
11, 1903: Bandleader Lawrence Welk (Yankton)
15, 1926: Vikings coach Norm Van Brocklin (Parade)
19, 1848: Marshal Wyatt Earp (Deadwood)
20, 1857: State's first white child John Stanage (Fort Pierre)
22, 1924: USA Today founder Allen Neuharth (Eureka)
25, 1867: Rushmore sculptor Gutzon Borglum (Hermosa)
29, 1928: Captain 11 Dave H. Dedrick (Sioux Falls)

29, 1942: Sen. Larry Pressler (Humboldt)
31, 1834: Dakota Chief Sitting Bull (Grand River)

APRIL

2, 1939: Gov. Frank L. Farrar (Britton)
6, 1932: Lt. Gov. Bill Dougherty (Sioux Falls)
9, 1912: Rushmore sculptor Lincoln Borglum (Hermosa)
9, 1952: Rodeo champ Paul Tierney (Piedmont)
11, 1889: Inventor Tom Fawick (Sioux Falls)
12, 1827: Pioneer reporter Annie Tallent (Sioux Falls)
17, 1915: Gov. Joe F. Foss (Sioux Falls)
20, 1935: Rancher James Sutton (Pierre)
22, 1876: Author Ole E. Rolvaag (Sioux Falls)
23, 1879: Gov. Tom Berry (Mellette)
27, 1938: Former First Lady Nancy Kneip (Sioux Falls)
30, 1858: Buffalo king Scotty Philip (Philip)
30, 1902: Nobel economist Theodore Schulz (Arlington)

MAY

1, 1843: Bishop Thomas O'Gorman (Sioux Falls)
4, 1930: *Dances With Wolves* translator Doris Leader Charge (Parmalee)
5, 1836: College originator Rev. Joseph Ward (Yankton)
6, 1948: Super 8 CEO Jack Pacak (Aberdeen)
9, 1786: Capitol namesake Pierre Chouteau, Jr. (Fort Pierre)
10, 1936: Announcer Gary Owens (Mitchell)
13, 1915: Artist Oscar Howe (Joe Creek)
14, 1945: Gov. Harvey L. Wollman (Frankfort)
15, 1856: Oz author Lyman Frank Baum (Aberdeen)
17, 1838: Bishop William Hare (Black Hills)
17, 1945: Journalist Steve Hemmingsen (Sioux Falls)
21, 1909: St. Louis Cardinal Ole Ward (Herrick)
23, 1877: Pioneer Grace Ingalls (De Smet)
26, 1937: Tony winner Ron Holgate (Aberdeen)
27, 1837: Marshal Wild Bill Hickok (Deadwood)
27, 1911: Vice President Hubert H. Humphrey (Wallace)
30, 1904: Bike Rally founder Pappy Hoel (Sturgis)

JUNE

3, 1900: Sen. Karl E. Mundt (Humboldt)
8, 1933: Quint mother Mary Ann Fischer (Hecla)
10, 1866: Scientist William H. Over (Clear Lake)
16, 1928: Mayor Ed McLaughlin (Rapid City)
18, 1930: Capitol muralist Paul War Cloud (Sica Hollow)
21, 1927: Pharmacist Bill Hustead (Colman)
23, 1842: First Gov. Arthur C. Mellette (Watertown)

24, 1789: Explorer Jedediah Smith (Black Hills)
26, 1926: Sculptor Ruth Ziolkowski (Crazy Horse)
30, 1938: Olympic Gold medalist Billy Mills (Pine Ridge)

JULY

2, 1909: Gov. Ralph Herseth (Houghton)
2, 1951: Actress Cheryl Ladd (Huron)
7, 1916: Miami Dolphins owner Joe Robbie (Sisseton)
8, 1902: Guam Gov. Richard Lowe (Madison)
16, 1821: Christian Science founder Mary Baker Eddy (Lead)
19, 1922: Presidential candidate George McGovern (Avon)
23, 1903: Gov. George T. Mickelson (Selby)
26, 1796: Artist George Catlin (Missouri River)
28, 1939: Singer Sherwin Linton (Volga)

AUGUST

1, 1770: Explorer William Clark (Missouri River)
6, 1882: Gov. Harlan J. Bushfield (Miller)
8, 1901: Nobel physicist Dr. Ernest O. Lawrence (Canton)
9, 1921: Nebraska Gov. John Exon (Geddes)
13, 1930: Composer John Cacavas (Aberdeen)
18, 1774: Explorer Meriwether Lewis (Missouri River)
21, 1908: Notre Dame coach Frank Leahy (Winner)
28, 1804: Chief Struck By The Ree (Wagner)
29, 1904: Wall Drug sign originator Dorothy Hustead (Sioux Falls)

SEPTEMBER

2, 1918: Chicago Cub Len Rice (Lead)
3, 1820: Homestake miner George Hearst (Lead)
6, 1908: Sculptor Korczak Ziolkowski (Crazy Horse)
6, 1954: State Attorney General Mark Barnett (Sioux Falls)
10, 1913: Gov. Nils A. Boe (Baltic)
12, 1944: Carpenter Leonard Peltier (Pine Ridge)
13, 1939: Gov. William J. Janklow (Pierre)
14, 1860: Pulitzer winner Hamlin Garland (Aberdeen)
14, 1963: Fischer quints (Aberdeen)
19, 1906: Congressman Ben Reifel (Parmalee)
20, 1822: Chief Red Cloud, and twin, Roaring Cloud (Pine Ridge)
28, 1935: Mayor Jackson White (Sioux Falls)
29, 1923: Quint physician Dr. Jim Berbos (Aberdeen)

OCTOBER

3, 1902: Pharmacist Ted Hustead (Wall)
3, 1911: Producer Joe Floyd (Sioux Falls)
3, 1944: Mayor Tim Rich (Aberdeen)
4, 1890: Sen. Gladys Pyle (Huron)

6, 1902: Congressman E.Y. Berry (McLaughlin)
10, 1904: Passion Play actor Josef Meier (Spearfish)
12, 1991: Surrogate twins Chelsea and Chad Uchytil (Aberdeen)
15, 1991: Siamese twins Kelly and Melissa Archer (Gettysburg)
19, 1856: Historian Doane Robinson (Watertown)
23, 1895: U.S. Secretary of Ag Clinton Anderson (Centerville)
25, 1948: State Auditor Vern Larson (Vivian)
29, 1913: Electrocuted killer George Sitts (Sioux Falls)

NOVEMBER

3, 1931: State Representative Joe Barnett (Sioux Falls)
4, 1876: Buffalo nickel designer Jim Fraser (Mitchell)
5, 1919: Accordionist Myron Floren (Roslyn)
8, 1950: Actress Mary Hart (Madison)
10, 1939: AIM activist Russell Means (Pine Ridge)
11, 1887: 3M industrialist William McKnight (White)
11, 1941: First Lady Linda Mickelson (Sioux Falls)
17, 1685: Explorer Pierre la Verendrye (Fort Pierre)
18, 1922: St. Louis Cardinal Kermit Wahl (Columbia)
19, 1898: Jockey Earl Sande (Groton)
19, 1964: Thrillers Coach Eric Musselman (Rapid City)
25, 1921: Lecturer Eleanor McGovern (Woonsocket)

DECEMBER

5, 1839: Lt. Col. George Armstrong Custer (Custer)
5, 1887: Vietnam War reporter Rose Wilder Lane (De Smet)
7, 1925: State Treasurer Homer Harding (Pierre)
8, 1850: Phone co-inventor J.L.W. Zietlow (Aberdeen)
9, 1947: Sen. Thomas A. Daschle (Aberdeen)
9, 1913: Ambassador Frances Galbraith (Timber Lake)
9, 1896: Sen. Francis H. Case (Custer)
11, 1882: New York Mayor Fiorella La Guardia (Fort Sully)
12, 1889: Pioneer Caroline Quiner Ingalls (De Smet)
12, 1923: Price is Right host Bob Barker (Mission)
26, 1914: Actor Richard Widmark (Sioux Falls)
28, 1946: Congressman Tim Johnson (Canton)
31, 1815: Brig. Gen. George Meade (Sturgis)
31, 1910: Gov. Archie Gubbrud (Lincoln County)

DEATH AND DISASTER

DEATHS

Alcoholism:
- Calamity Jane (Deadwood)

Blood poisoning:
- State constitution author Joe Ward (Yankton)

Breathing granite dust:
- Sole death during 14-year carving of Mount Rushmore (Keystone)

Burned:
- Guri Shobakken (Day County), April 17, 1884, state's first known death by prairie fire
- 17 patients at insane asylum (Yankton) Feb. 15, 1899

Cancer:
- Artist Harvey Dunn (Manchester)
- Gov. Archie Gubbrud (Alcester)
- Gov. Richard Kneip (Salem)
- Marshal Seth Bullock (Deadwood)
- Rodeo rider Casey Tibbs (Fort Pierre)
- Sheepman M.J. Smiley (Belle Fourche)
- Vice President Hubert Humphrey (Doland)
- L.A. Raider Lyle Alzado (Yankton)

Car Crash:
- First South Dakota Snow Queen Dorothy Lockington (Aberdeen)

Crushed:
- University president Dr. Ed Olson (Vermillion)

Dehydration
- Unknown prospector discovered by Boy Scouts atop Coffin Butte (Badlands) in 1936

Diphtheria:
- Guide Sa-kaja-wea (McIntosh)

Drinking wood alcohol:
- Two cavalry soldiers at Fort Meade, whose comrades erected a nine-foot tombstone

Drowned:
- Ole Gustopherson (Aberdeen), aboard the Titanic
- 236 people in 1972 Rapid City flood

Enlarged Heart:
- Jay Halverson (Sioux Falls), while taking a test to be a police officer

Falling:
- Native American boy, 400-years-old, discovered at Diamond Crystal Cave in 1929
- Stagecoach driver Harvey Fellows, from a stagecoach, during a parade

Frozen:
- 112 South Dakotans in Blizzard of Jan. 12, 1888

Gall bladder infection:
- Gov. Arthur Mellette (Watertown)

Gunpowder explosion:
- Fur trader Tom Sarpy (Scenic), when he stuck a candle into a 50-lb. keg to see what was in it, 1832

Hacked:
- Yellow Doll (Deadwood)

Hanged:
- Hickok murderer Jack McCall (Deadwood)

Head Crushed in Elevator:
- John Nichols (Lead)

Heart attack:
- Bigamist/economic director Bob Martin (Pierre)
- Bishop William Hare (Sioux Falls)
- Chief Red Cloud (Black Hills)
- Gov. Tom Berry (Belvidere)
- Gov. Coe Crawford (Huron)
- Notre Dame coach Frank Leahy (Winner)
- Sen. Francis Case (Custer)
- Sen. Karl Mundt (Humboldt)
- Sen. Peter Norbeck (Redfield)
- Sculptor Korczak Ziolkowski (Crazy Horse)
- Sculptor Gutzon Borglum (Hermosa)
- Vikings coach Norm Van Brocklin (Parade)

Influenza:
- 1,939 South Dakotans during 1918 epidemic

Malaria:
- Father De Smet (Fort Pierre)

Mountain Fever:
- Dr. Henry Newton (Deadwood), grandson of Sir Isaac Newton

Parkinson's Disease:
- Artist Oscar Howe (Vermillion)

Plane crash:
- Brig. Gen. Dick Ellsworth (Ellsworth Air Force Base)
- Ship namesakes John Waldron (Fort Pierre) and Ernest Hilbert (Quinn)

Pneumonia:
- Gov. Louis Church (Huron)
- Pioneer reporter Annie Tallent (Sturgis)

Scalped:
- 6 explorers with Ezra Kind (Black Hills), June 1834
- Mail carrier Charles Nolin, namesake of Dead Man Creek (Sturgis)

Shot:
- Chief Big Foot, 146 Dakota residents and 31 soldiers at Wounded Knee, 1890
- Chief Sitting Bull (Grand River)
- Chief Spotted Tail (White River)

- Dakota Territory Secretary Gen. Stan McCook, during heated railroad hearings in Yankton, 1873
- Explorer Meriwether Lewis (Missouri River)
- FBI agents Jack Coler and Ron Williams, and resident Joe Stuntz, at Wounded Knee, 1975
- Gaming hall owner Steve Sperlin, Deadwood's sole murder, 1990: shot by a sore loser
- Gen. George Custer (Custer)
- Land Office Registrar Jesse Wherry (Vermillion), after getting in a fist fight with Gov. Jayne
- Mayor Elmer Ladd (Sturgis)
- Outlaw Arkansas James Pooler (Pierre), by vigilantes
- Preacher Henry Smith (Deadwood), en route to church services
- Soldier playing cards with Poker Alice (Sturgis): she was found not guilty
- 65 South Dakotans in Spanish-American War
- 95 sailors aboard U.S.S. South Dakota during WWII
- 210 South Dakotans during WWI

Sports:
- Harry Jordan (Sioux Falls), during football, 1902
- State Representative Tom Young, playing basketball in Pierre, 1970

Stabbed:
- Chief Crazy Horse (Rapid Creek)
- Cleveland Hall (Wessington Springs), from wounds received 22 years earlier in Civil War

Typhoid fever:
- State's Attorney General John Pyle (Huron)

GRAVELY SPEAKING

For six decades the remains of Chief Sitting Bull rested in a neglected military cemetery in North Dakota. Late one night on April 8, 1953, 13 men secretly, quietly and efficiently exhumed the bones of Sitting Bull, placed them in a shiny box and raced back home to Mobridge, S.D. By dawn's early light the coffin had been reburied on a hilltop overlooking Mobridge and the Missouri River. To prevent grave robbing by North Dakotans, the coffin was encased in one ton of concrete. A marble bust of Sitting Bull topped the grave.

The highest grave between the Rockies and the Alps is that of Dr. Valentine McGillycuddy, the only person buried atop Mt. Harney. His ashes are under a brass plaque reading "Wasicu Wakan," which translates as "holy medicine man."

Ma Nash (Fort Meade) was buried in 1879 beneath a tombstone reading "Laundress." "Ma" Nash was really a man who wore a veil and had been married several times.

Sculptor Korczak Ziolkowski is buried in a granite tomb beneath the Crazy Horse monument. A crypt door sporting a brass door knocker is inscribed: "Storyteller in Stone—May His Remains Be Left Unknown." Ziolkowski planned to have a museum representing 50 nations built over his tomb.

After Chief Crazy Horse was stabbed to death, his family buried the body in an unknown location in South Dakota.

Chief Red Cloud is buried on the Pine Ridge Indian Reservation.

The first explorer to map Wind Cave (Black Hills) was 20-year-old Alvin McDonald, who is buried at the cave's entrance.

Years after Wild Bill Hickok was buried with his favorite rifle, his coffin was exhumed and moved to higher ground in Deadwood. An undertaker opened the coffin and poked the corpse with a stick. After no soft spots were found, the rumor quickly spread that Hickok had become petrified.

The marble base of Wild Bill Hickok's first tombstone was later used by a Deadwood bakery to roll candy on.

As a prisoner being escorted from a Sturgis prison, outlaw Curly Grimes tried to escape and was shot in the back. The one-time fastest gun in the West was buried on the road where he died.

At the Deadwood cemetery in 1876 Jack "Turkey Creek" Johnson was fired upon by his two mining partners. Johnson coolly shot them dead and later paid for their funerals. Their graves had to be blasted out of the frozen ground with dynamite.

A German who died and was buried in Deadwood in 1877 was dug up, boiled down to the bones and shipped back to relatives in Europe two years later.

The Singing Bridge (Mobridge) was built over a Native American graveyard. A tremendously loud humming sound, caused by tires on the bridge framework, led some to believe it was the chanting of spirits that were angry that the bridge was built.

Ten years after horsethief Lame Johnny was hanged near Deadwood, his head was shipped to the East Coast and the shackles that bound his legs were displayed in museums in Custer and Fort Pierre.

Only the skulls and large bones of the Woodland Dakota were buried. As was the custom on the Great Plains of South Dakota, the dead were first laid on scaffolds and at a later date the largest bones were buried in the earth.

The state Capitol (Pierre) is built over a cemetery.

Chinese had a clause in their Deadwood, S.D., labor contracts that after seven years their bones were to be shipped back to China. Each grave was later opened, each bone wrapped in muslin and placed in a narrow, metal-lined box and shipped to China.

A Chinese funeral procession in Deadwood included a gong, pink ribbons worn on arms of mourners, scattering colored paper along the funeral route and pouring whiskey over the grave.

Crystal Cave Park (Black Hills) contains the remains of an early explorer.

The first seven soldiers were buried in the Black Hills National Cemetery (Sturgis) in 1948. There are now 10,000 graves.

Native Americans in South Dakota buried their dead on elevated stands.

Seven years after Preacher Henry Smith was slain, another minister decided to move the body to a newer cemetery in Deadwood. An undertaker had to open 11 graves before he found Smith's. Eight years later the body was moved a third time, to the center of the same graveyard.

The Badlands are the world's largest animal graveyard.

Internal Revenue agent Andrew Dawson has two tombstones in Mount Moriah Cemetery (Deadwood) and nobody knows which one he is buried under.

Both corneas were removed from George Sitts, the first murderer to be put to death by electrocution in South Dakota, before his remains were buried in an unmarked grave near Sioux Falls, 1947.

Buffalo king Scotty Philip (Philip) died the day after relocating the graves of his five children and selecting his own burial site along the Missouri River.

Little Bighorn survivor Commanche (Fort Meade) was stuffed by Prof. Lewis Dyche for $450. The horse's internal organs were given a military funeral.

The parents of Chief Gall buried his heart in Wounded Knee Creek, St. Elizabeth's Mission (Mobridge), and the rest of his remains in an unmarked grave.

Sheriff Seth Bullock (Belle Fourche) requested that his tombstone carry only the word "Pioneer."

Himself mauled by a bear, explorer Hugh Glass dug a grave by hand to bury an elderly Native American grandmother he had come upon while he was crawling back to civilization to Fort Kiowa, S.D., 1832.

For three decades, 1902-34, Canton, S.D., was the site of America's only insane asylum for Native Americans. One hundred nineteen bodies of inmates are still buried under the town's golf course.

Boone May was guarding the Cheyenne-Deadwood Stage when ambushed by a crook named Frank Towle. May gunned down Towle and buried him on the spot. When May learned there was a dead-or-alive reward on Towle, he dug up the corpse, chopped off the head and tossed it on the desk of the Cheyenne bounty official, who then informed May the bounty was no longer in effect.

South Dakota's Medical School buries used cadavers in a plot at Bluff View Cemetery.

Phosphorescent lights have been reported over the graves of Tinton, S.D., miners who died violent deaths.

Jack McCall (Deadwood) was buried with the rope around his neck.

Dec. 29, 1890, two cavalry squadrons and a company of artillerymen met a band led by Chief Big Foot, who was shot once in the head. New Year's Day they pried the bodies from the snow and buried them.

Seventy-two years after she died, the bones of Little Big Horn survivor Marguerite Colby Allen were removed from California and reburied in South Dakota in 1991. Allen was a Dakota infant at the 1876 battle.

Explorer Meriwether Lewis (Missouri River) was fatally shot in 1809 and was immediately buried by a companion, Major James Neelly. No autopsy was performed.

America's only original cavalry post cemetery that has not been relocated is that of Fort Meade, S.D.

TITANIC PASSENGERS:
  • Beer salesman Ole Thorstenson (Aberdeen)
  • Housewife Mrs. A. Hewitt (Rapid City)

DEATH, BUT NO TAXES
Ten percent of Rapid City was destroyed when a four-foot wall of water hit the area, 1972.

Keystone, S.D., had been incorporated only one day when two-thirds of the town was destroyed during the 1972 Rapid City flood.

The only hunter killed while hunting in South Dakota during 1990 was shot by his companion.

Eighty-six percent of South Dakota hunting accidents are from hunters being shot by other hunters.

The most common accident among Black Hills gold miners was collapsing mines.

There were 97 murders and suicides during Deadwood's first three years.

Deaths at the 1990 Black Hills Motorcycle Classic (Sturgis) included a knife-wielding Australian, a camper inhaling carbon-monoxide in a tent and nine cyclists and car drivers.

A fire that swept through Deadwood Oct. 2, 1879, wiped out so many wooden buildings that brick became the building material thereafter. Over 100 businesses burned. The fire started in a bakery on Main Street run by baker Mrs. Ellsner. Moments later 8 kegs of blasting material exploded and showered the town with fireworks. The only death was Briton Casino Jack, who was deaf and burned to death in his room. The fire caused dogs to stampede all the way to Crook City.

To ensure that evil spirits could not pass through a tiny opening, Chinese laborers spread paper with tiny holes in them along funeral routes in Deadwood in the 1880s.

When the husband of Poker Alice died at their Sturgis ranch, Alice guarded the body from wolves as she journeyed three days in mid-winter to reach town. She sold her wedding ring to pay for his coffin.

A Crow prostitute being burned at the stake was the first person killed by Sitting Bull (Grand River). Sitting Bull, 17, shot her in the back with an arrow to keep her from suffering.

The state's first known case of arsenic poisoning occurred during August 1804 when explorer Meriwether Lewis nearly died of it near Elk Point, S.D.

Guide Hugh Glass was left for dead after a grizzly bear attacked him in South Dakota near the Missouri River. Glass made his way 170 miles across the plains of South Dakota. After he found the men who left him, he forgave them. Glass' life was later celebrated in verse and song.

Preacher Smith (Deadwood) was the first minister killed by Native Americans in the Black Hills.

Tom Brokaw (Yankton) appeared to choke up when reporting on TV the death of Princess Grace, but the journalist later insisted it was only a piece of popcorn lodged in his throat.

Calamity Jane (Deadwood) recited out loud at funerals the only prayer she knew, "Now I Lay Me Down to Sleep."

The largest funeral ever held in Deadwood was Calamity Jane's in 1903.

To keep souvenir hunters from snipping off souvenir locks of Calamity Jane's hair, the undertaker put a wire cage over the head of the corpse. Jane was laid out holding two six-shooters, but the undertaker removed the guns before burial.

In Hot Springs a vigilante group once hanged a known horse thief because they found a tree they couldn't resist.

Among Calamity Jane's pallbearers was George Leenan, the "best bartender in the Black Hills."

The Thoen Stone Monument (Spearfish) commemorates the Ezra Kind party's ill-fated discovery of gold in 1834. Native Americans killed the entire party, and their discovery was kept secret. In 1932 it was discovered that Kind had etched his discovery on a nearby rock.

After safely driving a stagecoach a world-record 300,000 miles, Harvey Fellows (Deadwood) died years later getting down from a flatbed truck carrying his Concord stagecoach during a Days of '76 Parade in 1929.

Cholera was introduced to South Dakotans by ill tourists arriving by steamboat in 1848. Hundreds of Dakota died.

When Sen. Francis Case died of a heart attack in the middle of his 1962 reelection campaign, it took the Republican Central Committee 20 ballots to select another candidate, Joe Bottum.

Murderer James Bell was lynched April 18, 1855, in Hughes County by a mob that tied his noose to a tall ladder that was leaned against the county flag pole.

When rampant disease caused death among hundreds of South Dakota pioneers, families would often lay their dead by the road so neighbors could take them to the cemeteries.

One South Dakota pioneer family ended up storing their dead little girl in a white casket in the attic until heavy snows melted and the ground softened in the spring.

Woodrow Nelson (Watertown), 73, dropped dead of a heart attack one day after South Dakota lottery officials notified him they had released the wrong numbers and he had not won $12 million, after all. His widow, Lois, later received $1,095 for the lottery ticket.

Seventeen people were murdered by the 13 men executed by capital punishment in South Dakota.

WILD BILL'S DEATH

Who's who in the August 2, 1876, murder of Wild Bill Hickok:

Gamblers playing poker: Wild Bill Hickok, Carl Mann, Frank Massie, Charles Rich

Murderer: Jack McCall

Saloon No. 10 owner: Carl Mann

Arresting sheriff: Isaac Brown

Dealer of the dead man's hand of two aces and two eights: Charles Rich

Defense attorney: Judge Miller

Trial judge: Judge Kuykendall

Prosecutor: Colonel May

Wild Bill Hickok (Deadwood) carried two ivory-handled pistols in his belt, not a holster. Even though shot in the head, Hickok was able to draw his Smith & Wesson .32-caliber pistol.

Wild Bill Hickok once gunned down nine people during a robbery. Three were innocent bystanders.

While a crowd was debating whether or not to hang Jack McCall for Hickok's murder, one man dropped dead of drinking poor whiskey.

Displayed in the Adams Museum (Deadwood) are the pipe Wild Bill Hickok was smoking when he was shot, a stone found in his boot, and a leaf from his grave.

Gunslinger Wild Bill Hickok never wore a holster. He kept his two ivory-handled .44 caliber pistols in his belt, drawing them crosswise. Hickok was carrying a Smith & Wesson .32-caliber pistol when slain in 1876.

Hickok had been married less than five months to circus owner Agnes Lake before being killed in Deadwood.

Hickok owed a $50 drink tab to Saloon No. 10 at the time of his murder. Hickok's possessions were auctioned off to pay for his funeral.

SITTING BULL'S DEATH

Sitting Bull was shot in the back, on the left side. Sitting Bull's body was transported to Fort Yates under a pile of wood on a supply wagon. Seven members of Sitting Bull's bodyguards were also slain and buried in a common grave by the Rev. T.L. Riggs and some Christian Native Americans. The four slain police were buried in a Catholic cemetery. Sitting Bull was not a Catholic or a Christian so soldiers buried him, without ceremony, in a rough wooden box in a corner of the cemetery at Fort Yates. When rumors spread that Sitting Bull's bones had been sold to souvenir hunters, his grave was opened. His skeleton was found intact. When the fort was abandoned, all graves, except Sitting Bull's, were moved.

MEN WHO SECRETLY REMOVED SITTING BULL'S REMAINS FROM NORTH DAKOTA TO MOBRIDGE, S.D.,1953:
- Dick Andrews
- Martin Beffart
- Ray Claymore
- Marvin Dietrich
- Charles Grey Eagle
- Dan Heupel
- Alvin Heyd
- Louis Huber
- Slim Lindgrin
- Al Miles
- Charles Spencer
- Walter Tuntland
- George Walters

"QUOTE (AND UNQUOTE)"

"I do not choose to run for president in 1928." — **Calvin Coolidge, while vacationing in the Black Hills, 1927.**

"That's the first time I've ever literally floored a listener." — **Harry Truman, when a reporter fell backwards while photographing Truman eating a pheasant sandwich at the train depot in Aberdeen, 1944.**

"They were born together — they are one and I will make them twins." — **Benjamin Harrison, after shuffling the proclamations creating North Dakota and South Dakota, so no one would know for sure which came first, 1889. Not even he knew.**

"I suppose____ Edmunds better be appointed Governor of Dakota. Get the name and send it with this, to the Secretary of State." — **Abraham Lincoln, in a memo to his Secretary of Interior on the casual appointment of Newton Edmunds, a clerk whose first name the president did not even know, 1863.**

"If you didn't know you were vice president 30 days ago, maybe you're too stupid to be vice president." — **Lyndon Johnson, to Hubert Humphrey (Huron), 1964.**

"Until ten minutes ago, I had no conception of its magnitude, its permanent beauty and its importance." — **Franklin Roosevelt, upon seeing Mount Rushmore for the first time, 1936.**

"In our public discussions we sorely need a kind of honesty that has often been lacking...the honesty of straight talk." — **Richard Nixon, in dedicating the Mundt Library (Madison), 1969.**

"The key to this century is power—power on the farm, as well as the factory—power in the country as well as the city." — **John Kennedy, upon dedicating the Oahe Dam, 1962.**

"I wanted those Britishers to see my typical ideal American." — **Teddy Roosevelt, on why he sent Sheriff Seth Bullock (Deadwood), as his emissary to Great Britain.**

"The Black Hills of South Dakota are the best damn place in the world to live." — **Dwight Eisenhower, in Lakota, as he was inducted into the Singing Tribe of Wahoo (Custer), 1953.**

"He never lays down his arms in the presence of an enemy." — **William McKinley, in Aberdeen, to First South Dakota Regiment troops returning from war, 1900.**

"Jack, don't forget to water the tree." — **George Bush, to Mayor Jackson White (Sioux Falls), at an arbor ceremony at Terrace Park.**

"We're not going to pull the rug out from under them while they're struggling to get on their feet." — **Ronald Reagan, promising to help farmers in Sioux Falls, despite having policies disastrous to agriculture.**

"When he first visited me in the Oval Office, I felt that he should have served there." — **Jimmy Carter, at the funeral of Hubert Humphrey (Doland).**

"NEARLY THE PREZ"

"We'll talk to you a little later on. Can we do that, when we know here? All right, we'll give you a ring later on. Bye, bye Bill." — **Robert Kennedy, in his final phone conversation, to Bill Dougherty (Sioux Falls), June 4, 1968. Kennedy, awaiting results of California's presidential primary, would be slain an hour later.**

"I am one thousand percent for Tom Eagleton, and I have no intention of dropping him from the ticket." — **Presidential candidate George McGovern (Mitchell), July 26, 1972, right before he dumped Eagleton.**

"What separates a good nation, from a great nation, is the way it treats its poor, its elderly and its disabled citizens." — **Hubert Humphrey (Huron).**

"Stay out of bed as long as you can. Ninety percent of all the people die in bed." — **Advice to Hubert Humphrey, from his father.**

"Gene really doesn't want to be president, and I do." — **McGovern, on what separated his presidential candidacy from that of Gene McCarthy, 1968.**

"SCIENTIFICALLY SPEAKING"

"Our storage capacities are being taxed to their maximum." — **Anatomy Department Chairperson Wesley Parke, when the University of South Dakota discovered they had an over-abundance of cadavers and needed to start charging an acceptance fee of $300, 1981.**

"A very old individual who obviously led a long and perilous life." — **Black Hills Institute of Geological Research, in describing the world's largest Tyrannosaurus rex remains, discovered in Faith, S.D., in 1990.**

"Hey, get your big feet out of the way!" — **Captain Albert Stevens, as his copilot abandoned the rapidly falling world-record balloon launched over Rapid City, 1934.**

"Deeply concerned about the need and poverty in the world, and engaged in finding ways out of underdevelopment." — **Royal Swedish**

Academy, when announcing why Ted Schulz (Arlington) was awarded the Nobel Prize in Economics, October 17, 1979.

"When I was in school nobody even thought of going to Mars." — **NASA engineer Don Mlady (Sioux Falls), who coordinated the scientists who launched the 1976 Viking missions.**

"Region deserves better name." — *National Geographic*, **about the Badlands, 1947.**

"The entire region seems void of all wild animal life." — **Official Badlands game survey, 1919.**

"I am satisfied that gold in satisfactory quantities can be obtained in the Black Hills." — **Gen. Custer, when prospector Horatio Ross discovered gold, 1874.**

"The climate in the Black Hills is so healthy that you have to kill a man to start a cemetery." — **Pioneer George Aryes (Deadwood).**

"Get away from it." — **Advice from state snake eradicator Ed Cronk (Philip) on what to do when encountering a live rattle snake.**

"GOLD: The Land of Promise. Glittering Treasure found at last, a Belt of Gold Territory 30 miles wide." — **1876 headline in Chicago newspaper, about the Black Hills.**

"I'd give a lot to know where I picked that up." — **Troy Palmer (Hill City), when an auto mechanic discovered a big chunk of gold in Palmer's car chassis, 1956.**

"The houses are filled with bed-bugs, fleas and rats." — **An inspector to Fort Sully (Pierre), whose logs were eventually used for steamboat fuel.**

"FRIENDLY FACES AND PLACES"

"Piss on North Dakota." — **Response by one of the 13 Mobridge, S.D., men who removed Sitting Bull's remains from North Dakota in the dead of night, 1953.**

"Beer." — **Original beverage suggestion for naming community of Tea.**

"Call it Dante's Inferno, for all I care." — **H.T. Mayo, storeowner who suggested Dante, S.D., be named after his favorite author.**

"We'll call the damn thing 'Rushmore'." — **Prospector Bill Challis, in response to a question by New York attorney Charles E. Rushmore as to the name of an unnamed granite mountain in the Black Hills, 1885.**

"A thousand years from now and this may be another enigma like the Sphinx or the heads on Easter Island." — **Sculptor Lincoln Borglum**

(Hermosa) on why the Hall of Records should be completed at Mount Rushmore.

"Î have reached the hunter's highest round of fame." — **George Custer, after shooting a bear in South Dakota, 1874.**

"South Dakota, where men are men and steaks are three inches thick." — *Time* **Magazine, 1945.**

"I lied. I lied to you. I lied to my family. I lied to a lot of people for a lot of years when I said I didn't use steroids." — **L.A. Raider Lyle Alzado (Yankton), who started taking steroids while attending college in South Dakota.**

"A gambler, part-time gunman and full-time liar who worked in all three professions." — **Watson Parker, in a book about Wild Bill Hickok.**

"A good horse will last, but I can't get more than a couple years out of a pickup." — **Badlands rancher quoted in** *National Geographic*, **1981.**

"If you can see an Indian up there, that's fine." — **Sculptor Lincoln Borglum (Hermosa), in response to an Italian film crew's claim in 1977 that shadow formations caused a fifth face, that of a Native American, to appear on Mount Rushmore.**

"I felt a carved needle would look too much like a totem pole." — **Sculptor Gutzon Borglum (Hermosa), on why he selected Mount Rushmore, over the Needles.**

"People who do not take their hometown paper are brain dead anyway, and their passing away has no news value." — **A West River publisher who refused to publish obituaries of non-subscribers.**

"I never graduated from anything." — **Laura Ingalls Wilder, who at age 15 began teaching school for three years in De Smet.**

"I was the last guy on the totem pole with the Lakers. Magic made me feel as though I was as important as everybody else." — **Skyforce coach Kevin McKenna (Sioux Falls), who played 243 NBA games over six seasons on four teams.**

"Judging from the delegation of boozy individuals around town, one would suppose that a delegation of Black Hillers had arrived." — **Laramie** *Daily Sentinel*, **May 1876.**

"Miss Anthony is a tiresome old lady." — **Irene Cushman, after hearing suffragist Susan B. Anthony speak in Deadwood in 1890.**

"I was considered the most reckless and daring rider and one of the best shots in the western country. Why don't the sons of bitches leave me alone and let me go to hell my own route?" — **Calamity Jane, when someone tried to tame her drinking.**

"My life has been involved in this ever since I came out here. I wouldn't know what else to do." — **Ruth Ziolkowski, who, since the death of her husband in 1982, instructs seven of her 10 children in the carving of Crazy Horse.**

"CRIMES AND MISDEMEANORS"

"A nude body displayed in public was not only bad taste but would have a bad effect on the community's moral values." — **One commentary which forced the city of Sioux Falls to have a nude statue of Michelangelo's David face away from traffic, and be surrounded by trees, 1972.**

"'Take that, damn you." — **Jack McCall, as he fatally shot Marshal Wild Bill Hickok (Deadwood), 1876.**

"It came down after the second play after the Rams got the kickoff." — **Witness Tom Brown (Hoven) on seeing a plane with $18 million worth of marijuana land outside town on Super Bowl Sunday, 1980.**

"The keys to your cell are in your mouth." — **Judge Andrew Brogue, to imprisoned pregnant witness Joanna LeDeaux, who had her baby in jail because she refused to testify at the Leonard Peltier trial in Rapid City.**

"Mount Rushmore is the most beautiful, stolen mountain in America." — **CBS Sportscaster Pat O'Brien (Sioux Falls).**

"Them oily cowards. If it's the last thing I do, I'm gonna live long enough to kill the both of 'em." — **Hugh Glass, who despite a ripped up back and broken right leg, crawled 200 miles through hostile country, and later hunted down—but did not kill—two companions who abandoned him in the wilderness of South Dakota.**

"He was the most deadly shot with rifle and pistols that ever lived." — **Buffalo Bill Cody, about Wild Bill Hickok.**

"I shot him before my tears could blind me." — **Army scout Solomon Two Stars (Fort Sisseton), after shooting a fellow Native American who had murdered an entire family.**

"Remember Custer and the Little Bighorn." — **Shouts by soldiers as they gunned down Native Americans at Wounded Knee, Dec. 29, 1890.**

"I knew we were never going to get out unless somebody in the room took action." — **Senior Christopher Ericks (Rapid City) after disarming a fellow student who fired 10 shots and held 22 fellow students hostage in school, 1991.**

"If I go down there's going to be a lot of grease spots in Britton." — **Comment the FBI attributed to Britton banker Robert Marx, found guilty on eight counts of bank fraud, 1991.**

"THAT'S ENTERTAINMENT"

"Her hope is to teach English and give piano and voice lessons." — **Sioux Falls *Argus Leader*, about 1970 Miss South Dakota, Mary Hart.**

"Ladies and gentlemen, next we have a new member in our band, Alvin Ashby, from Evansville, Indiana. Alvin, step right up here and tell the people who you are, and where you come from." — **Lawrence Welk (Yankton), during a live TV broadcast.**

"Who threw that?" — **Elvis Presley, whose collarbone was hit by a frisbee tossed on stage during his final South Dakota concert, in Sioux Falls, 1977.**

"Lars: 'Ole, you better keep your window shades down. Last night I valked by your house and you vas chasing Lena around da bed.' Ole laughed, and said: 'Da yoke's on you! I vasn't even HOME last night!'" — **Favorite joke of Red Stangland (Sioux Falls), who has written 16 Norwegian joke books since 1973.**

"To draw or not to draw attention to one's anatomy? Isn't that the question?" — **Mary Hart (Sioux Falls).**

"Don't try to hum along." — **Advice to Tom Brokaw (Yankton) from his three daughters, when they learned he would host a live opera anniversary in 1991.**

"Personnel must be conservative and conduct in keeping with religious productions." — **Job description for applying to be in Passion Play (Spearfish).**

"All the good Moslems go to Mecca and all the good cyclists come to Sturgis." — **Malcolm Forbes, while at the Black Hills Classic Cycle Rally (Sturgis).**

"Three hundred moccasins packed with gumbo and horseshit that we scraped for days." — ***Dances With Wolves* Technical Advisor Cathy Smith, about a South Dakota thunderstorm pelting 150 movie extras.**

"Never step on a white line." — **Sparky Anderson (Bridgewater), on a superstition he has successfully employed while winning 100 baseball games in two national leagues.**

"I wish I knew how to control The New York Times best-seller list, because if I did, my book would still be on it." — ***USA Today* founder Allen H. Neuharth (Eureka).**

"I got myself really drunk one night and had my husband film it. When I saw myself later, I was appalled and fascinated. One never sees oneself the same way other people do." — **Cheryl Ladd (Huron), on how she readied herself for the role of an alcoholic nurse.**

"Best company on a desert island, best company on a dessert, best company, best. Whew!!!!" — *Time's* **comments, June 9, 1941, for painting of a nude woman by Harvey Dunn (Manchester).**

"This is Dan Rather, reporting from Sioux Falls, South Dakota." — **Dan Rather, in a 1986 broadcast closing that bothered many residents. Most local viewers felt the city was so well-known that the name of the state didn't need to be mentioned.**

"They call me lucky little rich boy, got everything, He's the son of a Cotton King." — **Sung by country western legend Sherwin Linton (Watertown), in his No. 1 hit "Cotton King," which has sold over 200,000 copies since first released in 1966.**

"If you want to put your state on the map, make sure that Kevin Costner films a movie in your state." — **Super 8 President Jack Pacak (Aberdeen), on the boom his motels are enjoying from** *Dances With Wolves* **publicity.**

"It really doesn't matter because they don't know where either state is located anyway." — **Watertown deejay Jim Aesoph, when East and West Coast residents, whom he randomly calls live on the air, confuse North Dakota and South Dakota.**

"I don't like the way Teddy Roosevelt is looking at me." — **Cary Grant, in Hitchcock's** *North by Northwest,* **the first motion picture filmed on location at Mount Rushmore.**

"I would like to see all animals out of entertainment." — **Emcee Bob Barker (Mission).**

"A wiry imp with an athletic walk, a lopsided grin and a supremely self-confident air." — *Time,* **about Allen Neuharth.**

"I hope the film shows young people on our reservation, where self-esteem is low, that you have to do the best you can and be proud of yourself." — *Dances With Wolves* **dialect coach, Doris Leader Change (Rosebud).**

"The majority of owners I have met are like Joe Robbie of Miami, real devotees, men and women to whom the building of a respectable team becomes a passion, and they add luster to the sporting scene." — **James A. Michener, about the Sisseton-native.**

"I don't think there is anything that can stop me." — **Allen Neuharth.**

"It was the saddest hour I have experienced in America." — **Author Ole Rolvaag (Elk Point), upon learning his novels weren't selling up to expectations.**

"It has been a long time since I have read a novel as distasteful, absurdly violent, and luridly melodramatic." — **Critic Victor Haas, about *King of Spades*, by Frederick Manfred (Vermillion). The novel is about a Black Hills miner who unknowingly falls in love with his own mother.**

"These people are so all-noble they're as implausible as the savages in old Westerns." — ***People* Magazine, in reviewing the Native Americans in *Dances With Wolves*, filmed in South Dakota.**

"Covering a drowning in Minnesota taught me one very important lesson: always ask one more question." — **KELO-Land's Steve Hemmingsen (Sioux Falls), whose resourcefulness as a young deejay covering a tragedy, earned him national Associated Press honors.**

"It's surprising to me that kids at that age think we go around in chauffeured limousines." — **First Lady Linda Mickelson (Sioux Falls), who drives herself, reacting to a common response of children.**

"I think women are wonderful, and we should have a woman president and a plurality of women in our legislature." — **Author Frederick Manfred (Vermillion).**

"I'm convinced I'm the most envied man on earth: I get to play Santa Claus 12 months a year." — **Dave Dedrick (Sioux Falls), whose celebrity as Captain 11 has given pleasure to three generations of children.**

"You have to play what the people understand." — **Lawrence Welk.**

"He's a stubborn German and I'm an equally stubborn Norwegian." — **Accordionist Myron Floren (Roslyn), about Lawrence Welk.**

"Nobody got shot yesterday or last night. It's getting dull." — ***Black Hills Daily Times*, May 4, 1878.**

"Everybody knows the sky's the limit." — **KTWB station owner Lee Axdahl, when 100 listeners showed up to hear a free Randy Travis concert at Howard Wood Field on April Fool's Day, 1991. All fans got for the station's joke was a bottle of pop.**

"Their image of South Dakota is that we probably, barely have running water and shoes on our feet." — **Mary Hart, about her friends.**

"NATIVE AMERICANISMS"

"Does Federal Express come to the reservation?" — **Question put to college professor Doris Leader Charge (Parmalee), by Hollywood** agents who wanted to send her the script for *Dances With Wolves*, so she could translate it into Lakota.

"This is a good day to die." — **Crazy Horse (Moreau River), as he rode unarmed into the Battle of Little Bighorn.**

"Caress a mountain so that the white man will know the red man had great heroes, too." — **Chief Henry Standing Bear, to sculptor Korczak Ziolkowski (Crazy Horse), in 1939.**

"I used to party with him. I used to sleep at his house." — **AIM activist Russell Means (Pine Ridge), of Gov. Bill Janklow.**

"When the white man found gold in the Black Hills, it was something like a modern corporation striking oil under the floor of the Vatican." — *National Geographic*, **1981.**

"I will not have my people robbed." — **Chief Sitting Bull (Grand River), as the government took his lands in South Dakota.**

"Indian art can compete with any art in the world." — **Oscar Howe (Joe Creek).**

"My lands are where my dead are buried." — **Chief Crazy Horse.**

"No newspaperman as much as said hello to me." — **Billy Mills (Pine Ridge), after winning a Gold Medal on a soggy, 10,000 meter track during the 1964 Olympics in Japan.**

"There are no Indians left but me." — **Chief Sitting Bull, when other chiefs signed another treaty giving more of South Dakota to the whites.**

"The Sioux will kill you." — **Sitting Bull, of a warning he believed was said to him by a bird, just days before the Chief was killed by a fellow Native American.**

"One great robe." — **An anonymous Dakotan, about the 75 million buffalo that once roamed through South Dakota.**

"It's towns in rural Mississippi, or Indian Reservations in South Dakota, or low income neighborhoods in the inner city that most doctors simply don't want to go to." — **Mike Wallace, on "60 Minutes".**

"While D.C.'s boys must have felt a little like Custer did back in 1873, we stood proud. When the race was over, we were fifth as a team and two of our runners had infiltrated the Indian superiority of this day, and finished in the top 15." — **Basketball coach Don Greenfield (Doland), giving comments which got him suspended from the bench in 1991.**

"You shall have the land as long as the waters run and the grass grows green." — **Governmental statement, during signing of 1868** later gold was discovered, and the Native Americans were kicked out.

"GOVERNMENT AT WORK"

"I can't send a white-haired old lady to prison." — **Gov. Bulow, on why he pardoned 75-year-old gambler Poker Alice (Sturgis).**

"Best fatman water skier in South Dakota." — **Gov. Bill Janklow, describing himself.**

"South Dakota is fiftieth in everything: quality of life, services, you name it. My slogan is 'when you wake up in South Dakota, you're still in South Dakota'." — **Minnesota Gov. Rudy Perpich, in a feud with South Dakota Gov. Bill Janklow.**

"I've got one 'X', and the oil company has two. They're the 'double-cross' boys." — **Nebraska Sen. James Exon (Lake Andes), when people confuse his last name with the Exxon oil company.**

"If he had been a white man, there's no question he would have gotten the chair." —**Gov. Frank Farrar, when he commuted the death sentence of murderer Thomas White Hawk in 1969.**

"The only contest I ever lost was to an elderly grandmother." — **Gov. Richard Kneip, when TV viewers selected a grandmother, over him, to return as guest host of NBC's "Saturday Night Live."**

"We absolutely do not approve of the party that was held in our house Nov. 28." — **Gov. George Mickelson, April 13, 1990, with wife, Linda, at his side.**

"When I sell the movie rights I will pick someone with a pimple on his nose to play Pressler." — **Marilyn Bill, a surgeon's wife who helped set up the FBI ABSCAM sting in which Sen. Larry Pressler refused the bribe.**

"Wild Bill is ours. He's here to stay. And possession is nine points of the law." — **Mayor R.L. Ewing (Deadwood) when Abilene, Kans., wanted to exhume and move the grave of gunslinger Wild Bill Hickok.**

"Noise that would annoy the sensibilities of an ordinary person, is banned." — **Ordinance passed by Brookings City Council, September 1991.**

"Here is the state of South Dakota. We reflect a little more deeply and celebrate a little more proudly." — **Gov. George S. Mickelson, at Mount Rushmore.**

"I need to untangle these official poles or it will be my official ass." — **Secret Service agent, as he readied fishing tackle for use by President Bush in the Black Hills, 1991.**

"Minnesota's government has strangled the opportunity to prosper." — **Bill Janklow, who worked in Minnesota following his term as South Dakota governor.**

"Governor Carlson is Dakota-izing Minnesota." — **Ex-Minnesota Gov. Perpich, about his successor.**

"It was spent to save the American system of government." — **Sen. Harlan Bushfield (Miller), when asked by the press what became of $17,000 that mysteriously disappeared after being left over from his 1940 campaign.**

"We should consider electing persons in the prime of their lives rather than in the twilight of his or her career." — **Sen. Larry Pressler, at the onset of his four-month presidential campaign, 1979.**

"Excuse me, I think I'll go home and get a clean handkerchief." — **Rev. Rolf Lium (Hermosa) when informed that U.S. President Coolidge would be worshipping within minutes at his church, 1927. The Secret Service supplied a fresh handkerchief.**

"It's not very gentlemanly." — **Small Business Association Administrator A.Vernon Weaver, upon learning Gov. Bill Janklow had legally taped their phone conversations.**

"Before I only had to worry about streetlights and barking dogs." — **Deadwood Mayor Bruce Oberlander, who had to increase the town's police force from five to eight after legalized gambling hit town in 1989.**

"The automobile is a plaything for idle minds and hands. It is also a very successful contrivance for killing people." — **South Dakota gubernatorial candidate Abe Osdel, in 1892.**

"FAMILIES"

"My belly was so hard in those days my wife could dance on my stomach with high-heeled shoes." — **Driller Hap Anderson, at the golden anniversary of Mount Rushmore, 1991.**

"He was a son-of-a-bitch and an angel." — **Anne Ziolkowski, daughter of the late Crazy Horse sculptor, about her dad.**

"She just needed to borrow my uterus." — **Surrogate Grandmother Arlette Schweitzer (Aberdeen), about daughter, Christa.**

"I don't see why I should pick up with you since it doesn't look like you're going to amount to anything." — **Miss South Dakota Meredith Auld, in a note to journalist Tom Brokaw, in their school days.**

"The communications gap grew wider. I would ask a question, get a short answer, then silence." — **Loretta Neuharth, ex-first wife of USA Today founder Al Neuharth (Eureka).**

"He's charming, rich, challenging, and inspiring—a great catch, as long as you don't mind riding a roller coaster with a snake." — **Sen. Lori Neuharth, ex-second wife of *USA Today* founder Allen H. Neuharth (Eureka).**

"This is a very spiritual place. I feel Dad is here to protect and guide me. And I feel Crazy Horse is with him." — **Casimir Ziolkowski (Crazy Horse).**

"When Ray came home and told me he had purchased the Padres, I said it was nice that we were getting into a religious thing." — **Joan Kroc (Rapid City), the McDonald's hamburger heiress, upon learning her husband bought a San Diego baseball team.**

"I made up my mind when the babies were born that they were going to grow up in a normal family atmosphere, and to do that means a lot of work." — **Quint mother Mary Ann Fischer (Aberdeen).**

"Christmas and birthdays is about the only time I see them." — **Andrew Fischer (Aberdeen), who divorced his wife when their quints were 17.**

"Quintini." — **A double martini drink featuring four olives and an onion, created by an Aberdeen bartender following birth of the Fischer Quints.**

"FINAL EXIT"

"We will go north and fight until not a white man is left." — **Last words of Crazy Horse (Moreau River).**

"Gone to Crook City to preach, and if God is willing, will be back at 3 o'clock." — **Last words of Preacher Smith (Deadwood).**

"I am not going." — **Last words of Sitting Bull (Grand River).**

"It's all in the draw." — **Last words of Poker Alice (Sturgis).**

"Bury me next to Bill." — **Last words of stagecoach driver Calamity Jane (Deadwood) .**

"I am hit." — **Last words over the walkie talkie by FBI Agent Ron Williams, slain at Pine Ridge.**

"In all my experience, this is the first time the authorities ever helped me escape prison." — **Last words of cop killer George Sitts, executed in Sioux Falls, 1947.**

"You must work on the mountain—but slowly—so you do it right." — **Last words of sculptor Korczak Ziolkowski (Crazy Horse).**

"Oh, God." — **Last words of Jack McCall, hanged in Yankton, S.D., for murder of Wild Bill Hickok.**

SIGNS OF THE TIMES

"I wish I had legs like Mary Hart." — **Message on a bib worn by a teddy bear in dressing room of Mary Hart (Sioux Falls).**

"I'd rather be in North Dakota." — **Mount Rushmore's Teddy Roosevelt on billboards rented throughout South Dakota by the North Dakota Department of Tourism, 1982.**

"Get a soda/Get a beer/Turn next corner/Just as near/To Highway 16 and 14/Free ice water/Wall Drug/" — **Original three-foot-long Wall Drug (Wall) signs advertising free ice water, July 1936.**

"Until some divine authority determines a better method, we will continue to call this the approximate center." — **Message on official state historical marker overlooking center of North America in Hughes County.**

"+ S" — **Symbol painted on houses that had been checked for bodies and were safe for occupancy following Rapid City flood, 1972.**

"Hi, Nixon" — **Message disced into his fields by farmer Ival Meyers (Wentworth), to welcome the president. Nixon saw the greeting as he helicoptered from Sioux Falls to Madison, 1969.**

"Slow: Men at Work." — **Sign posted by Korczak Ziolkowski on Crazy Horse, S.D., mountain, 1960s.**

"Great Faces. Great Places." — **Message on South Dakota license plates.**

"No dogs or Indians allowed." — **Sign seen in Scenic, S.D., in 1980.**

"Bad whiskey. Gored by buffalo. Eating 14 hard boiled eggs. Hanged. Run over by stagecoach. God knows. Struck by bar glass. Broken thumb." — **Official causes of death posted for some of the folks buried in Mt. Moriah Cemetery (Deadwood).**

"You ain't seen nuthin' yet." — **Message on official state historical marker overlooking Slim Butte.**

"G.C. U.S. 74" — **Graffiti carved by Gen. George Custer on a granite rock in the Black Hills, 1874.**

"South Dakota honors her sons and daughters who served their country in time of war." — **Inscription on Flaming Fountain (Pierre), August 1967.**

"Here the West begins." — **Fairgrounds (Huron).**

"Don't snore loudly. If you must drink share the bottle. Forbidden topics of discussion are stagecoach robberies and Indian uprisings." — **Stagecoach rules posted throughout South Dakota during 1870s.**

"Dancing and records." — **Hobbies listed by Tom Brokaw in his 1957 Yankton high school yearbook.**

"Thistle while you work" and "Pet tumbleweeds, complete with leashes." — **Bumper stickers seen in Mobridge, S.D., when town was invaded by car-size tumbleweeds, 1989.**

"Aberdeen: Home of the Fischer Quints." — **Billboard greeting once welcoming travelers.**

"In Prosperity, Be Joyful." — **Motto of world's only Grain Palace, which lasted nine years until burning in Aberdeen.**

"See South Dakota Last." — **American Indian Movement (AIM) campaign ad, 1970s.**

"McPaper of fast-food journalism." — **Label by competition when Allen Neuharth unveiled *USA Today*, 1982.**

'A1ANA2" — **License plate of Lawrence Welk (Yankton).**

"Here lie the bodies of Allen, Curry, and Hall. Like other horse thieves they had their rise, decline and fall." — **Epitaph atop Hangman's Hill (Rapid City), from triple executions on June 21, 1887. Actually, short nooses caused the three to die of strangulation.**

"The first son-of-a-bitch who disturbs our stakes is liable to be cannibalized immediately thereafter." — **Sign by gold mine in Rochford, signed by prospectors C.B. Strong and A.B. Striker, 1878.**

"Death and the Management of the Dying Patient." — **Title of Hill City, S.D., workshop being attended by 400 physicians, clergy and social workers the day a 1972 flood killed several hundred people in nearby Rapid City.**

"Phoenix-like it will rise from its ashes with augmented stateliness and beauty." — **Postcards sent by students to their families and friends after the only building composing Dakota State College burned to the ground, in 1886.**

"Pard we will meet again in the happy hunting ground to part no more." — **Message on tombstone of Wild Bill Hickok (Deadwood).**

"Got all the gold we could carry. Our ponies all got by Indians. Have lost my gun and nothing to eat and Indians hunting me." — **Explorer Ezra Kind, 1834, on tablet discovered in 1887 in Black Hills by Louis Thoen.**

"Come home, America." — **Theme of McGovern's 1972 presidential campaign.**

"It takes a semi-load of corn to get your picture taken with Reagan." — **Sign appearing on farm truck outside Arena (Sioux Falls) where** thousand-dollar donors got their photo taken with the President, 1986.

"Hurry Back, Harvey." — **Button worn by staff of Gov. Harvey Wollman, who lost the 1978 primary. He never did make it back.**

"You have a choice, Sherwin Linton for President." — **Bumper stickers distributed by the country western singer from Watertown.**

"Congratulations on your assignment to Ellsworth AFB. Once you find out where Ellsworth is located, images of snow and cold will probably come to mind." — **From manual given new residents of Ellsworth Air Force Base (Rapid City), 1991.**

GOVERNMENT

OLD GLORY
The first American flag flown in Deadwood, S.D., on July 4, 1876, was sewn from underwear.

The first American flag flown at Fort Sod (Sioux Falls) was made from flannel shirts.

The American flag flown highest over the United States, 13.7 miles, was aboard the Explorer II balloon launched from Rapid City in 1935, a record that held 22 years.

America's largest flag was unveiled from Mount Rushmore by President Bush in 1991. The 120-by-80-foot flag, sewn by Aerostar Inc. (Sioux Falls), was destroyed by high winds as it was lifted off the monument by a balloon.

Explorers Lewis and Clark wrapped a Dakota lad in the America flag when they arrived at Fort Pierre in 1804; the boy, Strike the Ree, grew up to be chief of the Yanktons.

By an Act of Congress, the American flag flies day and night over Deadwood's Mt. Moriah Cemetery.

The first flag flown over Mount Rushmore when it was dedicated in 1925, was from France.

The French flag flies 24-hours a day near Fort Pierre, in honor of the day in 1743 when French explorers claimed the land for France, and buried a lead plate.

ODYSSEY FOR THE OVAL OFFICE:
For three consecutive presidential elections a South Dakotan was on the ticket. All were Democrats, white males and U.S. Senators. Humphrey, as vice president, was the only one to win.

- 1964, Lyndon Johnson/Hubert Humphrey (Huron) won with 43,126,506 popular votes and 486 Electoral Votes. They beat Barry Goldwater/William Miller.
- 1968, Hubert Humphrey/Edmund Muskie lost even though they received 31,275,166 popular votes and 191 Electoral Votes. Winners were Richard Nixon/Spiro Agnew.
- 1972, George McGovern (Mitchell)/Sargent Shriver also lost to Nixon/Agnew, receiving 29,170,774 popular votes and 17 Electoral Votes.

HHH
In order to motivate Johnson to select him as his 1964 running-mate, Humphrey clipped the cover of LIFE magazine, made a paper campaign button baring his and the president's pictures and slipped it under LBJ's orange juice at a White House breakfast.

After being elected vice president, but before he was sworn in, Humphrey was having dinner with friends in a posh Washington, D.C., restaurant, when he impulsively draped a white towel over his arm and pretended to be the maitre d'. He seated several couples, without any of them giving him a second glance.

Democrat Humphrey twice asked Republican Gov. Nelson Rockefeller to be his 1968 running mate, but was turned down. On the day Humphrey picked his running mate, he favored Gov. Richard Hughes, educator Terry Sanford and Sen. Fred Harris. But at the last minute Humphrey settled on his fifth choice, Ed Muskie.

Humphrey presented vice presidential cuff links to Soviet Secretary Alexei Kosygin, with instructions to wear them as a symbol of a new spirit of kinship with the United States. For years afterwards, Humphrey examined every news photo of Kosygin, and never did spot those cuff links.

Humphrey learned the lesson of greed when he would hang his Christmas stocking up the day after Christmas, expecting more candy. It was always refilled with corncobs.

While running for president in 1968, Humphrey jumped up and kissed the TV set showing his wife during the Democratic National Convention.

Muriel Humphrey sold sandwiches for a dime each to help her husband, Hubert, get through college.

At midnight on New Year's Eve 1968 Humphrey entered his bathroom and flushed his toilet. This symbolic action was his way of flushing away the worst year of his life.

Humphrey's final speech was to have been about Dr. Martin Luther King, Jr., but HHH died the evening before he was to deliver it.

LBJ'S INSTRUCTIONS TO HHH, AS VICE PRESIDENT:
- Never share secrets with wife, Muriel
- Never publically disagree with LBJ
- Never lobby for special interests
- Clear speeches with White House
- Publically support LBJ on all decisions

MCGOVERN
Democratic Presidential candidate George McGovern was a Republican until changing his mind while painting a house in 1952.

McGovern's 1972 presidential campaign manager was Gary Hart.

When McGovern became head of the South Dakota Democratic Party in 1953, the Democrats held no state office and occupied only two of the 110 legislative seats.

McGovern's first presidential campaign, lasting 18 days in 1968, was as a replacement candidate for the slain Robert Kennedy.

Out of over a quarter million votes cast, George McGovern won the 1962 U.S. Senate race by 583 votes.

During a Wisconsin campaign dinner, opponent Ed Muskie was five minutes into his speech when Gary Hart paid a band $50 to immediately strike up with "Happy Days Are Here, Again," as McGovern walked into the hall.

McGovern was America's first Food for Peace director.

While based in Africa during WWII McGovern flew 35 combat missions over Europe and was awarded the Distinguished Flying Cross.

McGovern occupied John Kennedy's Senate office.

In 1980 McGovern was one of five liberal senators targeted for defeat by the National Conservative Political Action Committee. After three terms, McGovern lost.

During WWII, McGovern was shot down on his 30th mission over Austria.

McGovern bought a Connecticut inn, and later declared bankruptcy.

MEN WHOM MCGOVERN ASKED TO BE RUNNING-MATE, 1972:
- Sen. Ted Kennedy: declined three times
- Sen. Tom Eagleton: accepted, then resigned
- Sen. Abe Ribicoff: declined
- Sen. Hubert Humphrey: declined
- Gov. Reuben Askew: declined
- Sen. Ed Muskie: declined
- Peace Corps director Sargent Shriver: accepted

FAMILY AFFAIR
George T. and George S. Mickelson are South Dakota's first father/son governor-team.

In 1978 Gov. Harvey Wollman took his oath of office from his brother, Justice Roger Wollman.

Ralph Herseth served as South Dakota's governor and his wife, Lorna, later served as secretary of state.

MORE GOVERNMENT AT WORK

The first royalty to visit the state was Prince Paul Wartenburg, of East Prussia. The 45-year-old prince spent three days in March 1830 at Fort Pierre while on a hunting trip out West.

Shortly before the Civil War, Israel Green (Mitchell) led a detail of 12 men who stormed the arsenal held by John Brown at Harper's Ferry.

Dakota was a territory for 28 years.

South Dakota's first post office, at Ponce's Agency, was established March 14, 1860.

In the Nixon White House, Sen. Larry Pressler (Humboldt) was legal aid to U.S. Secretary of State Henry Kissinger

Donations from children built the Soldiers and Sailors War Memorial in Pierre, S.D.

The first visit to South Dakota by the King and Queen of Norway was Flag Day, 1939.

The first legislature of Dakota Territory met in Yankton in 1861. The upper house met in William Tripp's house, while the lower house met in the Episcopal chapel.

In 1991 South Dakota had 22 Cabinet posts, of which four (18%) were run by women.

America's Populist Party, composed of stressed farmers, harassed by taxation, seeking to better their condition, was born in Huron, S.D. on June 10, 1890

South Dakota is among seven states with no individual income tax.

Rose Wilder (DeSmet) hated FDR to such an extent that in 1944 the journalist announced she was giving up writing so her taxes wouldn't help finance the New Deal.

South Dakota is administered by 67 counties, 310 towns and 1,050 townships.

South Dakota's permanent installations were Forts Meade, Randall and Sisseton, although all three were ultimately abandoned.

CONGRESS, O CONGRESS

Because his congressional district is the entire State of South Dakota, Congressman Tim Johnson (Canton) spends three months each year living in motels.

His first year in Congress, Congressman Tim Johnson is credited with passing eight different pieces of legislation, including three South Dakota water projects.

At one time South Dakota had three Congressional districts. Now the state has one.

Sen. Tom Daschle (Aberdeen) accepts an average of three of the 40 dinner and reception invitations he receives each week.

Sen. Tom Daschle receives an average of 700 letters and 400 phone calls from South Dakotans, each week.

James Abdnor (Kennebec) was the state's sole bachelor U.S. Senator.

Senators Jim Abourezk (Rapid City) and James Abdnor were both sons of Lebanese immigrants who had sold wares on West River ranches.

Sen. Larry Pressler (Humboldt) is a National 4-H winner and a Rhodes Scholar.

Sen. Larry Pressler vowed to and succeeded in shaking 500 hands a day during his 1974 Congressional campaign.

Karl Mundt (Madison) served a record third of a century in Congress: five House terms, and four Senate terms.

Ben Reifel (Sisseton) was the only Native American in Congress during the 1960s.

South Dakota's first two U.S. Senators were R.F. Pettigrew and G.C. Moody.

STATE'S WOMEN U.S. SENATORS:
- Gladys Pyle (Huron)
- Vera Bushfield (Miller)
- Muriel Humphrey (Doland), represented Minnesota

FIRSTS BY GLADYS PYLE (HURON):
- South Dakota woman elected to the state legislature
- Woman elected to state's constitutional office
- Woman U.S. Senator in nation

WHITE HOUSE WOES
At age 27 William H.H. Beadle (Sioux Falls) commanded the honor guard as Lincoln gave his second inaugural address. A month later Beadle accompanied Lincoln's funeral train from Washington to Illinois.

Captain John Todd was able to get his cousin, First Lady Mary Todd Lincoln, to persuade her husband to locate the first Dakota Territory capital in Yankton, where the captain held land.

Sixty-two Black Hills cowboys loudly and jovially crashed the 1905 inaugural parade of their buddy, Teddy Roosevelt, in Washington, D.C. They amused themselves by roping police and female parade watchers, staged a shoot-out on an ambassador's lawn, and easily galloped, guns and all, past the Secret Service to ride up to the President and shake his hand at the White House.

President Grover Cleveland signed the Admission Act for North and South Dakota Feb. 22, 1889, but they didn't become states until the new president, Ben Harrison, signed the proclamations that Nov. 3.

President Teddy Roosevelt sent three of his sons to spend summers in Deadwood with Seth Bullock, where the lads learned how to ride, hunt, shoot and live in the rugged outdoors.

Republican Sen. Larry Pressler (Humboldt), 37, was virtually ignored in his 1980 presidential bid.

The first monument in the U.S. to honor Teddy Roosevelt was a tower built on Mount Roosevelt (Deadwood), by Seth Bullock.The memorial was dedicated July 4, 1919.

Clinton Anderson (Centerville) is the only South Dakotan to serve as a Cabinet member. Anderson was Truman's Secretary of Agriculture, 1945-1948.

Lyndon Johnson attended the groundbreaking of the Big Bend Dam (Chamberlain), 1960. John Kennedy dedicated Oahe (Pierre) two years later.

The only entire First Family to visit South Dakota has been President and Mrs. Nixon and daughters Tricia and Julie, in 1969, for the Karl Mundt Library dedication in Madison.

Sen. Karl Mundt (Madison) was one of 12 advisors whom Richard Nixon called upon the night of his 1968 nomination, to suggest a vice presidential running mate. Spiro Agnew was later picked.

While campaigning for president in South Dakota in 1968, Richard Nixon said his deep ties to the state were through land owned by relatives of his wife, Pat.

William McKinley was the first sitting president to visit South Dakota, October 14, 1899. Earlier, Benjamin Harrison was a U.S. Senator from Indiana, during his first visit to the state, July 1885.

The first national presidential convention held in the state was May 9, 1900, when Populists gathered in Sioux Falls to chose

William Jennings Bryan and Charles Towne as their party's candidates.

Because the state was low on law officers, President Kennedy was guarded by 50 additional military police from Kansas, and a coast guard crew from Missouri, when he dedicated the Oahe Dam, 1962.

President McKinley made certain he was in Aberdeen, S.D., to welcome home the South Dakota veterans of the Spanish-American War. Not only did the president greet them there, but his special train hurried on ahead of the soldiers to Redfield, Huron, Sioux Falls and Yankton where he repeated his welcome and words of appreciation.

President Benjamin Harrison intentionally shuffled the papers making North and South Dakota states Nov. 2, 1889, so that one state would not be superior to the other. Since North Dakota is alphabetically first, it is the 39th state while South Dakota, claims it is 40th.

Sylvan Lodge (Custer State Park) served as the summer White House to presidents Coolidge and Eisenhower.

Seth Bullock (Belle Fourche) organized Teddy Roosevelt's Rough Riders.

STATE'S WHITE HOUSE VISITORS:
- George Bush
- Calvin Coolidge
- Dwight Eisenhower
- Gerald Ford
- Ben Harrison, as senator
- Herbert Hoover
- John Kennedy
- Lyndon Johnson, as senator
- William McKinley
- Richard Nixon
- Ronald Reagan
- Franklin Roosevelt
- Teddy Roosevelt
- William Taft
- Harry Truman, as senator
- Woodrow Wilson

BALLOTS
The first election in the Northwest was held August 22, 1804, at Elk Point, S.D., when explorers Lewis and Clark picked their sergeant, Patrick Gass, to replace a man who had died the previous evening.

South Dakota has three electoral votes in 1992.

Mamie Shields Pyle (Huron) was the state's first woman nominated as a presidential elector.

IT'S THE LAW

The first divorce laws in South Dakota granted a divorce to a married person without notification of the spouse.

The state's second set of divorce laws granted divorce only for adultery or life imprisonment.

The first session of the Territorial Legislature at Yankton, passed laws prohibiting hogs to run wild, forced Native Americans to possess a pass to leave the reservation, outlawed whorehouses and established ferries in South Dakota.

A bill to ban blacks from South Dakota passed one house in the first legislature, but was narrowly defeated in the other.

South Dakota did not establish a mental health agency until 1947.

In 1991 Brookings, S.D., banned three or more beer kegs at a single address.

Missionary Joe Ward (Yankton) drafted a code of school laws, composed the state motto "Under God the People Rule," wrote the description for the state seal and was known as the Father of Congregationalism in the Dakotas.

Seth Bullock (Belle Fourche) introduced the legislation to establish the nation's first national park, Yellowstone.

Bills allowing women to vote in South Dakota surfaced (and were defeated) eight times, until all women got the vote, in 1920.

Women were not allowed to serve on juries in South Dakota until 1947.

South Dakota was the first state to pass Initiative and Referendum legislation, Jan. 27, 1897. Resolution No. 101 had passed voters the previous November.

The 24th Amendment (outlawing poll taxes) to the U.S. Constitution became law when South Dakota ratified it in 1964.

CAPITAL WORK

At twice over budget, the state's third, and current, Capitol (Pierre) opened in 1910, featuring the following:
- one two-foot ball atop dome
- six marble drinking fountains
- 33 clocks
- 58 rugs
- 65 phones

* 119 rooms
* 193 doors
* 200 radiators
* 690 brass cuspidors
* 2500 keys
* 250,000 feet of wire
* 3 million bricks

South Dakota's first Capitol was a white wooden structure built by the city of Pierre in 1890. The "temporary" building lasted through 11 legislative sessions.

Capitol Lake (Pierre) is 10 acres. Originally, goldfish were stocked in the lake. The lake features a Flaming Fountain.

All exterior stones used on the state Capitol arrived by train.

While excavating the Capitol in 1907, workers uncovered a group of pine coffins containing the remains of outlaw James "Arkansaw" Putello, who was gunned down in Pierre on a cold night in November 1884. Arkansaw's skull was placed on display with the South Dakota Historical Society.

The first Capitol was a wooden structure erected in the middle of raw prairie near a deep gulch, which was filled and became Capitol Lake, home to hundreds of mallards and Canadian geese.

Miniature dolls of South Dakota's First Ladies are in Pierre.

CAPITOL'S EXTERIOR STONES:
* Bedford limestone
* Black Hills sandstone
* Kettle River sandstone
* Marquette raindrop sandstone
* Meade County granite
* Ortonville granite
* Sioux Falls jasper

A CAPITOL IDEA
During the 1850s Sioux Falls, S.D., was under serious consideration as state capital of Minnesota.

Pierre, S.D., is one of three U.S. Capitals not on any interstate highway. Others are Juneau, Alaska, and Honolulu, Hawaii.

South Dakota's capital was named after a fur trader who kept Native American slaves.

If it had not been for the bitter and protracted arguments over the choice of a capital city, North Dakota and South Dakota would have been a single state.

During the 1890s it cost Pierre, S.D., over a half million dollars to keep its status as state capital from going to either Huron or Mitchell.

Aberdonians did not want Dakota Territory divided because the town was likely going to be the capital city when Dakota became a state.

Immediately after Congress established Dakota Territory in 1861, with Yankton as capital, both Vermillion and Bon Homme submitted bills to become the capital. Not until 22 years later did Pierre make its first bid to become the permanent capital.

In the 1885 statewide election for selecting a permanent capital, Huron beat four other towns. Congress, however, claimed the state's Constitution had no legal status, so the election was void. In another election four years later, after the Constitution was legally drafted, Pierre was the top voter-choice.

Twice between 1889 and 1903, Mitchell and Huron tried to wrestle the state capitol title away from Pierre. Finally, in 1904, Pierre was made permanent capital.

Pierre's status as capital has been challenged by six other towns.

South Dakota had two territorial capitals, Yankton and Bismarck.

The building that Watertown unsuccessfully offered in order to lure the permanent capitol to town, became a night club.

GOVERNORS

Gov. Joe Foss (Sioux Falls) won the Congressional Medal of Honor from President Roosevelt, May 18, 1943.

Gov. Joe Foss was the sole dignitary to stand at attention for every military group passing the reviewing stand during a sweltering, 2.5-hour Fourth of July parade in Rapid City in 1991.

One of the first acts of Joe Foss when he got elected governor was to replace the entire Board of Charities and Corrections because it had supported someone else for governor.

Coe Crawford (Huron) was the only South Dakota governor known to speak Latin.

Captain John Todd, cousin of First Lady Mary Todd Lincoln, expected to become the first governor of Dakota Territory. Just as President Lincoln was about to officially name him, however, Todd's business partner, Dan Frost, attacked a Union arsenal and joined the South as a general. Under the circumstances, Lincoln turned to a loyal friend and family physician, Dr. William Jayne, to be the first governor.

South Dakota has had only four Democratic governors: Bulow, Herseth, Kneip and Wollman.

Gov. Andrew E. Lee was South Dakota's sole Populist governor.

Gov. Peter Norbeck was a driving force in the establishment of Mount Rushmore.

Gov. W. J. Bulow was the first Democratic governor of South Dakota.

Gov. Bill Howard used his own money to open an insane asylum in Yankton.

Peter Norbeck was the state's first native-born governor.

Gov. Bill Beadle laid the cornerstone to the state Capitol in 1908.

Richard Kneip (Salem) was the first governor of the state to serve more than two terms. In fact, he had to go to court in order to be allowed to run for his third term.

Gov. Peter Norbeck, an oil driller, introduced small deep artesian wells into the state by developing a process for putting down such wells.

Places named for Gov. Kneip (Salem) include a library, park and state office building.

Charles Herreid (Aberdeen), as presiding officer of the South Dakota Senate, was the only lieutenant governor to never have had a ruling questioned or decision appealed.

Gov. Bob Vessey (Wessington Springs) was the first governor to compel candidates to make expenses public. He also gave railroads authority to build connecting tracks.

South Dakota's governors have been born in three countries: the USA, Norway and Canada.

The only governor to homestead in South Dakota was Frank Byrne (Faulkton).

Six months before the rest of the nation repealed Prohibition in 1933, Gov. Tom Berry had the state legislature legalize the sale of beer in order to create a new source of tax revenue.

When Gov. Kneip resigned July 24, 1978, to become Ambassador to Singapore, Harvey Wollman (Frankfort) became the first lieutenant governor to move into the governor's office.

Harvey Wollman was governor the shortest length of time, six months.

Whenever bachelor Gov. Nils Boe needed a hostess, one of his sisters helped out.

The first action Gov. Andrew Lee took upon assuming office was to order all state funds brought to Pierre and physically counted.

Deciding his first obligation was as governor, Gov. Frank Byrne turned down his election to the U.S. Senate in 1913.

Gov. Nils Boe (Baltic) gave away souvenir pieces of the old state Capitol's copper dome to visitors.

Arthur C. Mellette (Watertown) was the final governor of Dakota Territory, and the first governor of South Dakota (1889).

CONSTITUTIONAL OFFICERS, 1992:
- Attorney General Mark Barnett
- Auditor Vernon Larson
- Gov. George Mickelson
- Lt. Gov. Walter Miller
- Secretary of State Joyce Hazeltine
- Treasurer Homer Harding

BY THE NUMBER

WHO WATCHED WHAT ON TV?

1 billion - *The Wizard of Oz*, by Frank Baum (Aberdeen); world's most-watched film

100 million — Pat O'Brien (Sioux Falls), announce 1991 World Series

100 million — Super Bowl XXIX, at Miami stadium named for Joe Robbie (Sisseton)

89 million — Hubert Humphrey (Huron) nominated for vice president, August 28, 1964

70 million — Texan Phyllis George beat 1970 Miss South Dakota Mary Hart

26 million — Gary Owens (Mitchell), on *Laugh-In*, 1968

22 million — Catherine Bach (Faith), on *Dukes of Hazzard*, 1981

21 million — Cheryl Ladd (Huron), on *Charlie's Angels*, 1977

20 million — Mary Hart (Sioux Falls) on *Entertainment Tonight*, 1991

18 million — Lawrence Welk (Yankton), 1965

14 million — Tom Brokaw (Yankton), 1991

200,000 — Steve Hemmingsen, Doug Lund on KELO-Land News (Sioux Falls), 1992

WHO TOURS WHAT EACH YEAR?

2.1 million — Mount Rushmore (Keystone)

2 million — Wall Drug (Wall)

1.1 million — Crazy Horse (Thunderhead Mountain)

1 million — Badlands

500,000 — Corn Palace (Mitchell)

300,000 — Motorcycle rally (Sturgis)

250,000 — Reptile Gardens (Rapid City)

250,000 — State fair (Huron)

80,000 — Mammoth Site (Hot Springs)

67,000 — 1880 train (Hill City)

60,000 — Passion Play (Spearfish)

2,000 — Petrified Park (Lemmon)

WHO WITNESSED WHAT?

150,000 — Contestants dig for prizes during KELO-Land Gold Rush, in Manchester, S.D., 1961

125,000 — National Cornpicking Contest in Sioux Falls, Nov. 3, 1938

100,000 — President Bush rededicate Mount Rushmore, July 3, 1991

75,000 — Billy Mills (Pine Ridge) win Gold Medal at Olympics in Japan, 1964

51,531 — Sparky Anderson (Bridgewater) coach his first World Series, 1970

30,000 — World's largest balloon launched from Rapid City, 1934

20,000 — President McKinley welcome soldiers back from Philippines, in Aberdeen, 1900

10,000 — President Nixon dedicate Mundt library in Madison, 1969

9,456 — DakotaDome (Vermillion) host state's largest basketball crowd, February 11, 1989

8,189 — Elvis during his final South Dakota show, in Sioux Falls, 1977

7,390 — Skyforce play Thrillers in their largest game, Jan. 24, 1992, in Rapid City

7,000 — Captain 11 Dave Dedrick honored, Madison, Nov. 1, 1990

3,000 — First Lady Pat Nixon attend memorial service for victims of Rapid City flood, 1972

1,700 — Gutzon Borglum start carving Mount Rushmore, 1927

1,000 — "Baby Face" Nelson rob a Sioux Falls bank, 1934

150 — Josef Meier perform first Passion Play (Spearfish), 1938

42 — George Sitts fry in the electric chair, Sioux Falls, 1947

WHO DOES WHAT?

147 million— Bought *Little House* books by Laura Wilder (De Smet)

9 million — Receive seed catalogs from Gurney (Yankton)

6 million — Read column by Allen Neuharth (Eureka)

3 million — Bought books by Fred Manfred (Vermillion)

1.2 million — Bought Norwegian joke books by Red Stangland (Sioux Falls)

696,004 — Live in South Dakota, 1990

600,000 — Bet in Deadwood, 1990

138,000 — Attend the state's 915 schools, 1990

98,268 — Lived in South Dakota when it became a state, 1889

95,000 — Live in poverty in South Dakota, 1991

64,842 — Subscribe Sundays to *Argus Leader* (Sioux Falls), 1991

64,000 — Served South Dakota during WWII

35,000 — Farm in South Dakota, 1992

32,000 — Served South Dakota during WWI

20,000 — Visit Wall Drug each day

15,000 — Served under the command of Chief Sitting Bull

6,720 — Work for federal government in South Dakota

5,000 — Drink free ice water daily at Wall Drug

2,500 — Guarded Rapid City following 1972 flood

1,405 — Sit in adult prison cells in South Dakota, as of Oct. 31, 1991

1,200 — Queen candidates who annually vie for South Dakota Snow Queen title

1,000 — Soldiers accompanying Gen. Custer to the Black Hills, 1874

1,000 — Dakota who danced the Ghost Dance (Scenic)

800 — International members of National Buffalo Association (Ft. Pierre)
600 — Huron's fair staff, including eight full-time
398 — Licensed barbers, in South Dakota, 1991
390 — Workers who carved Mount Rushmore
200 — Seized Wounded Knee, 1973
190 — Cast of Passion Play (Spearfish)
168 — Made laws in first state legislature, 1889
150 — Movie extras acting in *Dances With Wolves*
95 — Sailors named on plaque at U.S.S. South Dakota memorial (Sioux Falls)
15 — Largest family to emigrate to state, 1915
13 — Men who relocated Sitting Bull's remains, 1953
4 — Crew members of each B-1B bomber, Ellsworth AFB, 1987
1 — Lived in state's smallest town, White Rock, 1991

HEIGHTS:

7,242 feet — Harney Peak, tallest point between Rockies and Alps
563 feet — Crazy Horse (Custer)
450 feet — Mount Rushmore (Keystone)
242 feet — Oahe Dam (Pierre)
96 feet — Rotunda in Capitol (Pierre)
28 feet — Pheasant statue (Huron)
14.6 feet — State's tallest tunnel (Keystone)
7 feet, 2 inches — High jump by Nick Johanssen (Miller), 1991

LENGTHS:

2,250 miles — Oahe shoreline
370 miles — South Dakota
120 miles — Black Hills
19 miles — Spearfish Creek (Black Hills)
14 miles — Needles Highway (Black Hills)
680 feet — U.S.S. South Dakota (Sioux Falls)
200 feet — Bicentennial mural (Rapid City), largest in western U.S.
120 feet — Flag unfurled July 3, 1991, over Mount Rushmore
120 feet — Yellow Stone, first ship in state
66 feet — Minuteman II missile (Badlands)

AREAS:

77,116 square miles — South Dakota
13,500 square miles — Underground missile silos (Badlands)
160.1 square miles — Francis Case, state's largest lake
30 square miles — Rapid City, largest town (in area) in state
1.7 million acres — forest covering state

69,004 acres— Custer State Park, state's largest

WEIGHTS, VOLUMES:

92 million yards — Oahe Dam (Pierre), state's largest construction project

8.3 million tons — Granite removed from Crazy Horse sculpture

41,000 tons — U.S.S. South Dakota (Sioux Falls)

2,100 tons — petrified wood used to build Petrified Park (Lemmon)

245 tons — Pathfinder nuclear reactor (Sioux Falls) removed for burial, 1991

220 tons — Cyclotron, by Nobel Winner Dr. Ernest Lawrence (Canton)

40 tons — cement cover on each of the 150 Minuteman II silos (Badlands)

22 tons — Crazy Horse scaffolding

17.8 tons — Gold mined annually at Homestake (Lead)

3.5 tons — David statue (Sioux Falls)

3 tons — Wounded Knee sculpture

9.7 pounds — Garbage generated daily by each Sioux Falls resident, 1991

STEPS:

741 steps — Crazy Horse

723 steps — Jewel Cave National Monument (Black Hills)

450 steps — Wind Cave (Hot Springs)

29 steps —Grand Staircase, state Capitol (Pierre)

WIDTHS:

Box Elder Creek (Rapid City), normally **25 feet** wide, was **155 feet** wide following the 1972 flood.

South Dakota's widest tunnel (Keystone) is **42 feet** wide. The narrowest is **8 feet, 7 inches** (Sylvan Lake).

South Dakota is **210 miles** wide.

DEPTHS:

Lake Francis Case, the state's largest lake, is **140 feet** deep.

Big Stone Lake is the state's lowest elevation, at **962 feet**.

FAMILY, HEALTH, RELIGION

SOUTH DAKOTANS AND THEIR NUMBER OF CHILDREN:
- Sharpshooter Calamity Jane, none
- Author Laura Ingalls Wilder, one
- Sculptor Gutzon Borglum, two
- Journalist Tom Brokaw, three
- Vice President Hubert Humphrey, four
- Rapid City Mayor Ed McLaughlin, five
- Coach Norm Van Brocklin, six
- Poker Alice Tubbs, seven
- Gov. Richard Kneip, eight
- Carpenter Leonard Peltier, nine
- Sculptor Korczak Ziolkowski, ten
- Parent Mary Ann Fischer, 11 (including quintuplets)
- Activist Russell Means, 17

HONEY BUNS
When South Dakota Economic Development director Robert Martin dropped dead of a heart attack in October 1976, two wives and nine children showed up for the funeral. Martin was a bigamist supporting two families in towns some 200 miles apart. Wife No. 1, Mary Lou, and their four children, lived in Pierre. Wife No. 2, Pat, and their five children, lived in Sioux Falls. Neither had known of the other's existence.

Calamity Jane, married 12 times, always claimed she was Mrs. Wild Bill Hickok.

Gov. George S. Mickelson met his wife, Linda McCahren, at church in eighth grade.

In 1912, a full half century after they had last seen each other, childhood sweethearts Charles Stillwell (Tyndall) and Kate Noble got married in her New England house in the presence of his four, and her four, children.

Steroids had so weakened the tendons of Los Angeles Raider Lyle Alzado (Yankton) that even though he had torn his biceps completely in half, he limped through his 1991 marriage ceremony.

FAMILY AFFAIR
On May 22, 1956, Pioneer George Walker (Nowlin) died at the age of 106.

South Dakota is 90 percent white, seven percent Native American, and three percent black, Asian and Hispanic.

Adopted in 1971 by Rev. and Mrs. Ken Moreland (Faulkton), Shaun Nguyen Moreland was the state's first Vietnamese child.

Mrs. L.M. Stavig (Sioux Falls) was the 1964 National Mother of the Year.

The first white child born in Dakota Territory was John Sanage (Fort Pierre). Sanage and his father hauled hay for Gen. Custer when he camped near Yankton en route to Little Bighorn. Sanage, a bachelor, lived to be 77-years-old.

USA *Today's* Al Neuharth (Eureka) met his first wife when both were cheerleaders performing at a basketball tournament in South Dakota. Neuharth met his second wife at an Apollo moon launch, near the Kennedy Space Center.

South Dakota's Hutterite Colonies are made up of families who find peace in a life-style alien to the society around them. Hutterites reject some modern conveniences and practice a type of isolation from people of different faiths.

HEALTHY WEALTHY & WISE

In 1991 Los Angeles Raider Lyle Alzado (Yankton) announced he was suffering from brain cancer he claimed was caused by steroids he took in college in South Dakota. Steroids had caused Alzado's weight to balloon from 190 to nearly 300 pounds.

The first governor of Dakota Territory was Dr. William Jayne, President Lincoln's physician.

Pharmacist Hubert Humphrey was coincidentally born over a drug store in Wallace, S.D. While serving as America's 38th vice president, Humphrey was not allowed to legally dispense medicine.

An early remedy used by South Dakota pioneers bit by rattlesnakes, was to suck out the venom, then cut off the head of a small animal and apply the hot blood to the wound. (Not recommended.)

The first vaccine for small pox in the Black Hills arrived by Pony Express.

When an unexpected blizzard hit Yankton in April 1873, Elizabeth Custer not only cared for her feverish husband, but used her new rugs to wrap some dozen frozen soldiers who stumbled into her unheated quarters.

Because it was suspected that any steamboat traveling into South Dakota between 1847-1853 brought cholera into the state, every boat was washed out and disinfected on the Big Sioux River.

In 1900, Mother Joseph Butler (Aberdeen) offered her convent as a shelter for victims of black diphtheria. Despite their lack of formal training, all the nuns went into homes to care for the sick.

As a result, a banker gave them money to open St. Lukes's hospital.

Despite a disabling stroke in 1969, Sen. Karl Mundt (Madison) represented South Dakota in Washington for four more years.

South Dakota had 85 AIDS cases between 1985-1991.

At any given moment, a maximum of 5,037 patients may be cared for in the state's 64 hospitals. Sioux Falls has five of the hospitals, with 407 beds in McKennan (Sioux Falls) the state's largest hospital, while Douglas County Memorial (Armour) is the smallest, with nine.

Two Sioux Falls hospitals cared for the most and least amount of patients during 1990. McKennan Hospital treated 12,471 patients while Crippled Children's cared for 26.

The most occupied hospital in South Dakota is Crippled Children's (Sioux Falls), whose occupancy rate in 1990 was 91.7 percent. Holy Infant (Hoven) had the state's lowest: six percent.

McKennan Hospital (Sioux Falls) delivered 880 babies in 1990 while 12 hospitals in South Dakota delivered none.

South Dakota has an infant mortality rate of 10 babies out of every one thousand births. Nine out of every one thousand pregnant women in South Dakota, have an abortion.

A caravan of South Dakota ambulances delivered petitions about the high cost of health care to Washington officials in 1991.

Black Hills Rehabilitation Hospital (Rapid City) is the only rehabilitational hospital between Denver and the Twin Cities.

Grigsby's Cowboys were a volunteer cavalry led by attorney general Melvin Grigsby (Sioux Falls). The dozen men were scheduled to join Teddy Roosevelt in Cuba during the Spanish-American War, but many got sick from typhoid.

One-sixth of South Dakota's residents are uninsured.

In 1832, the first people vaccinated in South Dakota, by a Missouri physician, were fur traders and their Dakota friends.

When a relative died without medical care in 1956, Hans P. Peterson donated his ranch to start a hospital in Philip, S.D..

DeSmet Hospital's emergency room was shut down by federal authorities for nine months in 1990-1991 because the two doctors were unable to physically comply with the rule requiring them to be on call 24 hours a day.

South Dakota is among the dozen states who have no accredited, free-standing long-term care facilities.

HOLY WATER, HOLY COW!
In 1920 three visiting ministers got lost in the Black Hills in "Go to Hell Gulch."

A Yankton manufacturer named his new cigar the "Mary Paul," in 1882, after a disgraced nun who married a Soviet physician.

Evan's Plunge owner Fred Evans donated the land for every church in Hot Springs.

More South Dakotans are Catholic than any other religion.

Naming the town of Faith had nothing to do with religion. One theory is that it was named after Faith Earling, whose father owned the railroad that came through town.

Native Americans would place stones in the forks of trees atop Bear Butte (Black Hills), as a form of worship. Over the years the stones have become ingrown in the trees.

Shrine of the Nativity (Piedmont) contains Bethlehem Cave, where perpetually lighted lamps from the U.N. are maintained by the Benedictine order.

Charles Martin, who was not a minister, taught the first Sunday School class in South Dakota, at a Presbyterian church in Vermillion, on June 14, 1861.

Praying for a miracle to rid the state of grasshoppers, Father Pierre Boucher placed four huge, wooden crosses along an 11-mile pilgrimage near Jefferson during May 1876. The grasshoppers left.

President Grant issued a peace policy that only one religious denomination was allowed on each South Dakota reservation.

The Bishop of Sioux Falls declared special dispensation for Catholics visiting President Kennedy at the Oahe Dam dedication, 1962, allowing them to eat hotdogs and hamburgers sold by vendors.

Calamity Jane's first visit to a church was at her own funeral, at Deadwood's Methodist Church.

In order to increase their space 50 percent, St. Luke's Hospital (Aberdeen) bought Lincoln Hospital, 12 blocks away, and moved it next to their site. It took seven months for horses and tractors to pull the 4,000-ton, four-story Lincoln Hospital on rollers over a solid bed of nails in 1940-1941.

The Episcopal Church of All Angels (Spearfish) was curiously built in the memory of Alexander Hamilton. For years, Hamilton's

granddaughter sent a Christmas gift to each child in the Sunday School.

Benedictine monks built the Blue Cloud Abbey (Marvin) to further Native American education. It is the state's sole monastery.

When South Dakota's Hutterites, who did not believe in violence, refused to support the American war effort during WWI, their property was seized and sold for war contributions.

Huron is home to St. Anthony's, the "Cathedral on the Prairie," a small-scale copy of a thousand-year-old German church.

Native Americans considered a hackberry tree, growing out of a rock near Madison, sacred.

Two huge Latin crosses, carved over the centuries by wind and rain, appear in the Black Hills.

Medicine Rock (Mobridge) bears impressions that Native Americans consider to be a symbol of great powers.

Medicine Rock, a 20-ft. wide stone near Gettysburg, is believed to be sacred by Native Americans because of the deeply ingrained footprints.

Father Hoecken baptized 25 children in the first known baptism in the state, June 12, 1840, in the Bad River, near Fort Pierre.

Religious groups operate the state's two Native American schools. Jesuits educate Oglala Sioux near Pine Ridge while the St. Joseph Indian School (Chamberlain) helps keep the Dakota heritage alive.

The oldest Lutheran Church in South Dakota is Vagen Church (Mission Hill).

Rev. Stephen Riggs preached the first Christian sermon in South Dakota on September 29, 1840, at Fort Pierre.

The first nuns in South Dakota arrived in August 1880 to work with Native Americans on Standing Rock Reservation.

Father De Smet introduced Catholicism to the Dakota of South Dakota, but it was Benedictine abbot Martin Marty who firmly established the missionary work among the Native Americans.

John Raver helped build the schoolhouse at Cold Springs, S.D., married there, celebrated his 50th wedding anniversary there, and is buried right outside.

South Dakota Bishop Martin Marty (Sioux Falls) presented a decorated buffalo robe to Pope Leo XIII. A Dakota artist decorated the fur with Native American history, including Custer's Last Stand. The pontiff also blessed a gold medallion.

The only structure still standing at Fort Randall, S.D., is the chapel.

While aboard the steamboat Yellow Stone in 1823, Explorer Jedediah Smith gave the first public prayer in South Dakota,.

The state's largest shrine is to Our Lady of Lourdes (Philip), erected in 1957 by Rev. P.J. O'Connor.

Gov. Janklow battled the American Civil Liberties Union for several Christmases, because he wanted a Nativity displayed at the state Capitol.

The first mass in South Dakota was held by Father Ravoux, on the James River in Brown County, 1842.

Father John DeSmet refused an offering of a bag of gold from the Black Hills in 1848, and warned the Dakota to keep quiet about it, or whites would invade.

Jedediah Smith spoke the first Christian prayer in South Dakota near Mobridge in 1823. The state's first sermon wasn't delivered until 17 years later, by Rev. Steven Riggs. Presbyterians built the first church in South Dakota two decades after that, in Vermillion.

Prayer Rock is near Britton, S.D.

NATIVE AMERICANS

SITTING BULL.........AND CUSTER
Sitting Bull (Grand River) and Gen. George Custer never saw each other at the Battle of Little Bighorn in neighboring Montana.

Native Americans called the Battle of Little Bighorn, "Samarra."

To demonstrate courage before his tribes attacked Custer at Little Bighorn, Chief Sitting Bull had medicine men paint his hands and feet red, and blue stripes, across his shoulders. Sitting Bull's son cut a piece of skin off of the chief's right wrist. Fifty knife cuts went up the chief's arms. Sitting Bull then prayed, collapsed and saw a vision of army troops being defeated.

While holding a revolver and a Winchester rifle, Chief Sitting Bull watched the Battle of Little Bighorn from atop a hill. Sitting Bull prepared himself for battle by holding a mink stuffed with 10 herbal remedies. Gen. George Custer, without any permission from any Dakota, was authorized to explore the Black Hills in 1874, which he did.

Dakota believed Gen. Custer and his troops were doomed because they climbed the sacred Bear Butte in the Black Hills in 1874. Two years later Custer and his infantry were slaughtered. And the photographer who photographed the Butte committed suicide.

After being missing for 40 years, photographs of nine Native Americans who survived the Battle of Little Bighorn in 1876 were finally given to Custer Battlefield National Monument in 1991.

Sitting Bull became a chief in his thirties. By June 1876 Sitting Bull had assembled 15,000 Dakota at his Montana base, one of 60 of his camps. Their tipis, near Little Bighorn, stretched three miles.

Custer originally came to South Dakota in 1874 to select a spot for a fort, deep in Dakota territory.

A Black Hills scout named White-Man-Runs-Him was the first Custer scout to spot the distant Dakota camp at Little Bighorn. So clear and precise were his recollections that they were studied by military students, for years.

Sitting Bull, covered with yellow, would raid enemy camps on a horse painted red.

Sitting Bull had a vision of blue coats falling. A few days later Gen. Custer marched his tired troops right into Sitting Bull's camp at Little Bighorn. Since Sitting Bull was miles away at the time, Crazy Horse, Crow King and Gall led the afternoon attack that slaughtered Custer and his three commands in less than an hour.

Sitting Bull fled to Canada following the victorious Battle of Little Bighorn. Sitting Bull returned to America when the government promised a full pardon. Instead, the chief was thrown in a military prison for two years.

Because so many of his women and children had been killed by cavalry bullets in the Battle of Little Bighorn, Chief Gall, from that moment, used a hatchet to kill enemies.

Sitting Bull was teaching his Dakota people the Ghost Dance in 1890, when tragedy struck the state. Efforts were made to curb Ghost Dancing, or the Messiah Craze, which terrified white settlers. A number of unarmed Native Americans, like Sitting Bull, including women and children, were killed at Wounded Knee in the Messiah War.

When Buffalo Bill heard that his good friend Sitting Bull had been arrested in 1890, he tried to free him, but government agents kept Cody away. Sitting Bull was murdered within days. Sitting Bull was buried in an unkept grave in Fort Yates, N.D.

WOUNDED KNEE

Two days after the 1890 massacre at Wounded Knee rescuers discovered four babies still alive, wrapped in blankets near their slain mothers. Armed Native Americans seized Wounded Knee, S.D., during 1973 for 71 days. Two deaths and 300 arrests followed.

On Feb. 27, 1973, the American Indian Movement, AIM, took over a trading post and a church at Wounded Knee in order to draw attention to the plight of Native Americans.

Russell Means (Pine Ridge) was beaten when he accused Oglala President Dick Wilson of taking funds, Feb. 27, 1973. Means and 200 supporters then seized Wounded Knee. April 24, 1973, Means negotiated a stand-down. The remaining 120 Native Americans surrendered to authorities May 8, 1973. Means was then indicted on 10 federal felony charges. Means wore resplendent Native American regalia to his trial, Feb. 12, 1974. His attorney was William Kunstler. Charges were dismissed Sept. 16, 1974.

STATE'S SEVEN RESERVATIONS, NINE TRIBAL COUNCILS:

- Cheyenne River: Blackfeet, Minneconjou, Two Kettles, Sansa Arc bands
- Crow Creek: Lower Yanktonai and Hunk Pati bands
- Flandreau Santee Sioux Tribal Council: Santee
- Lower Brule: Lower Brule band
- Pine Ridge: Oglala
- Rosebud: Burnt Thigh and Upper Brules bands
- Sisseton-Wahpeton: Sisseton and Wahpeton bands

- Standing Rock: Blackfeet, Hunk Papa and Upper Yanktonai bands
- Yankton Tribal Council: Yankton

RESERVATIONS

Today there are 7,000 Native Americans living on Rosebud, but they do not have full civil rights. Individual plots of land may not be sold to anyone outside the tribe, without consent of the federal government. Common land usually needs the approval of Congress to be sold.

The Oyate, the Dakota Nation, is made up of seven tribes and within each tribe are seven bands which are further broken down into several Tiyospaye or family units. Seven feathers or seven council fires are used to symbolize the Nation and the strength of unity.

Eighty-percent of South Dakota's Native American reservations border the west bank of the Missouri River.

Today, 12,000 Dakota live on Pine Ridge. Sixty percent of their youth drop out of high school. Eighty-seven percent of adults don't have jobs. At Pine Ridge's hospital one in four babies is born shaking with delirium as the result of their mother's drinking during pregnancy. The suicide rate is double the national average. In 1990 the 11 exhausted doctors handled 9,636 cases.

The million-acre Pine Ridge Indian Reservation is governed by the Oglala Sioux Tribal Council headed by a Tribal President. All are elected. The Oglala Sioux is the largest of 7 tribes that comprise the Teton Lakota Nation, and claims some of history's greatest Native American leaders.

CRAZY HORSE

Crazy Horse (Moreau River) posed for no photos, signed no treaties and was stabbed to death by a fellow Native American.

Crazy Horse never kept possessions for himself, and was beloved by hundreds of Dakota for his charity.

When a cocky officer named Captain William Fetterman boasted he could ride through Crazy Horse's hostile turf with only 80 soldiers, Crazy Horse proved Fetterman wrong. All 81 were wiped out, 1866.

In 1876 Crazy Horse lead the first organized battle employing mounted and armed Native Americans in American history.

Russell Means

Over his career, Native American activist Russell Means (Pine Ridge) has seized Plymouth Rock; led a prayer vigil atop Mount Rushmore; renamed the Bureau of Indian Affairs the 'Native American

Embassy'; sued the Cleveland Indians for using Chief Wahoo as their mascot; and forced a federal standoff at Wounded Knee.

During Christmas of 1967 Russell Means escorted a white Santa Claus around the Rosebud Indian Reservation, distributing gifts to children. The Santa was future Gov. Bill Janklow.

Russell Means, who founded AIM, the American Indian Movement in Minneapolis in September 1968, lost the 1974 election for tribal presidency.

During April 1981 Russell Means and AIM set up Camp Yellow Thunder in the Black Hills. The camp was named for a young Native American killed after being forced to dance naked for whites.

Russell Means forced the government to successfully investigate the murder and molestation of Native American women, during February 1972.

Russell Means announced the Trail of Broken Arrows, November 1972.

Russell Means lead 78 Native Americans on a day of mourning for the stabbing of Wesley Bad Heart Bull, Feb. 6, 1973.

In 1992, Russell Means got good reviews for his featured role in *The Last of the Mohicans*.

Government matters

Gov. Andrew Faulk negotiated the Treaty of Laramie, which moved Native Americans westward and opened the Black Hills to white settlers.

In 1991 a United Nations official arrived in South Dakota to hear claims of Native American violations.

Chiefs Crazy Horse and Sitting Bull did not want to sell the Black Hills to the whites. Chiefs Red Cloud and Spotted Tail did.

In 1980 eight Dakota tribes were awarded $122 million when the U.S. Supreme Court ruled that 100 square miles of the Black Hills had been improperly taken from Native Americans a century earlier.

Red Cloud was the first chief to sign a treaty selling the Black Hills.

Dakota chiefs signed treaties by touching a quill pen to the document. They thought that their word should have been sufficient. The government successfully acquired nine million acres of South Dakota and surrounding states, in 1889, by secretly meeting with all Dakota chiefs — except Sitting Bull.

Chief Red Cloud joined other chiefs in signing the Fort Laramie Treaty in November 1868. The treaty allowed Native Americans to hunt and live quietly in the Black Hills. The government enforced the treaty until Custer discovered gold there six years later.

SUCCESSIVE 'OWNERS' OF THE BLACK HILLS:
- Crow Nation
- Poncas Nation
- Cheyenne Nation
- Dakota Nation
- France
- Spain
- England
- France
- United States

DAKOTA MEANS 'FRIEND'
Native Americans in South Dakota prefer to be called Dakota or Lakota, which means friend, rather than Sioux, which is a put down, meaning a snake in the grass.

Native Americans living near the Black Hills used to hear distant rumblings, which stopped in 1830. The thunder sounds came from coal deposits.

In 1862 South Dakota legislators considered conferring the right to vote to Native Americans until somebody discovered they outnumbered the whites. It was then proposed to allow only Native Americans who could read and write to vote, but that proposal also fell through.

Returning Desert Storm troops were presented an eagle feather in 1991 and honored in Mission, S.D., with a ceremonial war dance, last done after WWII.

The major Native American tribes of South Dakota include Arikara, Cheyenne and Dakota, or Sioux.

Moundbuilders left traces of their culture along the Missouri River in South Dakota as early as 800 A.D.

Dakota were driven into South Dakota by the Chippewa of northern Minnesota. The Dakota displaced the Arikara.

In 1823 the Arikara fought — but lost to — fur traders near Mobridge, S.D.

A prehistoric village, Firesteel Creek (Mitchell) was an ancient Native American village with a population of about 1,000 living in 70 lodges. Each lodge housed up to 20 villagers. It existed 1000 years ago.

Mitchell, S.D., features a 1,000-year-old Mandan Indian village.

The Dakota made up the Lakota, Dakota and Nakota districts and have kept the religion, virtues and culture alive and flourishing on all Native American reservations in South Dakota.

Buffalo chips, or wood of the cow, were good fuel for Native Americans and South Dakota pioneers.

Before beads were introduced by European traders on the Northern Plains in 1800, most decoration on clothing was done with paint and porcupine quills. Long ago quilling was done only by women who were members of certain quilling societies. Glass beads had been a part of every Native American trader's inventory since the time of Lewis and Clark in 1805. Traditionally the Dakota have used a technique called Lazy Stitch for sewing beads to a hide.

The Federal Bureau of Indian Affairs Office, covering three states, was established in 1949 over an Aberdeen shoe store.

The nation's largest Native American newspaper is the *Lakota Times* (Rapid City). The 10,000 subscribers have been enjoying the publication since the first issue, July 1981.

The earliest written record of the Black Hills and the Badlands is a winter skin showing Chief Standing Bull. He took back to his Plains people a pine tree unknown to them.

Earliest inhabitants were nomads who hunted the Great Plains for giant bison and woolly mammoths 12,000 years ago. They buried their dead in long, low mounds.

Around 1200 A.D. the Mandans and Arikara brought farming to the region. They built earth lodges and grew crops along the Missouri River, until the Dakota drove them out into North Dakota in the late 1700s.

Dakota were the most powerful residents of the Great Plains — about 20,000 strong at their peak — during the 1800s. Dakota were well-equipped with firearms and filled with the spirit of conquest. Dakota drove both the Omahas and Iowas from their hunting lands as they swept towards the Black Hills, where they overcame the Kiowas and the Cheyenne. By 1822 the dominance of the Dakota extended over eastern Wyoming.

Aberdeen, S.D., is home to one of 11 BIA offices in America.

As a farm agent with the BIA, Ben Reifel (Sisseton) used an ABC chart, his own symbols and translations, and his command of the Lakota dialect to explain federal policies to Native Americans on reservations. Reifel's talks were so successful he was

made a Field Agent in charge of BIA seminars throughout five states.

Appointed by President Ford in 1976, Ben Reifel was the nation's final Commissioner of Indian Affairs. After Reifel retired, the office was assumed by the Department of the Interior.

While vacationing summers in South Dakota, Presidents Coolidge and Eisenhower were inducted into the Dakota tribe. Coolidge was even named chief.

South Dakota did not pass its first state holiday honoring Native Americans until 1990, the same year it granted the Dr. Martin Luther King Jr. holiday.

Dakota in South Dakota did not have a written language, but their personal and tribal histories were preserved in picture drawings on animals skins, which were called "winter counts."

Native Americans in South Dakota originally used dogs — not horses — to haul their goods.

The original Lakota language in South Dakota was composed entirely of words of a single syllable.

Dakota were impressed with the first gun brought into South Dakota. Lewis and Clark had an air gun that took 300 pumps for 16 shots.

The first Native American police officer in South Dakota was Captain George "Man Who Carries His Sword" Sword, Pine Ridge, 1878.

Chief Red Cloud lived to the age of 120.

So convinced were the Dakota that the Ghost Dance would soon eliminate all whites that they did not retaliate for the murder of Sitting Bull.

Lewis and Clark interviewed two women in South Dakota before selecting Sacajawea as their guide.

Dakota initially did not want miners to be in the Black Hills because the Native Americans felt the smell of the white people would ruin the buffalo hunting.

Silk top hats were the universal article of trade among Dakota in the Black Hills in 1875.

BELIEFS
Dakota and Cheyenne tribes fought for possession of Hot Springs, S.D. They believed the water was a cure for all ills.

A prophecy in South Dakota says that seven generations after arrival of the whites, Dakota will mend the damage to their culture, become a great nation and be leaders in the fight to protect the environment.

Dakota believed the Needles were the home of great spirits who ruled the universe.

The seven sacred rights in South Dakota are bravery, fortitude, generosity, honesty, humility, respect and wisdom.

Spirit Mound (Vermillion) is a 70-ft. high knoll.

Bear Butte (Sturgis) is a 4,422-foot high volcanic bubble considered sacred by the Dakota. Bear Butte was once a sacred Native American shrine and guidepost for pioneers, considered a geographical power spot. Because this unique power belongs to the Universe, all tribes respect a prayer pilgrimage to Bear Butte regardless of the national identity of the seeker. Possessing a symbol of Bear Butte serves to remind the owner of the vastness, complexity and harmony of the Universe. This symbol also reminds each individual that he or she is the Center of his or her universe.

Dakota still hold prayer fasts atop Bear Butte.

In the old days there were two kinds of flutes. Medicine Men called Elk Dreamers, who had dreamed of and received power from elk, made flutes that produced a single sharp note. Their flutes were made of ash in the shape of a crane with an open mouth.

Buffalo Dreamer flutes were cedar branches which had been split, hollowed out and glued together with hide or hoof glue. They had six finger holds and another hole nearer the mouthpiece covered by a block of wood representing a horse.

Visitors to Spirit Mound, S.D., are encouraged to drop a friendly note down a pipe to appease the belligerent little people who live in the 70-ft. hill.

Dakota believe everything on earth came from inside the earth.

Black Elk (Little Powder River) took his first scalp, at age 13, at Little Bighorn. Three years later he heard voices, and was proclaimed an Oglala Dakota holy man. Voices helped him escape being slaughtered at Wounded Knee.

Dakota believed a terrible Thunder Bird lived atop Harney Peak, home of the gods. The bird created storms and lightning from its eyes.

Native Americans believed their Great Spirit made foot prints in Medicine Rock near Gettysburg, S.D.

PLACES

BLACK HILLS

The Black Hills, once under an ocean, are older than the Alps, Himalayas or Rocky Mountains.

In 1945 the Black Hills was considered as permanent site for the world headquarters of the United Nations. Greece was the only country to support the concept. Architect Luvine Berg planned a city named America Center in the Black Hills. Berg's plans called for 170-foot wide avenues encircling a one-million sq.-foot capitol and 20,000-seat auditorium. The 30-story capitol would support a huge globe. A World Highway would stretch from Alaska, through the Black Hills, to South America, then over to Africa.

Black Hills National Forest is 1.3 million acres that also embraces an 111-mile Centennial Trail.

BADLANDS

The Badlands were once a portion of a giant salt water sea. A volcano pushed up the floor of the Badlands. Thirty-eight million years ago rivers rushed down from the newly risen Black Hills, and spread their mud, gravel and sand on the Badlands. The floodplain built up with spires, ridges and pinnacles covering an area 100 miles long and 50 miles wide.

The Badlands was home for thousands of dinosaurs, about 25 million years ago. Their fossils became preserved in the soggy marshlands.

President Franklin Roosevelt proclaimed the Badlands a national monument in 1939. In 1978, President Jimmy Carter made it a national park, its purpose being to preserve the scenery, wildlife, fossils and plants.

The Badlands will be completely eroded in one million years.

HOME SWEET HOME

Hugging the east side of the Badlands is the only sod house remaining in South Dakota.

The state's lowest zip code is 57001 (Alcester); the highest, 58538 (Standing Rock).

The gray, two-story Governor's Residence (Pierre) was built in 1936 as a WPA project. The fireplaces were made of petrified wood from the Badlands. Among the 18 rooms is a Native American Room.

Col. W.C. Boyce bought Fort Sisseton and used it as his lavish, private estate.

Spearfish was South Dakota's fastest growing town during the 1980s.

The largest home in South Dakota is the 82-room residence of Ruth Ziolkowski (Custer).

During 1944-45, 200 German POWs were held at Fort Meade. Gen. Rommel's African Corps had to work in nearby sugar beet fields during the day. Most of the Germans were older masons and carpenters and were also used to help reconstruct the fort's original buildings.

The entire state of South Dakota was obtained by five major treaties between the federal government and Dakota people.

A hidden city with a stone wall spanning 1,200 feet was discovered in a Black Hills cow pasture in 1927. Farmer C.H. Reich was plowing south of Rapid City when he uncovered portions of the wall. The farmer took a piece to a gypsy who said the stone was part of a "temple of gold." Since the wall merged into a nearby hill, it was believed that the city was concealed inside. Even President Coolidge paid the 50-cent fee for a curious visit. By the 1930s the Hidden City was the top tourist attraction of South Dakota. Geologists then proclaimed it a natural series of dikes. Traffic began shifting to the new Mount Rushmore carving. By WWII the Hidden City had closed to tours.

There are eight South Dakotans to the mile.

Fort Pierre is the state's oldest continuously inhabited white settlement, established in 1817.

Sioux Falls was founded in 1856 and maintains it is the oldest town in South Dakota, even though it was abandoned in 1860 and destroyed by Native Americans.

In 1876 Deadwood was the largest community in South Dakota, with 25,000 prospectors.

EVENTS/TOURS

Belle Fourche, S.D., is home of the Black Hills Round-Up.

Hot Springs hosts the Miss South Dakota pageant each June.

Murdo, S.D., has the world famous Pioneer Auto Museum featuring over 200 cars.

Museum of Geology, South Dakota School of Mines (Rapid City) includes 1,200 different minerals, including meteorites and gold nuggets.

Terry Peak (Lead) can accommodate 6,000 skiers every hour.

Reptile Gardens (Rapid City) offers alligator wrestling, rattlesnake milking and an Enchanted Animal Village.

Marine Life (Rapid City) has the state's only live killer shark.

The Arne B. Larson Collection of Musical Instruments (Vermillion) is the world's largest musical collection.

The Cheyenne River Sioux Indian Reservation (Eagle Butte) has the Sioux Culture Center.

The Chapel in the Hills (Rapid City) was built in 1969. It is an exact replica of the famous 840-year-old Borgund Church of Norway.

Enchanted Doll Museum (Mitchell) has 4,000 dolls.

The South Dakota Korean and Vietnam War Memorial (Pierre) opened in 1985.

Tyndall, S.D., has a balloon museum.

The state's oldest museum is W.H.Over (Vermillion).

Fort Sisseton, S.D., is a restored 1864 Army frontier post.

The first fair in South Dakota was held in Huron in 1885. After another year in Huron the fair board began a rotation system among towns. In 1905 Huron's railroad barons deeded 85 acres to the state for use as a permanent site. A grandstand arrived from Yankton. By 1991 the fair had grown to 83 buildings on 170 acres.

Western Woodcarvings, Custer, S.D., houses the world's largest collection of animated Old West wooden figures.

The South Dakota Cowboy and Western Heritage Hall of Fame, is in Fort Pierre, S.D.

Deadwood, S.D., hosts "Days of '76."

The Flintstone's Bedrock City is in Custer, S.D.

WATER, WATER EVERYWHERE
One billion tons of water are controlled by South Dakota's Missouri River dams.

Wall Drug (Wall) serves 78,000 gallons of free ice water to customers each summer.

Of the three greatest waterfalls in the Black Hills, one is lost, one is buried in a mountain and one is completely dry. The lost waterfall is called Forsyth Falls and was photographed by the 1874 Custer Expedition. Thunderhead Falls is 600 feet inside a mountain where the waters of Rapid Creek travel over a 32-ft. precipice. Spearfish Falls is bone dry. At one time the biggest falls in the Hills was so great that it was nicknamed "Baby Niagara." But in 1917 Homestake Mine diverted the waters into a hydroelectric pipeline.

Evans Plunge (Hot Springs) is the world's largest natural warm water indoor swimming pool. The slide stretches 164-ft. There is an inflow of 5,000 gallons of water-per-minute, with a complete change of water 16 times daily.

Soldiers named the lakes near Lake City, S.D., according to how close they were to Fort Sisseton: Two Mile, Four Mile, Six Mile and Nine Mile Lakes still bear those names.

Roughlock Falls got its name from pioneers having to chain their wagon wheels together in order to descend the nearby road.

The Little White River (Rosebud) is South Dakota's steadiest flowing stream.

French trappers did not like the name of Handy's Lake (Charles Mix County) so the name was changed to Lake Andes.

The falls in Sioux Falls drop 90 feet over the distance of a mile.

Sheridan, once the county seat of Pennington County, is now at the bottom of a lake, with its only visitors being scuba divers and fish.

South Dakota has 33 creeks officially known as "Dry."

Lake Kampeska has a beach 2,000-ft. long.

Big Stone Island Nature Area is accessible in the summer only by boat and only by ice in the winter.

Long Lake (Watertown) has buried treasure somewhere under its eastern banks. A sack of gold coins taken from a train robbery was hidden by a Native American named Gray Foot.

Lake Poinsett is the largest natural lake in South Dakota, 7,866 acres.

A ferry operates between Running Water, S.D., and Niobara, Neb.

The Missouri River Bridge over Lake Francis Case is the longest span between the Mississippi and the Pacific.

South Dakota's Red River is one of six American rivers that flow north.

Deep artesian wells provide the water for the Flaming Fountain at the state Capitol in Pierre.

In 1955 the entire town of Pollock was moved to higher ground. What couldn't be moved was leveled. Lake Pocasse covers what was the town.

The Missouri River drains a 529,350-sq.-ft. basin.

South Dakota has 15,000 artesian wells.

DAMS (CITY), YEAR BUILT, LAKE FORMED
- **Big Bend** (Fort Thompson), 1966, Lake Sharpe
- **Fort Randall** (Pickstown), 1956, Francis Case
- **Gavin's Point** (Yankton), 1956, Lewis and Clark
- **Oahe** (Pierre), 1962, Oahe

AREAS, BUILDINGS
Chute Roosters, Hill City, S.D., has the world's only museum/supper club. Guests eat in an 1886 barn.

Big Stone Power Plant (Milbank) is jointly owned by three investor-owned utilities. Despite the fact it uses 9,000 tons of coal each day, it is a pollution-free operation.

Rapid City, S.D., was originally laid out with a simple compass, in 1876, by Long John Brennan.

Charles Mix County, S.D., spent two years as part of Nebraska.

Verendrye Hill Monument (Pierre) is made of stones from every county in the state.

Pierre, S.D., is at the westernmost drift of the glaciers.

OUT OF SITE!

Butte County, S.D., is the geographical center of the U.S.: Latitude 44 degrees 58' North, Longitude 103 degrees 46' West.

South Dakota has one area code, 605, and two time zones: East River, Central, and West River, Mountain.

As of 1992 South Dakota had three nature areas, 13 state parks, 24 recreational areas and 40 lakeside areas.

The states of Montana, Nebraska, North Dakota, South Dakota and Wyoming can be seen from atop the 7,076-foot Terry Peak (Lead).

There are over a dozen cities in the United States with populations greater than the entire state of South Dakota. Some South Dakota counties, however, are larger than some states.

Rapid City was started in 1876 by a group of unsuccessful miners, to provide supplies for the gold fields.

PARK IT

Seth Bullock (Belle Fourche) wrote the legislation that resulted in Congress establishing Yellowstone National Park.

SOUTH DAKOTA HAS:
- Three national grasslands (Buffalo Gap, Fort Pierre, Grand River)
- Two national parks (Badlands, Wind Cave)
- One national memorial (Mount Rushmore)
- One national landmark (Wounded Knee)
- One national monument (Jewel Cave)
- Zero national historical battlefields, parks or sites

STATES WHOLLY OR PARTIALLY INCLUDED IN THE ORIGINAL DAKOTA TERRITORY:
- Montana
- North Dakota
- South Dakota
- Wyoming

Carl Grupp's Bet On It! Trivia Myths:
UNSUNG HERO

FORT PIERRE, MARCH 23, 1910:
NEARSIGHTED COWBOY CODY WILLIAMS MISTAKES
MONTSTRO THE BULL FOR THE FAMILY MILK COW
AND INADVERTENTLY INTRODUCES
A BRAND-NEW RODEO EVENT.

NAMES

WHO WAS WHO

- Sparky Anderson (Bridgewater): **George Anderson**
- Catherine Bach (Faith): **Cathy Bachman**
- Gutzon Borglum (Hermosa): **John Borglum**
- Calamity Jane (Deadwood): **Martha Jane Canary Burke**
- Crazy Horse (Moreau River): **Curly**
- Deadwood Dick (Deadwood): **Nat Love**
- Fischer Quints (Aberdeen): **A, B, C, D and E**
- Gall (Mobridge): **Pizi**
- Pappy Hoel (Sturgis): **John Hoel**
- Lame Johnny (Deadwood): **Cornelius Donahue**
- Mary Hart (Sioux Falls): **Mary Jo Harum**
- Wild Bill Hickok (Deadwood): **James Hickok**
- Cheryl Ladd (Huron): **Cheryl Stoppelmore**
- Frederick Manfred (Vermillion): **Feike Feikema**
- Mother Joseph (Aberdeen): **Mary Ellen Butler**
- Poker Alice (Sturgis): **Alice Tubbs**
- Potato Creek Johnny (Deadwood): **John Perrett**
- Preacher Smith (Deadwood): **Henry Weston Smith**
- Clint Roberts (Presho): **Clint Nye**
- Red Stangland (Sioux Falls): **Eider Stangland**
- Sacajawea (Mobridge): **Bird Woman**
- Sitting Bull (Grand River): **Slow**
- Spotted Tail (Black Hills): **Jumping Buffalo**
- Uncle Torvald (Sioux Falls): **Robert Johnson**
- Mamie Van Doren (Rowena): **Joan Lucille Olander**

NATURAL FORMATIONS THAT LOOK LIKE THEIR NAMES

- Altar (Badlands)
- Battleship (Castle Butte Canyon)
- Bishop (Badlands)
- Cathedral Spires (Custer)
- Cleghorn's Flower (Rapid City)
- Elephant's Head (Hot Springs)
- Hogback (Roberts County)
- Needles (Black Hills)
- Notches (Hot Springs)
- Old Man in the Butte (Corson County)
- Saddle Horn (Harding County)
- Traffic Cop (Needles Highway)
- Twin Sisters (Pringle)

NAME SUGGESTIONS FOR SOUTH DAKOTA, 1883:

- Dakota
- Garfield
- Lincoln
- Magatanka, Dakota for "Big Country"

- Maya-Wakan, means "God's Country"
- Mazatinka, means "Land of the Prairie"
- Miniese Wakpa, means "Missouri River"
- Tinta-Maka, means "Prairie Land"
- Waca-Tinta, means "Prairie Flower"

BANDS OF LAWRENCE WELK (YANKTON):
- America's Little Band
- Champagne Music Makers
- Honolulu Fruit Orchestra
- Hotsy Totsy Boys
- Peerless Entertainers
- Novelty Orchestra

NAME ODDITIES:
Holy Terror Mine (Keystone) was named after the owner's wife, who always complained the family mines were never named in her honor. The 1874 mine, ironically, soon yielded $70,000 worth of gold each week!

KELO-Land (Sioux Falls) was dubbed when a staff member sarcastically suggested the station reverse the sound of "Land O'Lakes," an early sponsor.

South Dakota means "friend."

Native Americans knew the Black Hills as "Paha Sapa" and the Badlands as "Maico Sico."

Frustration Spire, Cathedral Spires, Shaft of Light and Teeter Totter Tower are some of the Needles in the Black Hills.

Oahe is Dakota for "firm foundation."

In order to not be confused with the well-established Motel 6 chain, some Aberdonians named their new motel the Super 8, with original rates at $8.88-per-room, 1974.

Nemo was named by a miner who spelled "omen" backwards. A chunk of quartz rolled backwards down a hill and he didn't want to change his luck.

Homestake Mine (Lead) was started by miners who hoped to "stake" a claim that would yield them enough money to build a "home".

Hisega was named after the first letters of six girls who picnicked there in 1908: Helen, Ida, Sadie, Ethel, Grace and Ada.

Ellsworth Air Force Base (Rapid City) was previously called Rapid City and Weaver. Eisenhower named it for a plane crash victim.

Gen. W.S. Harney never saw the peak named in his honor in South Dakota.

EROS (Sioux Falls) stands for Earth Resources Observation Systems, and houses satellite photos.

Terry Peak was named for Gen. Alfred Terry.

Fort Meade (Sturgis) was named for the commander of the Army of the Potomac in the Civil War. Gen. Sheridan selected the site and laid out the camp by personally riding around the area and pointing with his sword the location of each building.

Caverns and passages in Jewel Cave (Black Hills) include the names of $, !, ?, Confucius Chimney, Hippodrome, King Kong's Cave, MacGee's Closet, No Passing Zone, Hell Canyon, Torture Room, Hurricane Corner, Mighty Tight Street, Einstein Tube, Grief, Sunburn Haven and Easy Street.

Horse Thief Lake (Mt. Rushmore) is named for Lame Johnny, since he kept his stolen horses near by.

Saddle Creek (Faulk County) was renamed "Nixon."

Yankton held the title of "Cement City" for 19 years, until the British owners shut the plant down in 1909.

Four cowboys killed near Grindstone, S.D., in 1877 were the namesakes of Deadman's Creek.

Fool Soldier Band was the name of a skirmish in a hay field near Sioux Falls when 11 Native Americans rescued some Europeans from being scalped, in 1862.

Pathfinder Atomic Plant (Sioux Falls) was named in honor of explorer John C. Fremont.

Sen. Karl Mundt (Madison) coined the term "pumpkin papers," from the State Department papers hidden by Whittaker Chambers in his Maryland pumpkin patch.

The first 100 miles of the Yellowstone Trail are named in honor of J.W. Parmley (Ipswich).

The first white to claim South Dakota for anybody was French explorer Robert Cavelier, who claimed a huge chunk of the Midwest for Louis XIV, calling it, "Louisiana," in 1682.

Enemy Swim (Day County) was named for Chippewa who managed to escape nearby Dakota by swimming away.

L. Frank Baum (Aberdeen) created the mythical land by looking at the letters on a two-volume set of encyclopedia, "O-Z."

Lewis and Clark gave the Missouri River tributaries in South Dakota their names.

The largest donation by a foundation to the preservation of Mount Rushmore was The Gannett Foundation, headed by Allen Neuharth (Eureka). The foundation changed its name to The Freedom Forum the day after it completed giving $1 million towards the monument.

Over half of the state's counties are named for white, males prominent in government at the time the territory was formed. Most of the 25 counties named for legislators were never visited by their namesakes. Also found among the county names are seven Civil War heroes, a French peasant (Bon Homme), a Roman goddess (Aurora) and the King of Norway (Haaken).

Some 6,000 locations in South Dakota have place names.

In 1900 a railroad survey crew stopped by a small shack for a coffee break. Because of the good brew, the crew dubbed the site "Java." That October the nickname became the town's official name.

A valley near Custer is named America Center.

E.H. McIntosh platted Mound City in March 1885 and called it Mound City because the small hills to the north, were referred to as "bachelor mounds."

The first three counties created in South Dakota: Dakotah, Wabasha and Wahnahta, formed the entire half of the state.

Early French explorers called the lands of South Dakota "prairie" which was their term for meadow.

The Coolidges were so popular in South Dakota that during their 1927 visit Squaw Creek was renamed Grace Coolidge Creek, and a nearby peak was renamed Mt. Coolidge.

SOME TOWN NAMES:
Akaska means "a Native American woman who lives with several men."

Andover was named by foreign railroad officials as "end over," which slurred into "and over."

Artas is Greek for "bread."

Bancroft was named for an insurance agent who spent many hours in the town mystifying the citizens with card tricks and magic.

Beebe was one of four South Dakota towns named for bankers.

Bradley was named for a visitor who saved the life of the chief engineer in charge of construction, during a local labor fight.

Bruce was named for New York's black U.S. Senator B.K. Bruce.

Canton was named by settlers who believed the town was situated diametrically opposite Canton, China.

Cavour was named for Italy's father of their railroad system.

Columbia was named after the popular song, "Hail, Columbia."

De Smet was named for Father Peter De Smet, Apostle of the Native Americans.

Faith, according to one version, was named after a rich girl with that name. Others claim pioneers had to have it, in order to live there.

Fort Pierre is the oldest continuous white settlement in the state.

Hayti is named for the twisted hay tied and used as fuel.

Hecla was named for an Icelandic volcano.

Hosmer is the maiden name of a Captain Arnold's wife.

Howard was named for a lawyer who had recently died, Howard Farmer.

Kadoka is Dakota for "hole in the wall," an entrance to the Badlands.

Marvin was named after a Marvin Company safe in the nearby post office.

Mobridge is derived from a telegrapher's contraction for MO (Missouri) and bridge.

Ordway was named for the governor of New Hampshire.

Philip was named after Scotty Philip, owner of the world's largest buffalo herd.

Pukwana was named for Longfellow's word for peace pipe, in "Hiawatha."

Roscoe was named for a U.S. Senator from New York.

Tular was slurred from "Two liars," in honor of two brothers who told tall tales to entertain passengers when a train stopped nearby.

Wall is for the wall of the Badlands.

Winner won the struggle to establish a town on the railroad right-of-way.

NAMES OF FOLKS:

Gov. George Speaker Mickelson received his middle name because his father was South Dakota's Speaker of the House.

George McGovern (Mitchell) named his son, Steve, after Adlai Stevenson.

Todd Allen (Sioux Falls) was named Miss Gay South Dakota, 1991. Todd and Allen are his first and middle names.

McGovern's Secret Service code name in his 1972 presidential campaign was "Redwood." Eleanor McGovern was "Redwood II." Eleanor traveled on commercial air flights under the name "E. Morgan."

Always found chomping on a cigar, Poker Alice (Sturgis) earned her nickname and a reputation as the most notorious Faro dealer and madam in the Black Hills.

An angry lad named Anderson (Bridgewater) threw a basketball opponent through two glass doors and earned the nickname "Sparky."

Hickok got his nickname when a woman shouted "Good for you, Wild Bill," when Hickok calmed down a lynch mob.

Since Explorer William Clark had difficulty pronouncing Sah-Cah-Gar-We-Ah, he called her Jane.

Calamity Jane said she earned her nickname after rescuing a captain on her horse during a daring enemy attack. A high class madame, Dora DuFran, however says the nickname was picked up from sick folks saying, "where calamity was, there was Jane." Historian Watson Parker suggests a third version: the nickname came from the fact that Calamity Jane's male friends picked up a venereal "calamity" from her.

Vice President Humphrey (Doland) was known as "Lightning," by the Secret Service.

Gen. Sam Sturgis named the county and the town of "Sturgis" after his son, Jack, slain in the Battle of Little Bighorn.

NICKNAMES OF FOLKS:
- **W.H.H. Beadle** (Sioux Falls): Savior of the School Lands
- **Ben Black Elk** (Black Hills): Fifth Face of Mount Rushmore
- **Tom Brokaw** (Yankton): Duncan the Wonderhorse; Buttonnose
- **Muriel Humphrey Brown** (Doland): Bucky
- **Calamity Jane** (Deadwood): Champion Swearer of the Black Hills; Queen of the Wild West; White Devil of the Yellowstone
- **Everett Comstock** (Aberdeen): Mr. Golf of South Dakota
- **Jack Crawford** (Black Hills): Poet Scout

- **Myron Floren** (Roslyn): Mr. 7:15
- **Hamlin Garland** (Aberdeen): Dean of American Letters
- **Hugh Glass** (Black Hills): One-bite cannibal
- **Niels Hansen** (Brookings): Burbank of the Plains
- **Wild Bill Hickok** (Deadwood): Prince of Pistoleers, Duck Bill
- **Hubert Humphrey** (Huron): Happy Warrior; Pinky
- **Fiorello LaGuardia** (Fort Sturgis): The Little Flower
- **Jack McCall** (Deadwood): Broken Nose
- **J.W. Parmley** (Ipswich): Father of Yellowstone Trail
- **Scotty Philip** (Philip): Buffalo King
- **Poker Alice** (Sturgis): Queen of the Women Gamblers of the Old West.
- **Earle Sande** (Groton): The Dutchman; Handy Guy
- **Norm Van Brocklin** (Parade): The Dutchman
- **Lawrence Welk** : Liberace of the accordion
- **Laura Ingalls Wilder** (DeSmet): Half-Pint
- **Korczak Ziolkowski** (Crazy Horse): Storyteller in stone

NICKNAMES OF PLACES, THINGS:
- **Aberdeen**: Hub City
- **Aces and Eights** held by Wild Bill Hickok when he was killed: Dead Man's Hand.
- **Clint Anderson's home** (Centerville): Lazy V Cross
- **Ellsworth Air Force Base staffer**: Black Hills Bandit
- **Black Hills National Cemetery** (Sturgis): Arlington of the West
- **Brookings**: American Siberia
- **Badger Clark's home** (Custer): Badger Hole
- **Black Hills gold miner**: Pilgrim
- **Buffalo Gap** (Custer): buffalo highway
- **Chamber award** (Aberdeen): George
- **Deadwood, Lead**: Twin Cities
- **Deadwood**: Boss City of the Black Hills
- **De Smet**: Little Town on the Prairie
- **Eureka**: Wheat Capital of the World
- **Pacific unit of Gov. Joe Foss** (Sioux Falls): Joe's Flying Circus
- **Gayville**: Hay capital of the world
- **Groton**: Sunflower Capital of World
- **Humphrey's home**: Triple H
- **Huron**: Gateway to the West
- **McGovern's campaign plane**: Dakota Queen II
- **Minuteman II missiles** (Badlands): Birds
- **Missouri River**: Old Misery, Big Muddy
- **Mobridge**: Bridge City; Oasis of Oahe; Walleye Capital of the World
- **Mount Rushmore**: Shrine of Democracy; Four Faces
- **1930 Morrell strike** (Sioux Falls): Bloody Friday
- **Allen Neuharth's home** (Eureka): Pumpkin Center
- **Pick-Sloan Missouri River Basin Project**: state's four dams

- **Pierre cattle trail**: The Strip
- **Pine Ridge FBI murders**: ResMurs, for Reservation Murders
- **Rapid City**: Gypsum Camp; Hay Town
- **Replacing nuclear missiles (Badlands)**: Force Modernization
- **Sioux Falls**: Divorce Capital, Queen City of the Plains
- **Sitting Bull's village**: Flying By
- **South Dakota**: Sunshine State; Coyote State; Land of Infinite Variety; Rushmore State
- **Sturgis**: Scoop town
- **Unsuccessful Black Hills miner**: Gopher
- **U.S.S. South Dakota**: Battleship X; Big Bastard
- **Webster**: Buffalo Republic
- **Yankton**: Mother City of the Dakotas; Cement City

FISCHER QUINTUPLETS

WHO'S WHO

Fischer Quints (Aberdeen) were born September 14, 1963, at St. Luke's Hospital. Since the names were too long for bracelets, nurses, who were nuns, labeled the babies A, B, C, D and E:

- **Mary Ann**, named for her mom
- **Mary Magdalene**, for paternal grandmother
- **Mary Catherine**, for St. Luke's hospital administrator, Sr. Catherine Davis M. Stephen
- **James Andrew**, for father, Andrew Fischer, and physician Dr. James Berbos,
- **Mary Margaret**, for head baby nurse R.N. Marguerite Doran

Dr. James Berbos had delivered 3,607 babies by the time he delivered the Fischer Quints.

At the time of their birth, the father of the Fischer Quints, Andy Fischer, was a $76-a-week shipping clerk.

Until Mary Ann Fischer gave birth to quints, the only other mention of her name in a newspaper, had been her bowling scores.

COUNTING BY FIVES

The day before Mary Ann Fischer gave birth to healthy quintuplets in 1963, she milked a cow, canned dill pickles and hoed her garden. The 197-pound expectant mother was so large that she had to pick up a bucket of milk, take a single step, set the pail down, pause, pick up the bucket, take a single step, etc.

Mary Ann and Andy Fischer met while bowling in Aberdeen.

Mary Ann Fischer won the 100-yard dash at an All-State Track meet.

Mary Ann Fischer was Protestant until two years into her marriage, when she became a Catholic.

Because husband, Andy, refused, Dr. James Berbos had to inform May Ann Fischer she would deliver multiple births.

Andy Fischer had never been interviewed by a reporter until the quints were born.

Andy "Shine" Fischer, was so nicknamed because, as a youth, he worked at a Sunshine Grocery Store.

Mary Ann Fischer had only one store bought dress before the quints were born.

SPECIAL DELIVERY

The Fischer Quints are the first surviving quints in American history, the fourth known quints born in the Western Hemisphere, and the 50th known set in the world.

The odds of Mary Ann Fischer giving birth to quints in 1963 were one in 57 million.

The Fischer Quints, four girls and a boy, also had four other sisters and a brother.

The quints were born two months premature; all were nonsurgical births.

Mary Ann Fischer gave birth without an anesthetic.

Because the South Dakota Birth Certificate only had room for triplets, it had to be custom altered to accommodate the Fischer Quints.

Quintuplets Jimmy and Mary Ann each developed from a single egg. Girls Cathy, Margie and Maggie are identical triplets.

Mary Ann Fischer remained conscious through the birth of her quints.

The Fischer Quints were delivered in one hour, 3 minutes.

The first purchase by the father of the Fischer Quints was two cows.

Dr. Berbos delivered the Fischer Quints free of charge.

Two isolettes arrived from Minneapolis, by car, to hold the Fischer Quints.

The first meal eaten by the Fischer Quints was glucose and water drained through tubes inserted in their noses.

St. Luke's Hospital did not charge the Fischers beyond what their insurance covered, for the delivery of the Quints.

The Fischer Quints were the second set of quints born in the Western Hemisphere in eight days. The others were Venezuelan.

In order to escape all the media attention drawn by the birth of his quints, Andy Fischer hid out in Sacred Heart Catholic Church.

Twelve medical personnel delivered the quints.

A FISH BOWL OF LIFE

President Kennedy sent the Fischers a congratulatory telegram from Rhode Island. Pope Paul VI sent five gold medallions.

The quints were featured on four separate covers of the Saturday Evening Post.

As highest bidder, Curtis Publishing bought exclusive rights to photograph the Fischer Quints.

During a single day — September 23, 1963 — bandleader Lawrence Welk visited the quints, their mother went home from the hospital, James got his first try at milk from a bottle, and all five quints were inducted into the Dakota Native American tribe.

Sen. George McGovern introduced a bill into Congress exempting the Fischers from federal taxes until the quints were 21. The IRS said no way, but did decide all gifts were tax-free.

The Fischers built a new house west of Aberdeen. When the family moved into the 17-room home, it had eight bedrooms, three bathrooms and an entire wing that could be sealed off.

Whenever photographers showed up to photograph the quints, Mary Ann Fischer wanted an accounting of each roll of film.

A reporter, dressed as a nun, once visited the quints and successfully sneaked off with several recipes of Mary Ann Fischer.

BABIES...NOT QUINTS
Mary Ann and Andy Fischer always called their quintuplets "babies," never "quints."

The quints were one week old before they were weighed.

The Fischer Quints were baptized and confirmed on the same day.

When the quints turned 21 in 1985, most were still living at home in Aberdeen.

In anticipation of tourist traffic due to the quints, Highway 12 was widened near Aberdeen.

Through faith, persistence and lots of common sense, Mary Ann Fischer raised her 11 children out of the public eye.

While teenagers, the four girl quints were forbidden to date and each had to undergo corrective eye surgery.

Mary Ann Fischer never read any of Dr. Spock's books about raising children.

Mary Ann Fischer gave birth to six children in less than 13 months: quints in September 1963, followed by daughter, Cindy, in September 1964.

Four days after he delivered the Fischer Quints, Dr. James Berbos delivered a baby to a Mrs. Rodney Fischer, no relation to the family.

Over 25,000 tiny pins used in a Quint Parade were painstakingly painted pink and blue by Girl Scout Troop No. 66.

The Fischer's new house did not have any room called the "nursery."

In 1980, when the quints were 17, parents Mary Ann and Andy Fischer were granted a divorce.

FISCHER FICTION

Over the years the media claimed the Fischers received Midas-sized piles of cash, all of which was false, said Mary Ann Fischer in 1992.

What usually happened in most instances is that promised gifts never materialized, or donations were much smaller than reported.

Early stories, which weren't worth the paper upon which they were published, claimed the Fischers received:

- $250,000
- $125,000 house
- $75,000 in services
- $45,000 for each quint upon graduation from high school
- $8,000 for TV rights
- $4,000 for 24-hour exclusive TV rights
- 500 shares of various corporate stock
- 15 different college scholarships

GOLD

ALL MINE

Homestake Gold Mine (Lead) is the largest-producing gold mine in the Western Hemisphere.

Homestake has yielded over 35 million ounces of gold.

Each year the mine produces 570,000 ounces — that's 17.8 tons of gold, folks!

Except during WW II, Homestake has operated continuously since 1876.

Homestake was discovered by Fred and Moses Manuel April 9,1876.

Homestake is a modern hard rock mine that employs over 1,300 miners and other workers whose work area is often 1.5 miles below the surface.

Homestake needs 2,500 tons of ore to process a 27.4-pound bar of gold.

An underground fire in 1907 in the Homestake Mine took 80 million cubic feet of water to put out.

Areas of Homestake that caved in were nicknamed "Sinking Gardens."

In 1934 Homestake provided South Dakota with one-third of the state budget.

Homestake Mine shut down for two months during 1901-1902 when union miners refused to work with non-union workers.

Two-thirds of Homestake's 1,300 employees were raised in South Dakota.

Homestake was started by Henry Harney, the Moes Brothers and Red Manual. The group sold the mine to George Hearst who made a fortune which helped to finance the newspaper empire built by his son, William Randolph Hearst. In the 1870s George Hearst pioneered modern gold-mining techniques while working for 18 months on his 4.7-acre Homestake Gold Mine.

Between 1876 and 1945 40 million tons of gold ore were removed from the Open Cut (Lead). The Open Cut will eventually be 960 feet deep, 1,800 feet wide and 4,500 feet in length.

Few Homestake Gold miners ever see the gold they mine. A ton of ore yields barely enough gold for a wedding ring.

During WWII Homestake Mine made hand grenades.

North America's richest gold mine has shafts plunging 8,000 feet.

Every ton of rock mined by Homestake yields a chunk of gold about the size of a marble.

The Open Cut is the only spot where Homestake Company's gold vein reached the surface.

Where once a solid mountain stood, The Open Cut of the Homestake Gold Mine is a man-made canyon hundreds of feet deep and 2,000 feet across created by removing 48 million tons of rock. As the gold ore was mined, the cut got bigger and Lead's business district diminished. Five full blocks no longer exist.

Since WWII Homestake has given tours to two million tourists who are welcome to sample the ore. Because of this practice, the company gets rid of about 100 pounds of crushed rock every day.

GOLDEN TOUCH

A washtub holding $1 million worth of gold is buried somewhere in the Black Hills. In 1879, by working a rich claim near Newton Fork, two prospectors named Shafer and Humphrey managed to fill the tub with gold. Humphrey eventually took his share of the claim, and returned to his family in Ohio. Shafer, however, died, with no known relatives. Not a single nugget has ever turned up. The tub is still out there, and so is the gold.

One thousand soldiers accompanied Lt. Col. Custer when he escorted scientists to look for gold in the Black Hills in 1874. Gold was discovered in the Black Hills on July 27, 1874, by Horatio Ross, a miner with the Custer expedition. A sensational gold rush ensued, with papers claiming the ore vein "stretched 30 miles wide!" Custer himself minimized the discovery, giving it but brief reference near the conclusion of his report to the government.

Discovery of gold in 1874 nudged the first tide of white settlers into the Black Hills. During a single five-month period over 10,000 people flooded the area. Deadwood became the center of the Black Hills, as well as the wildest town in the wild, wild west.

The Black Hills gold rush, the last great gold rush in the United States, was soon followed by silver and tin booms in the Hills.

The custom of establishing legal gold claims in the Black Hills was adapted from German and Spanish laws.

Some were so desperate to claim areas in the Black Hills that one gold miner claimed a pine tree near Rapid City as his gold mine, saying its "bends, appurtenances and sinuosities" were to be used by him, for mining purposes.

The evening campfires of the record 75,000 gold miners in the Black Hills in 1876 were so close together that one soldier wrote that he could walk through the Black Hills at night without any difficulty.

In the early 1800s Father DeSmet warned the Dakota not to mention gold being discovered in the Black Hills. Native Americans kept silent for over seven decades.

During 1877 over $2 million worth of gold was mined in Deadwood, S.D.

The 1877 Black Hills gold rush was set off when prospector Potato Creek Johnny found a seven-ounce nugget in a creek outside Deadwood.

A wealthy English sportsman, Sir St. George Gore, had known about gold in the Black Hills, as early as 1854. While trout-fishing near Belle Fourche, Gore, who was rich already and only interested in sport, warned everybody in his fishing party never to mention it. As a result, another 20 years passed before another white, Gen. Custer and his men, discovered Black Hills gold, and sounded a world-wide alert.

BLACK GOLD
The first Black Hills Gold Jewelry was fashioned by New Yorker S.T. Butler (Deadwood) in 1878. Butler had followed the gold strikes from California to Montana to South Dakota, fashioning jewelry along the way.

Black Hills Gold was originally known as "Native Gold Jewelry."

Rings are the most popular Black Hills Gold jewelry items sold.

Original Black Hills Gold dies from the late 1800s are still in use.

Since 1969 Black Hills Gold has been owned by Betty and Lloyd West, F.L. Thorpe and Company.

The design of grapes and leaves honors the plant that once saved Butler, while lost in the forest, from starving. The distinctive colors follow the ancient Roman colors used in Biblical times.

Every six months the cigarette ashes and the sediment from Black Hills Gold wash basins are cleaned in order to recover the precious bits of gold dust that fall to the floor during the creation of jewelry.

BLACK HILLS GOLD COLORS:
- Gold
- Green
- Red
- Yellow

Carl Grupp's Bet On It! Trivia Myths:

EAST RIVER AND WEST RIVER, OR THE SAGA OF BARROWS AND GILTS

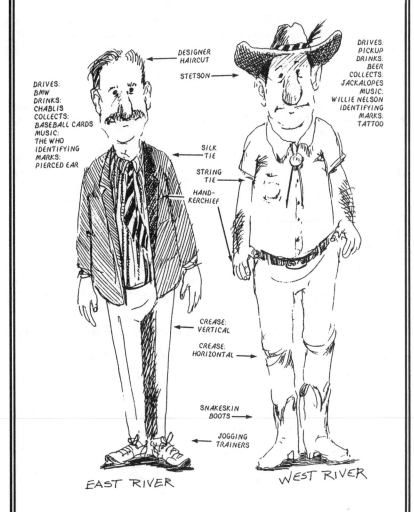

DRIVES:
BMW
DRINKS:
CHABLIS
COLLECTS:
BASEBALL CARDS
MUSIC:
THE WHO
IDENTIFYING
MARKS:
PIERCED EAR

DESIGNER
HAIRCUT

STETSON

DRIVES:
PICKUP
DRINKS:
BEER
COLLECTS:
JACKALOPES
MUSIC:
WILLIE NELSON
IDENTIFYING
MARKS:
TATTOO

SILK
TIE

STRING
TIE

HAND-
KERCHIEF

CREASE:
VERTICAL

CREASE:
HORIZONTAL

SNAKESKIN
BOOTS

JOGGING
TRAINERS

EAST RIVER

WEST RIVER

BARROWS AND GILTS, IDENTICAL TWIN BROTHERS, WERE SEPARATED AT BIRTH AND RAISED IN SOUTH DAKOTA ON EITHER SIDE OF THE MISSOURI RIVER. AMAZINGLY, WHEN FINALLY REUNITED AT THE AGE OF 40, THEY HAD NOTHING IN COMMON EXCEPT HEMORRHOIDS.

OOPS!

The wrong nose is carved on Washington's face on Mount Rushmore. Moreover, one of his eyes is five feet higher than the other.

One South Dakota scene had to be cut from *Dances With Wolves* when Kevin Costner's horse passed gas.

Upon the death of state economic director Robert Martin (Pierre) in 1976, it was discovered he was a bigamist with two wives and two families.

While interviewing 1959 Miss South Dakota Meredith Auld, Tom Brokaw (Yankton) thought his microphone was off when he told her he loved her. Thousands of listeners heard the announcement.

When too much snow melted on the fabric-supported DakotaDome (Vermillion), the roof sagged. In order to drain it, a university staff member used a rifle to shoot a couple holes in the ceiling. And it did drain. All over the indoor field.

So anxious was Dakota Territory to be recognized in Congress that it even rushed the election results of Midway County and its thousand healthy voters. Congress later discovered that Midway County did not exist. Nor did its thousand voters. In fact, the election was held in an area that had been evacuated because of a possible enemy attack.

Perhaps the longest night in South Dakota history was experienced by a zookeeper at the Reptile Gardens (Rapid City) when he accidentally locked himself in the Giant Python cage over night, with five 20-ft. pythons between himself and the door. No one knew he was in there until the rest of the staff showed up for work the next day.

Five days before his year-long sentence was up, Ray Drysden cut his way out of jail in Hot Springs, into the arms of Sheriff C. L. Johnson. A judge called Drysden "impatient," and sentenced him to 18 months in the state prison.

In 1953 tiny Igloo, S.D., was designated as part of the nation's strategic defense arsenal.

The communities of Haywood and Custer literally battled it out as county seat of Custer County, until surveyors discovered in 1881 that Haywood was two miles inside another county.

Only after Red Stangland (Sioux Falls) had 30,000 covers for a new Norwegian joke book printed, did he realize the printers did the wrong cover. Another time the wrong ink was used and Ole and Lena came out purple. Uffda!!!

The city of Lemmon, at one point, considered bulldozing down the historic Petrified Park, made entirely from ancient petrified rock, and hauling everything to the landfill.

Speaker of the House George Pinney (Bon Homme) got thrown through the window of a Yankton saloon by the Sergeant-at-Arms Jim Somers, because Pinney had earlier supported Vermillion, instead of Yankton, as state Capitol. Meanwhile at a restaurant across town, two other legislators, John Boyle and Enos Stutsman, flung bottles of ketchup and mustard at each other, over the same issue.

The U.S. Census officially counted 696,004 South Dakotans in 1990. More realistic estimates put the total at 714,000.

John Boyle (Vermillion) was the only person who was not a judge who was appointed to the State Supreme Court. Boyle managed to serve for two years, without ever writing a single opinion on any case. After he left the court, he joined the ministry.

Wild Bill Hickok (Deadwood) killed 36 outlaws as a lawman. Hickok was once fired after he accidentally shot his own deputy.

President Kennedy did not push any button, or throw a switch, to dedicate the Oahe Dam because worried officials thought the three billion kilowatts might electrocute him, 1962.

The post office of Greenwood, S.D., was originally located in Nebraska.

Super 8 Motels (Aberdeen) reports that one hunter gutted a deer in his motel room's bathtub, and never cleaned up the mess. When the cleaning lady showed up the next morning, she fainted from fright.

Worried that protesters would firebomb the 1970 White House Christmas tree from South Dakota, state officials failed in coaxing the Pentagon to fly the tree in a military cargo plane. Twice within six days the 73-year-old spruce tree was derailed. The jinxed tree eventually made it and was lit by the President on December 16, 1970 — in pouring rain.

Lawrence Welk (Yankton) bought dinner for a man he'd accidentally hit in the chest with a golf ball.

Believing he would never amount to anything, the entire band of Lawrence Welk walked out on him in Dallas, S.D.

Because the musicians of Lawrence Welk were billed as the Fruit Gum Orchestra, Welk handed out free gum to all dancers. Dancers, however, often dropped wads of gum on wooden dance floors, incurring the wrath of numerous dance hall owners.

When Lawrence Welk got his first job with a band he was unable to read music.

Lawrence Welk was fired from a succession of band jobs because he played loudly and off-key.

Among the written song requests received by Lawrence Welk were "Wheel Barrel Polka" and "Bear Bell Poke," instead of "Beer Barrel Polka;" "Jack the Knife," for "Mack the Knife;" and "Bronze Lullaby," for "Brahm's Lullaby".

South Dakota's prehistoric Forest City Man was exhibited before thousands of people at the Chicago World's Fair of 1893, and afterwards, throughout the country. Said to have been fossilized into limestone, the petrified body was discovered on a South Dakota farm. Only after the nationwide tour was the hoax discovered. A Redfield butcher had made a plaster body cast, enclosed bones obtained from a doctor, and poured in cement. The fake man was buried in a nearby field, to await discovery by a fellow also in on the scheme. The entire scientific community had been fooled.

George McGovern (Mitchell) was four hours late for his 1943 wedding, so the ceremony had to be delayed an entire day.

McGovern met his future wife, Eleanor Stegeberg (Woonsocket), when she beat him in a high school debate contest. The topic was Great Britain.

McGovern was once introduced by Johnny Carson on NBC's "The Tonight Show" as being from "North Dakota."

Wild Bill Hickok (Deadwood) read his own obituary three years prematurely in the Missouri *Democrat.* Hickok wrote a letter to the editor, correcting the error. Three years later Hickok was murdered while playing poker.

The gun of Jack McCall (Deadwood) was loaded with five defective bullets and only one good cartridge, the one that killed Hickok in a saloon. Outside the saloon, McCall vaulted into the saddle of a nearby horse, but the saddle cinch broke, and McCall fell to the street. He took off, but was captured inside a butcher shop.

Not only was South Dakota state Supreme Court Chief Justice George French not an attorney, he had never even studied law. French got the appointment because he was a buddy of President Grant and some congressmen.

Thirteen voters who listed Deadwood casino addresses on 1991 South Dakota voter registrations were investigated for fraud.

Because too many car accidents were being caused by a 30-ft., Center-of-North-America-monument in Hughes County, the South Dakota Highway Commission tore it down and built a new one over a mile away.

Lewis and Clark named a large South Dakota River, the Dog River. In French this translates to "Chien." English-speaking mapmakers thought they said "Cheyenne," which is what the river has since been labeled.

In order to get miners to stake out claims in the dry Balkan Mine (Rochford), promoters put pieces of gold in the tunnels. The scheme worked until a sharp miner discovered "E Pluribus Unum" on one of the fake nuggets.

Sam Brown rode 120-miles Paul Revere-style April 19, 1866, through several South Dakota and Minnesota communities warning of an imminent enemy attack. Upon learning the attack was false, Brown rode back through all the towns to rewarn the settlers, only to get caught in a blizzard and lose use of both legs due to frostbite.

Mary Ann Fischer (Aberdeen) was diagnosed as having triplets only four days before her healthy quintuplets were born in 1963.

In order to ensure large and enthusiastic crowds, Lieutenant Governor Bill Dougherty (Sioux Falls) erroneously told reporters that astronaut John Glenn was traveling in South Dakota with presidential candidate Robert Kennedy in 1968.

Early mapmakers thought "Black Hills" were not cheerful enough, and attempted to rename them "Purple Mountains" or "Magic Mountains," on early maps.

Al Neuharth (Eureka) bombed at creating *SoDak Sports* in 1952. Thirty years later he launched the successful *USA Today*, September 15, 1982.

After the 1989 autobiography of Al Neuharth had risen to fifth place on best-seller lists, his Gannett Foundation admitted it had spent about $40,000 to purchase 2,000 copies of Neuharth's *Confessions of an S.O.B.*

No one told banker Al Nystrom (Wall) about President Franklin Roosevelt's bank holiday, so Nystrom's bank was the only bank in America to remain open for business and in operation.

At a cost of $580,000 the U.S. Post Office decided to destroy 300 million stamps of Hubert Humphrey (Huron) because the side margin of the stamps said he became U.S. Vice President in 1965, rather than 1964.

In 1881 the first train through the Black Hills, the Black Hills & Fort Pierre, never came even close to Fort Pierre.

Artist Ed Simmons spent several thousand dollars applying gold-leaf in the Capitol Rotunda (Pierre) in 1910, but poor lighting made the expensive work difficult to see.

When Sen. Gladys Pyle (Huron) arrived at her first White House reception hosted by First Lady Eleanor Roosevelt, Pyle was embarrassed to discover both her white gloves were for the same hand.

In 1893 a psychic named "Johnstone" led a group of followers and skeptics in search of a hidden needle in Wind Cave. He found the needle, but joined the group in being lost in the maze of tunnels for two days.

William Howard Taft was the first president to visit the Black Hills, 1911. Taft was delighted at the large crowds which greeted him in Rapid City, unaware the people were there for the homestead lotteries.

One time two buildings in Lead accidentally fell 60 feet into an abandoned mine shaft.

The current state capitol was built with its base line three feet lower than the streets of Pierre. When the city refused to lower nearby Nicollet Street, the capitol commission ended up spending $2,000 to raise the foundation walls two feet, to meet the street's elevation.

Canistota, S.D., was named for Canastota, N.Y., but a mapmaker spelled it wrong.

Freeman and Menno had their names accidentally flipflopped when tired railroad workers put up town names at the opposite depots.

In 1979 the South Dakota Secretary of Game, Fish and Wildlife was caught with too many fish in his possession.

When President Teddy Roosevelt and New York Gov. Charles Hughes declined to dedicate the new state Capitol (Pierre), South Dakotans settled on an Iowa professor of agriculture.

In 1904 the government refused to register a 13-year-old girl who wanted to homestead near Rosebud. The government finally accepted her application when she provided documentation showing she was a divorcee and mother of a son.

Myron Floren (Roslyn) played the wrong version of "Yellow Rose of Texas" for President Eisenhower at the White House, January 26, 1959.

Flint Hill (Edgemont) contains quartzite, not flint.

Fort Sisseton, S.D., was to have been built west of the James River but a major and his soldiers confused directions and mistakenly built it 40 miles to the east.

One dark night during 1884 several Wilmot, S.D., citizens nudged a sleigh up to the back door of the Roberts Courthouse and stole all the records. Not to be outdone, Sisseton citizens stole the records at night from Wilmot — and hung on to them until Sisseton was confirmed as official county seat, in 1900.

A 17-mile water flume was built with hand labor in 1880 to carry water to gold miners at Rockerville. The $300,000 flume was a white elephant, constantly springing holes that miners unsuccessfully attempted to plug with horse manure. Also, little gold was discovered with it.

The children who found the historic Verendrye plate near Fort Pierre were going to sell the metal object for a nickel, but two legislators stopped them.

When Arthur Mellette began duties as the state's first governor, in 1889, he had no desk, no chair and no record books. South Dakota had to wait to transact any business until North Dakota officials finished copying all the record books.

Congress refused to acknowledge, or seat, South Dakota's first congressmen, Oscar Gifford and John Pickler, until they presented a Certificate of Election. The Certificate required an official State Seal, which was also delayed in its arrival to Pierre.

Sitting Bull was interrupted by applause and received a standing ovation when he addressed President Chester Alan Arthur at a railroad dedication in Dakota Territory in 1883. What the president and scores of white dignitaries did not know was that an interpreter was rapidly translating the chief's insults — "You are thieves and liars." — into friendly phrases. Sitting Bull proved so popular that the railroad invited him to Minnesota for a similar ceremony.

Beatle George Harrison ended up accidentally drenching Mamie Van Doren (Rowena) when he tossed a Scotch drink at an annoying photographer.

Because Naval commanders Malcolm Ross and M. Lee Lewis had not made prior arrangements with the National Aeronautic Association, their record 13.7-mile high balloon flight from Rapid City in 1956 was not certified as a world record.

When Andrew Oberg (Sioux Falls) reported that someone stole all the water in his well, officials were in the process of figuring out the theft when a well cleaning service notified Oberg that they had accidentally got addresses mixed up.

The State Soldiers Home (Hot Springs) was established in 1885 with the law stating it had to be managed exclusively by Civil War veterans. The law was later changed, when the state ran out of Civil War vets.

It took three years to create the 18-ft. bronze reproduction of Michelangelo's David and two years of wading through Italian red tape to get the statue to America, then Sioux Falls, and finally, erected in the Sunken Gardens. And then some folks demanded that officials face the nude male away from traffic.

Shortly after being launched the USS Huron was accidentally rammed by the USS Cooper and spent WWII fighting no one.

The biggest gold stampede in the Black Hills was perpetrated for profit on the sale of horses. In November 1876 Red Clark (Deadwood) arranged for false rumors to circulate that gold had just been discovered in the Wolf Mountains. Horses were suddenly in demand and Clark, and others sold some 1,500 horses within days to greedy prospectors.

So concerned that his arrival at the 1964 Democratic Convention would upstage that of Lady Bird Johnson and kill his chances at being picked to run for vice president, Hubert Humphrey (Doland) took an hour-long tour of Washington before flying to the convention in Atlantic City.

Dakota was divided into North Dakota and South Dakota because the greedy Congress wanted four, instead of two, more Republican senators.

After eight tries over 71 years, Viborg, S.D., voters finally approved on-sale liquor in 1991.

A mail pouch from 1952 was discovered 39 years later in Rapid City (in 1991) and sent to proper addresses.

An ill-timed flyover of four planes drowned out President George Bush at the exact moment he formally dedicated Mount Rushmore, July 3, 1991.

On December 3, 1919, the legislature convened in Pierre right before midnight, spent the next day, the Fourth, in full session, and adjourned right after midnight, thus fulfilling the legal requirement that a special session must last at least three days.

In 1886 the community of Lafayette built a saloon. When voters refused to grant a license, commissioners bought the building and turned it into the courthouse.

Just as Mayor Tim Rich (Aberdeen) was getting set to welcome convening educators, he discovered he was being introduced at an aviation convention. His Honor's staff had sent him to the wrong convention center.

Shine Street (Deadwood) was named by someone who could not spell "Cheyenne."

Jefferson, on Mount Rushmore, was dedicated twice. When President Franklin Roosevelt failed to show up for the program, sculptor Gutzon Borglum went ahead without him. When FDR did arrive, Borglum repeated the ceremony.

When the microphone of Hollywood cowboy star William Hart was cut off during a live broadcast of the unveiling of Roosevelt's face on Mount Rushmore in 1939, Hart began a loud, embarrassing shouting match with the radio technician. The argument was broken up by Mary Borglum, the sculptor's daughter-in-law.

Early tourists thought Mount Rushmore's Jefferson was Martha Washington.

Mount Rushmore sculptor Gutzon Borglum changed his birth date three times.

Workmen blasted too deeply on the original Jefferson on Mount Rushmore. When sculptor Gutzon Borglum returned from overseas in 1931, he had Jefferson destroyed and relocated on the opposite side of Washington.

Video stores say 15 percent—-98,000 out of 655,000—-of the *Dances With Wolves* videos are defective because manufacturers used a thinner video tape that snaps when rewound.

The first manuscript written by 65-year-old Laura Ingalls Wilder (De Smet), *Pioneer Girl*, was rejected by publishers. At that point her daughter, a newspaper reporter, pulled out one of the sections, relabeled it *Little House in the Big Woods*, and resubmitted it. The renamed book became an overnight best-seller.

Four months after it began flight operations in South Dakota, G.P. Express, of Grand Island, Neb., was officially grounded because of too few passengers.

IT'S A CRIME!

POT PLANE

An aging DC-7 cargo plane quietly landed in a pasture south of Selby, S.D., on Super Bowl Sunday, 1980. Nearby ranchers and fishermen reported to officials that they thought a crippled airplane had gone down. Much to the surprise of local lawmen, the plane, laden with 12.5 tons of marijuana worth $18 million, turned out to be the biggest drug bust in the state's history. Only the U.S. Defense Department was more alarmed: the world's largest transport plane had flown 3,000 miles from Colombia to South Dakota — completely undetected by radar!

- Six men were arrested and stood trial.
- A veteran Colorado pilot was paid $2,000 to remove the $150,000 plane.
- Five trucks hauled the weed south to the state capital, where it was guarded in an armory.
- State Treasurer David Volk wanted to sell the pot to the 14 states that use it for medical purposes, but health officials nixed the idea.
- The Attorney General's office saved 393 evidence samples, one from each bale.
- February 1980 the pot was ground through a Pierre tree shredder, soaked with 150 gallons of kerosene, and torched. Two armed DCI agents guarded the fire.

HOT SEAT

South Dakota's most recent public execution was held April 8, 1947, when cop killer George Sitts was executed in the electric chair in Sioux Falls.

The man who pulled the switch on cop killer George Sitts in 1947 was himself once tried for murder. Deputy sheriff Floyd Short (Lemmon) was later acquitted of the 1930 murder of a sheep rustler.

During the statewide manhunt for Sitts, the murderer hid out in the basement of the home of the Deadwood police chief, who was in the posse looking for Sitts.

Capital punishment in South Dakota:
- Hanging, done 12 times 1877-1913
- Electric chair, once, 1947
- Injection, on books since 1984

In 1915 South Dakota got rid of capital punishment. It took the gruesome murders of an Onida teacher and a Sioux Falls babysitter to shock the legislature into restoring it in 1939. South Dakota abolished capital punishment again in 1975, only to restore it a year later. It is still on the books.

BABY FACE

A thousand witnesses, including four police, saw gangster George "Baby Face" Nelson shoot an officer and kidnap four women tellers as he robbed the Security National Bank (Sioux Falls) of $56,000 on March 6, 1934. This was the first known time bullet proof vests were used in the state, and ironically it was on two of the robbers. The get-away cars were a Packard, Dodge and Lincoln.

As the Nelson gang switched cars south of Sioux Falls, Mrs. F.H.Faragher stopped to lecture the four women bank tellers on not wearing coats on such a cold day. The unknowing Mrs. Faragher suddenly had machine guns aimed at her and was told to move on. She did.

Kidnapped hostages:
- Alice Blegen
- Mildred Bostwick
- Emma Knabach
- Mary Lucas

PELTIER

The murder of two FBI agents on the Pine Ridge Indian Reservation, June 26, 1975, inspired the biggest manhunt in FBI history. Leonard Peltier (Pine Ridge) was convicted two years later and is serving two life sentences in Kansas.

Leonard Peltier, a grandparent, says he was protecting women and children at the time FBI agents were murdered on Pine Ridge.

Carpenter Leonard Peltier spends his time painting, in oils, while in Leavenworth Federal Penitentiary, in Kansas.

Peltier's Leavenworth Prison number is #89637-132.

SLAIN FBI AGENTS:
- Jack R. Coler
- Ronald Williams

NATIVE AMERICANS CHARGED WITH THE MURDERS:
- James Eagle, freed
- Darrell Butler, freed
- Leonard Peltier, imprisoned
- Bob Robinson, freed

PELTIER SUPPORTERS:
- Mikhail Gorbachev
- Sen. Dan Inouye
- Rev. Jesse Jackson
- Kris Kristofferson

- Willie Nelson
- Oliver Stone
- Robert Redford
- Bishop Desmond Tutu
- 27 tribal councils
- 80 Congressmen
- 17,000 Soviet citizens

ODD THEFTS

The most-stolen book from the Sioux Falls Public Library is *Chilton's Auto Repair Manual.*

According to Super 8 headquarters (Aberdeen), the most stolen items by guests are towels, ice buckets, ashtrays, blankets and washcloths.

It was crime that originally brought Laura Ingalls Wilder to South Dakota. In 1879 her father, Charles Ingalls, was hired by the railroad to guard surveyors' tools near Silver Lake, S.D.

Right after WWII the chandeliers from the state Capitol (Pierre) were stolen.

Selby became county seat of Walworth County, S.D., when citizens attacked the nearby county seat of Bangor, tore down its courthouse and removed the records.

In order to become the county seat, Belle Fourche citizens simply stole all the Butte County records in 1893.

Employee Daniel Bruce pleaded guilty in 1991 to taking $12,000 over a period of weeks from the Mission Convenience Store (Mission) and buying lottery tickets.

John McTigue (Deadwood) had his entire house stolen in 1878.

Mount Rushmore was built on sacred Native American land stolen for its gold.

While stationed in 1876 in Dakota Territory, Gen. George A. Custer appeared before congressional committees back in Washington and provided documented evidence that both President Grant's brother, Orvil, and the president's Secretary of War, Bill Belknap, were guilty of kickbacks. Belknap resigned, and the President was embarrassed over his brother's involvement. Thereafter, Grant refused to see Custer and was considering relegating him to some godforsaken post, when Custer decided to redeem himself in Grant's eyes by planning a daring raid at Little Bighorn.

State Treasurer William Taylor skipped the country with the entire state treasury, $367,020.59 in 1895. Taylor eventually ended up in the State Penitentiary, but little of the money was recovered. The state treasury still carries an account called "Taylor Lands" from which revenue is generated. Gov. Mellette turned his fortune over to the state, to pay for the losses caused by dishonest state treasurer Taylor.

One robber who held up a stage near Deadwood in August 1888 gave the victim a chance to win back his gold in a quick card game.

SIDESTEPPING THE LAW

Outlaw Arkansaw Joe Parker Putello was riddled with 20 bullet holes in less than 30 seconds the evening of Nov. 18, 1880, by a Pierre vigilante group seeking a $2,000 reward. After a hasty funeral, during which Arkansaw was viewed on a carpenter's bench in a saloon shed, he was buried on a nearby hill. Nearly a quarter century later, his remains were accidentally discovered when the foundation was dug for the current state Capitol.

The first inmates to occupy the South Dakota State Penitentiary (Sioux Falls) in 1882 came from Detroit, where territorial prisoners had previously been sent. Prisoners themselves provided the labor for continuing expansion of the prison.

South Dakota has three juvenile and two adult correctional facilities.

Wild Bill Hickok was shot in the No. 10 saloon while playing cards in Deadwood in 1876. Murderer Jack McCall also tried to shoot others in the bar, but his gun misfired. Hickok was able to pull out and cock both his pistols before dying.

After McCall was found innocent of shooting Hickok, Judge Kuykendall gave him 60 seconds to get out of town. Three months later, when McCall bragged about the murder, he was rearrested, taken to Yankton, retried, sentenced and hanged.

In order to force rioting miners out of a mine near Deadwood, Sheriff Seth Bullock once tossed burning sulphur down the shafts.

Gov. Bill Janklow (Pierre) told 93 South Dakota criminal defendants they could avoid prosecution if they moved to California.

During 1940 it was discovered that some $7,000 from the illegal sale of scrap metal from an old Sioux Falls bridge, and other items, had been paid for perks, parties and coffee for city workers.

The Sundance Kid robbed the Butte County Bank in Belle Fourche during September 1897. Arrested, Sundance escaped Deadwood's jail. Five years later he teamed with Butch Cassidy.

In 1971 President Nixon seriously considered naming Judge Sylvia Bacon (Watertown) to the U.S. Supreme Court.

Following their infamous bank robbery in Northfield, Minn., Sept. 7, 1876, brother outlaws Jesse and Frank James hid out in Sioux Falls. The brothers were the only members of the eight-outlaw gang to not get arrested or killed.

During the 1880s Wyatt Earp rode shotgun on gold shipments from Deadwood, S.D.

Mark Mickelson, son of Gov. George Mickelson, got two days in jail, was fined $300 and lost his driver's license for a month, after pleading guilty to DWI in August 1991. Mark's attorney said the 25-year-old did not get special treatment, even though he was released after only five hours in jail.

A seventeen-year-old Rapid City boy fired 10 shots and held 22 fellow high school math students hostage for nearly four hours on September 11, 1991, until being disarmed by a classmate.

Russell Means (Pine Ridge) was sentenced to a term in prison in Sioux Falls for rioting, November 1977.

The 1990 Hobo Day homecoming in Brookings, S.D., left $40,000 in damages.

AIM occupied Wounded Knee, S.D., from February 27-May 8, 1973. During the trial that followed, Judge Fred Nichol watched the prosecution call 79 witnesses over a 98-day period. The defense threatened to call 341 witnesses, but ended up calling only five, over a three-day period.

Joseph Iron Cloud, 30, stood trial in Rapid City in 1990 for biting the ear off a five-month-old baby.

As part of the prison-industries program, 20 inmates began working for Super 8 Motels, based in Aberdeen, S.D., taking phone reservations. The idea was dropped when inmates were discovered making bets and calling for drugs, over the phones.

Lynyrd Skynyrd keyboardist Billy Powell made several appearances in the Sioux Falls area in 1991, signing autographs, posing for pictures and doing media interviews but was nabbed by police when he signed a contract. Powell turned out to have been impersonated by Carroll Church, Jr., 33.

The triple murder trial of twin sisters and their boyfriend added a $50,000 bill to Perkins County taxpayers in 1991.

South Dakota has four U.S. District Courts.

The first courtmartial resulting from the Battle of the Little Big Horn occurred at Fort Meade, S.D., when Marcus Reno, who led the initial charge, was court-martialed and dismissed.

When a Watertown teacher refused an offer of marriage from Frank Pomhouse in 1912, he committed suicide with a gun in her classroom, in front of her pupils.

Fifty percent of South Dakota women get illegal haircuts in someone's home.

Gov. William Janklow sued *Newsweek* for printing alleged rape charges.

Wagon trains used to haul $250,000 in gold from Deadwood had strong boxes that were impregnable for at least 24 hours. Gold bricks weighed 200 pounds each, so it was harder for robbers to move them.

Wild Bill Hickok (Deadwood) gunned down seven men in gunfights in four states, the final one five years before his own death.

Al Swearingsen, manager of the Gem Theater (Deadwood) in the 1880s, used to lure innocent girls from the East Coast, to the Black Hills, with promises of acting jobs. Instead, the girls ended up as white slaves.

At age 27 Blanche Colman became South Dakota's first woman attorney in 1911.

South Dakota provided two companies of soldiers, the First Dakota Cavalry, for the Civil War.

During WWI German-born Hutterites living in South Dakota often had their cattle stolen by self-claimed patriots, in order to buy Liberty Bonds to fight Germany. A few Hutterites who refused to be drafted were imprisoned or had their houses hit with yellow paint. Restaurants dropped German dishes from their menus and some schools burned German books.

It was the fashion with the ladies of Deadwood in 1878 to carry guns in hip pockets.

"Fairy gold" is some $40,000 worth of gold bullion lost during an 1878 stage robbery near Deadwood.

In 1991 South Dakota began allowing female state penitentiary guards on duty in men-only sections of the Sioux Falls prison.

After being convicted of rioting in South Dakota, Russell Means feared for his life, so he sought refuge in California, where Gov. Brown refused to extradite him. When Brown left office Means fled to New York. In 1984 he returned to South Dakota, where he served a year in prison.

Black Elk (Mount Rushmore) was at the University of South Dakota's TV station when he learned JFK had been shot. Shaken, he immediately left, and sought privacy for two days.

Calamity Jane (Deadwood) was once thrown out of a brothel, for being a bad influence on the women residents.

All gold miners in the Black Hills in 1876 were technically outlaws, since the land was still owned by Native Americans.

A kidnapping attempt against Kermit Roosevelt, son of President Teddy Roosevelt, was thwarted when Marshal Seth Bullock (Belle Fourche) and his son, Stan, shot the two kidnappers dead.

While sitting in the Yankton jail for leading a vigilante group that hanged two horse thieves, Bill McKay was elected to the state legislature. McKay was permitted to sit in the state Capitol only when a police officer was present. McKay's case was later dismissed.

In 1905 the U.S. Supreme Court favored South Dakota when the state sued North Carolina for what it deemed $10,000 worth of worthless bonds. The judgment was $27,400, face value of the bonds.

During election night of the 1972 New Hampshire primary, a Howard Johnson Motel clerk received a bomb threat. She woke up Shirley MacLaine, who woke up Gary Hart, who woke up George McGovern. McGovern and his wife waited on a lower floor until police gave the all clear signal, and the tired McGoverns climbed on the fire escape in their bathrobes, then back to their room.

First three non-Native American women in the Black Hills, all of whom entered illegally:

- Gen. Custer's black cook, Sarah Campbell, who rode in on a wagon
- Reporter Annie Tallent, who walked in
- Calamity Jane, disguised as a male teamster bringing scientists

Carl Grupp's Bet On It! Trivia Myths:
OUTDOOR SPORT

ROGER BUSGALIA HUNTS PHEASANTS WITH A POWER MOWER TO GIVE THEM A FIGHTING CHANCE.

CREATURE FEATURES

WHERE THE BUFFALO ROAM

For filming the thundering buffalo stampede — four minutes on the screen — at the Triple U Standing Butte Ranch (Fort Pierre), the *Dances With Wolves* crew required eight days of shooting in 1989, and used one helicopter, 10 trucks, 20 cowboys, 24 bareback riders, 25 stuffed buffalo, 150 extras and 3,500 buffalo.

The American Society for Prevention of Cruelty to Animals gave *Dances With Wolves* high marks for the humane way it treated animals in South Dakota.

- Twenty-three mechanical buffalo, built at a cost of $250,000, were intermingled with real bison.
- Arrows were clipped to buffalo hair to give the impression of being shot.
- Fake buffalo were run on tracks on the Houck ranch.
- Stuffed buffalo were tossed from a truck, as cameras recorded their falling.
- The buffalo heart cut out by Wind in His Hair, was made of gelatin.
- All horse falls were performed by trick horses trained to fall. When Cisco was shot, he was actually doing a "lay down."
- When the wolf, Two Socks, was gunned down, a hidden tether actually pulled him down.
- A taxidermist's wolf was used to portray the dead Two Socks.

Lewis and Clark shot their first buffalo on August 23, 1804, in South Dakota.

As many as 1,500 buffalo roam Custer State Park, the second largest state park in America. Custer, the Buffalo Capital of the World, has America's largest buffalo herd.

Custer State Park sold 252 buffalo at their annual auction, 1991.

National Guard helicopters are used to herd buffalo during the annual roundup each September, at Custer State Park.

Tatonka, the great buffalo, was the most powerful animal faced by Native Americans in South Dakota. It provided food, clothing, shelter and medicine. Because Tatonka was believed to be directly related to the Great Spirit, buffalo skulls were central in sacred ceremonies.

Dakota in South Dakota believe White Buffalo Calf Woman brought the seven sacred rites and left a material symbol of the Creator's love, the eagle.

A thousand head of buffalo filed by their owner, Jim "Scotty" Philip (Philip), during his funeral.

In 1839 a herd estimated at millions of buffalo roamed through the Badlands. As settlers poured into South Dakota, the buffalo population rapidly decreased. By 1888 Texas longhorns had taken over buffalo grounds.

George Philip (Rapid City) took a couple buffalo to Mexico and entered them in a fight with Mexican bulls. The buffalo won.

Some scientists believe that waters from 30-feet of snow caused a huge flood in 1852 that exterminated most of the buffalo in the Black Hills.

When the steamboat Yellow Stone left South Dakota in 1831 it carried with it five tons of buffalo tongues.

Hugh Glass survived an 1823 buffalo stampede in central South Dakota because the lead bulls amazingly thought Glass's bear skin blanket was a bear, and took the thousand-bison herd completely around him.

The National Buffalo Association was established in Custer, S.D., in 1966, and moved to Fort Pierre in 1985.

The National Buffalo Association (Fort Pierre) offers eight-pound gourmet packs of buffalo steak, which contains 30% more protein and 50% fewer calories then regular steak.

Roy Houck (Pierre) was the founding president of the National Buffalo Association and owns the largest privately held buffalo herd in North America.

Standing Butte Ranch (Pierre) has no light showing through its corrals because if buffalo can see light through the fence, they will charge it.

Peter Dupree captured five exhausted buffalo on the state's last big buffalo hunt, near Grand River, in 1881. Dupree raised the buffalo among his cattle at his ranch, where they crossbred with native stock, ate well and prospered. When Dupree died in 1901, Scotty Philip bought the 57 buffalo and moved them to his ranch, at Philip.

In less than 30 years the number of Great Plains buffalo plunged from 50 million to a mere 551.

SNAKES ALIVE!
The Reptile Gardens (Rapid City) is the only place in the world featuring Barred Spitting Cobras on display.

The Reptile Gardens have 100 of 20 species of rattlesnakes. The snakes are given live mice and chicks every 10 days.

Since Earl Brockelsby opened the Reptile Gardens in May 1937, the only creatures that have escaped have been harmless garter snakes.

The Reptile Gardens features 800 animals, more than most U.S. zoos. Its the only place in the state where tourists may ride a 600-pound tortoise or view trained animals at the Bewitched Village.

The Reptile Gardens' longest rattler stretched 6.5 feet. The oldest lived 15 years.

Employees at the Reptile Gardens do not carry snake bite kits.

The Reptile Gardens has been rebuilt since losing the SkyDome and entire mezzanine reptile collection in an August 1976 fire.

The Reptile Gardens purchases its animal feed dead and frozen.

REWARD OFFERED BY REPTILE GARDENS FOR HEALTHY SPECIMENS DELIVERED ALIVE, 1992:
- $50,000 for 30-ft. anaconda or python, or 25-ft. crocodile
- $25,000 for 800-pound tortoise
- $20,000 for 16-ft. alligator
- $15,000 for 19-ft. King Cobra or eight-ft. rattlesnake

ANIMAL FEED CONSUMED AT REPTILE GARDENS DURING 1991:
- 130,000 mealworms
- 73,000 mice
- 68,000 crickets
- 18,000 chicks
- 6,000 rats
- 3,400 minnows
- 1,200 bushels of fruit
- 1,000 snakes
- 800 chickens
- 800 rabbits
- 500 hay bales
- 500 smelt
- 400 lizards
- 2 tons of fish

A Black Hills resident uses live rattlesnakes to make the molds for casting the rattler ashtrays sold at Wall Drug (Wall).

Historian W.H. Over (Vermillion) displayed live animals in Science Hall at the University of South Dakota. One day while defanging a rattler, it bit him. Over methodically took notes as he obtained medical help. Those notes were later published in national scientific journals.

Sacajawea (West River) drank a potion containing powdered rattlesnake rattles, to help with the difficult birth of her son.

South Dakota's sole rattlesnake is the prairie rattler.

The state's first snake eradicator, A.M. Jackley (Hot Springs), located over 600 rattlesnake dens.

Ed Cronk (Philip) captured over 13,000 rattlesnakes during a nine-year stint as the state's snake eradicator. Appointed by the Department of Agriculture, Cronk once captured 500 live rattlers in the largest snake cage in South Dakota. Cronk, who always carried two snake bite kits, was never bitten, never tasted rattlesnake meat and made some $300 a month selling live (yes, live) rattlesnakes, by the pound. His biggest client was the Reptile Gardens (Rapid City). Cronk's longest snake stretched four feet, four inches. The oldest was seventeen years.

OLD BONES

Fossils discovered in South Dakota include those for the camel, saber toothed tiger and three-toed horse. South Dakota was also inhabited by the giant pig, dinosaurs and a giant rhinoceros.

June 24, 1974, George Hanson was bulldozing on the south edge of Hot Springs, on land owned by Phil Anderson, when he noticed something white. It was a 7-ft. tusk. Nebraska Prof. Larry Agenbroad was brought in and concluded that 26,000 years ago some 100 mammoths got stuck while getting a drink. They starved or drowned. To date, 45 have been uncovered.

Hot Springs, S.D., has the world's only *in-situ* — being left as found — site for mammoths. At Mammoth Site, which is only 15% excavated, is the world's largest concentration of Columbian mammoth bones discovered in their primary context..

The biggest of only nine specimens of Tyrannosaurus rex ever unearthed — 40 feet long, weighing six tons in real life — was found in a sandstone bluff near Faith, S.D., during September 1990. Its femur, 54 inches long, exceeds by nine inches the famous specimen in the Museum of Natural History in New York. The new rex is robust, with a powerful, heavy build. According to the Black Hills Institute of Geological Research, which found the skeleton, the bones show evidence of injuries in the jaw and near the end of the tail, indicating a very old creature. After 15,000 hours of restoration, the skeleton will become the cornerstone of a new museum in Hill City, S.D.

The world's first Barosaurus dinosaur was uncovered near Piedmont by Prof. O.C. Marsh. The 50-ton dinosaur was found in the slopes of Piedmont Butte.

When Native Americans discovered the 15-foot long skeleton of a Titanotheres, they thought it to belong to a huge horse, Thunderhorse, who came to earth and killed buffalo during thunderstorms. The seven-ft. high Thunderhorse is currently displayed at the South Dakota School of Mines (Rapid City).

Rhinoceroses appeared in the Badlands 50 million years ago. These dog-sized creatures were called Titanotheres. The animal disappeared 23 million years ago, when the climate changed.

Only a paleontologist with a collector's permit may remove a fossil from the Badlands.

The South Dakota School of Mines (Rapid City) has skeletons of a crocodile, rhinoceros, three-toed horse, saber-toothed tiger, deer, camel, rodent and a 13-ft. fish that lived in prehistoric South Dakota.

Over 135 million years ago the Brontosaurus ate a simple vegetable diet in South Dakota. The creatures were 80 feet long and weighed 40 tons.

The world's finest Oligocene mammal fossil repository is in the Badlands.

The most common mammal in the prehistoric Badlands, was the oreodont, a pig-shaped ruminant. There were also ancestral horses, tapirs, camels, deer, rhinoceros and saber-toothed tigers. Hogs stood five-feet tall at the shoulder.

Lewis and Clark discovered a 90-ft. dinosaur skeleton, plesiosaurus, in South Dakota.

The camel originated in the Badlands and migrated to Asia.

CATTLE PRODS
Seth Bullock (Bell Fourche) was going to arrest what he thought was a cattle rustler one night, only to discover it was Teddy Roosevelt. The two became good friends. After becoming president, Roosevelt sent three of his four sons out to South Dakota, where Bullock broke them in as cowpunchers, teaching them to rope, throw and brand cattle.

Classic originator Pappy Hoel (Sturgis) used his motorcycle to herd cattle and check fence lines. He also had the nation's first motorcycle equipped with skis, which Hoel used to check on snowbound families and hungry Black Hills deer.

Now a ghost town, Le Beau, S.D., was once the busiest cattle-shipping point in America.

Pierre celebrates Oahe Days with a buffalo chip throwing contest each summer.

Castle rustlers and outlaws often hid out in Wessington Hills (Wessington Springs) because the long narrow range had wooded ravines and heights that enabled the bandits to see approaching visitors.

According to the National Livestock Association, Rancher Ed Lemmon (Lemmon) handled a world's record one million cattle in a lifetime. Lemmon also cut out, roped and carried to the branding fire a record 900 cattle in a single day.

Cowboys on the open ranges of South Dakota's West River country used to estimate the size of their herd from the tally made of new calves that were branded each spring, and divide the big herds by mutual agreement.

Despite the millions of cattle raised and moved through South Dakota during its history, the state did not create a Brand Board until 1939.

Pierre was originally built with sidewalks elevated two feet about the street to keep cows from splattering mud up on shoppers.

The grateful railroad named Murdo in honor of Texan Murdo Mackenzie, who in 1904 shipped thousands of Texas cattle to nearby Evarts to graze on South Dakota grass. Murdo was along the Fort Pierre/Custer stage run and the old Texas Cattle Trail, and became the cattle rail head of the Old West.

In 1886 a blizzard wiped out half of all cattle in South Dakota.

South Dakota State University (Brookings) announced in 1991 that research showed that shredded newspapers make better cow bedding than straw.

In 1952 U.S. Air Force planes dropped hay to stranded cattle in South Dakota.

Cattle associations met in Spearfish once a year to plan two roundups: one in the spring to cut calves for branding, and one in the fall to prepare animals for shipment to market.

The South Dakota Stock Growers Association organized the last big roundup, with 16 different roundup outfits, in 1904.

American livestock consumes 80 percent of South Dakota's corn crop.

The South Dakota Flying Farmers and Ranchers Club uses planes to inspect and herd their cattle.

BIRD BRAINS
Pringle, S.D., is home to the annual Chicken Strut, each July.

Naturalist John James Audubon catalogued 61 bird species during his first and only visit to South Dakota, 1843. Audubon brought his taxidermist along. The duo offended several tourists by his constant slaughter of birds and animals so they could be preserved permanently and painted later.

South Dakota has 300 species of birds.

The cowboy boots worn by Lt. Gov. W.D. Miller (New Underwood) are made of ostrich skin.

South Dakota had absolutely no pheasants (its state bird) until 1898, when Dr. Arne Zetlitz released two male and four female Chinese ringneck pheasants near Sioux Falls. The pheasant population eventually reached three million, giving South Dakota the title of "Pheasant Capital of the World."

Some 20 million pheasants were legally hunted in South Dakota during the first 20 years of legal hunting, 1919-1939.

In 1945 a record 7.5 million pheasants were harvested in South Dakota.

Huron, S.D., has the world's largest pheasant statue: 40-feet tall, 22 tons.

South Dakota's first pheasant season lasted a single day during 1919. Less than 200 pheasants were bagged, and hunters were confined to hunting only in Spink County.

South Dakota has 10 million pheasants.

As a teenager, country western singer Sherwin Linton (Watertown) felt so guilty about shooting a pheasant that he never went hunting again.

Country Side Wild Bird Farm (Lennox) started in 1979 with a few hundred quail. Today they are one of the largest producers in the Midwest.

In March 1991 over 1.2 million snow geese, en route to Canada, converged upon Sand Lake National Wildlife Refuge.

South Dakota, in 1991, offered hunting seasons for antelope, deer, dove, grouse, partridge, pheasant, quail, rabbit, squirrel, turkey and waterfowl.

Illegal pesticides killed seven bald eagles, eight geese, 13 ducks and snow geese near Pierre in 1991.

For the first time in nearly a century, two rare ospreys were hatched in the Black Hills in 1991.

In 1991 Huron began using noisy blasts to scare thousands of pesky blackbirds.

In 1916 international bird dog trials were held near Mobridge, S.D.

SOME SOUTH DAKOTA PHEASANT HUNTERS:
- Tom Selleck
- Clark Gable
- Billy Martin
- Dick Powell
- Bob Allison

HORSE SENSE
A special order kept anyone from riding Commanche (Fort Meade), the sole Army survivor of the Battle of Little Bighorn. The horse, owned by Captain Myles Keogh, was three-quarters American, and one-quarter Spanish. Two days after the June 25, 1876, battle, Lt. Henry Nowland found Commanche and helped rush the wounded animal 15 miles to an awaiting steamboat. Medics attended Commanche as the captain set a record of 53 hours while getting the ship back to Dakota Territory. After Commanche's seven bullet wounds healed, he was escorted in numerous parades; Fort Meade named one of its streets after the horse that received a lifetime Army pension. When the light-bay horse died of natural causes, Commanche was stuffed and put on display at Kansas University.

In 1876 Gen. George Crook (Platte) and his cavalry ended up eating many of their own horses after being stuck in mud near Deadwood during 11 continuous days of rain. Half the cavalry horses died of exhaustion when trying to cross the gumbo in a rainstorm near Slim Buttes.

Mounted members of the Pierre Polo Team directed the heavy traffic and parking for the crowds who came to see President Kennedy dedicate the Oahe Dam, August 17, 1962.

Chief Sitting Bull (Grand River) had a trick horse that was trained to raise a hoof and prance, at the sound of a gunshot. When the chief was gunned down, the horse began doing its tricks, a move that startled superstitious witnesses.

Following their infamous Northfield bank raid in 1876, outlaws Frank and Jesse James escaped from Minnesota and hid out near Valley Springs, S.D., where they unknowingly stole a pair of blind horses. A day later they stole stronger — and better seeing — horses near Canton, before fleeing back home to Missouri.

Fort Meade had America's only cavalry snow troop. During WWII the 4th Cavalry improved winter fighting skills by using tactics practiced by Native Americans in the 1800s.

Over 2,000 wild horses can be found roaming free among a 50,000-acre Black Hills Wild Horse Sanctuary in Hell's Canyon (Black Hills). The horses share the canyon with coyotes and deer. It is owned and operated by the Institute of Range and the American Mustang (IRAM), a non-profit corporation registered in South Dakota.

The prehistoric horse and camel originally arrived in South Dakota by coming from Asia, over the Bering Strait.

When the modern horse first appeared on the Great Plains, the Dakota had been using the dog as their pack animals. The Dakota called the horse, "Sunka Wakan," which meant "Holy dog."

Seth Bullock (Belle Fourche) introduced both alfalfa and thoroughbred trotting horses into the state.

The two horses brought to South Dakota by Lewis and Clark were ridden along the river banks.

South Dakota furnished 33,000 range horses for the Boar War in South Africa.

Horses used to pull gold ore trains through the Black Hills were nicknamed "hay-burners." The horse was replaced by compressed air locomotives. The last compressed air locomotive was retired in 1984.

The first Black Hills Roundup was held in Belle Fourche, S.D., July 4, 1918.

South Dakota's nickname, the Coyote State, came from an 1863 horse race at a fort. When a Dakota cavalry horse outran an entry by the Sixth Iowa Cavalry, the Iowans shouted, "Look at the 'kiote' run." The name stuck.

All present-day wild horses in South Dakota are descendants of ranch mounts turned loose by their bankrupt owners. The numbers increased as many ranchers lost their places during the Great Depression. By 1928 a large herd roamed the western part of the state. This Runyan Herd, named after race horses owned by a settler named Runyan, were often rounded up and sold by county officials desperate for revenue. By 1959 the Park Service was using airplanes to remove all horses from Badlands National Monument.

Redfield formed a volunteer fire department in 1890. During the day the city would use the horses on various projects, but when the fire whistle blew the horses would immediately recognize the signal and be ready.

When Chief Crazy Horse (Custer) is completed, his horse will be the largest sculpted animal on earth.

The Lakota Horse Dance Stick Bracelet, used by Native American braves in South Dakota, was made by the owner of a deceased horse. With this stick he was able to demonstrate his honor for the animal to the rest of the tribe.

Chief Crazy Horse (Moreau River) was 10 when he learned how to train wild horses, and 11 when he killed his first buffalo.

Gov. Tom Berry (Belvidere) raised Hereford cattle and saddle horses on his 30,000-acre ranch.

During the 1890s the fastest horse in South Dakota was named "Johnny Bee," owned by an ex-slave, Norval Blair (Onida).

Horse-mounted cavalry troops were used in the Black Hills until 1942. Up until WWII Fort Meade's 4th Cavalry held 1,180 military mounts. Over the next few years more soldiers were assigned to motorcycles and jeeps. The last troop to disband was F Troop.

BUG-EYED

South Dakota's official state insect is the honey bee.

The museum in Redfield, S.D., has 760 mounted butterflies.

Lewis and Clark logged daily complaints in their journals, about mosquitoes plaguing South Dakota.

Tarantulas are found throughout South Dakota.

FOUR-LEGGEDS

The only two Aberdeen, S.D., city employees immortalized in stone are mules, Kate and Maud, who hauled city garbage for over two decades. The marble marker rests in Aldrich Park, near where their water trough used to rest.

Peever, S.D., was home to a giant frogging industry, during the Roaring Twenties. Men, armed with long-handled nets, combed the sloughs, scooped up frogs, and crated them up. During a single day some 23 crates, plus two barrels of just frog legs, would be shipped to hungry folks on the East Coast. Froggers were paid 20 cents a pound.

Gen. George Custer needed 110 six-mule teams to transport his scientists, photographer and music band through South Dakota in 1874.

In 1876 a mule skinner named Phatty Thompson brought a wagon full of cats to the Black Hills, from Wyoming. Once in Deadwood, Thompson sold his 25-cent cats for up to $30 each,

making $1,000 in one afternoon. Most of the buyers were dance hall girls who sought cats as mouse catchers and pets.

The first domestic cats in South Dakota were brought by Manuel Lisa in 1812, to keep furs and pelts from being destroyed by mice.

During renovation of the Ohlman-Shannon Home (Yankton) in the 1950s, workers discovered a three-foot trench, filled with broken glass, that was dug to keep rats from boring into the foundation.

America's present Semitole bull stock is a direct result of rancher Dale Cutler (Aberdeen) obtaining Semitole semen from Switzerland and France for breeding with two bulls, Bismarck and Parisian, in the late 1960s.

South Dakota's official state animal is the coyote, found in all 67 counties.

The signature of Dakota Chief Sitting Bull (Grand River) was a drawing of a sitting bull.

Super 8 Motel headquarters (Aberdeen) reports that guests have left behind cats and pit bulls. Guests have also discovered alligators, moose, elk and grizzly bears wandering through Super 8 parking lots and lawns. South Dakota supports twice as many sheep as people.

A world-record 38-pound lamb was born April 7, 1975, in Howard, S.D.

South Dakota sheepmen used to place a tipi over a mother sheep and her baby to make sure the mother learned the smell of her lamb.

Sheep rancher M.J. Smiley hired Mexican gunslingers to help move his herd of 50,000 sheep across western South Dakota in 1904. When Black Hills cattlemen lined up to stop the herd, the lead cattleman was lassoed to the ground until everyone backed off. The sheep got through and Smiley used his money to start a sugar beet factory.

Professors at South Dakota State University (Brookings) developed a tailless sheep.

Huge mountain lions used to block the wilderness trails through the Black Hills, frightening the pioneers.

The Fort (Custer) features Black Bears named Bonnie and Clyde. Tourists may feed them apples and rolls. The Fort has South Dakota's largest teddy bear collection.

Bear Country U.S.A. (Rapid City) is the largest privately-owned collection of Black Bear in the world.

In 1874 Gen. Custer killed a bear near Custer.

A grizzly bear attacked explorer Jedediah Smith in the Black Hills in 1823, tearing off half his scalp. A friend crudely sewed the scalp back on. Thereafter Smith wore his hair long, to conceal the scars.

Explorer Hugh Glass was mauled by a grizzly bear south of Lemmon, S.D. Left for dead by his two companions, Glass crawled some 200 miles back to civilization. His adventure was later written into song.

John Morrell & Co. (Sioux Falls) could handle 6,000 hogs, 900 cattle and 2,000 sheep, each day. Every 20 hours 3,000 slabs of bacon pass through its 11 smokehouses.

In order to outfit its fire truck in 1991, the Hosmer Volunteer Fire Department sold raffle tickets for a live hog.

Holstein cow College Belle Wayne (Brookings) produced a record 824.3 pounds of milk in one week during December 1911. Her daughter later held second place in state-wide production.

A Holstein named Colantha Alewin, owned by the state hospital in Yankton, produced a then-record 15 tons of milk and half ton of butter shortly after her birth in 1916.

Back in 1925 federal prohibition agent "Two Gun" Hart (Aberdeen) and his unnamed dog successfully chased down moonshiners throughout the state.

Bachelor Gov. Nils Boe enjoyed the company of a "Beagle Boy" puppy given by South Dakota legislators.

Jefferson, S.D., has pari-mutuel dog races.

Great Plains Zoo (Sioux Falls) has over 300 animals.

Wall Drug has the world's only Jackalope you can ride.

The biggest tipi problem plaguing tipi dwellers in South Dakota, was mice.

Since 1988 Bob Barker (Mission) has refused to host the Miss U.S.A. pageant because fur coats were given contestants.

Deadwood Dick (Deadwood) kept a blue rabbit in a cage.

FISH TALES
The State Game, Fish and Parks Department stocked 2,600 rainbow trout into Horse Thief Lake one day before President Bush caught five fish there during an hour of fishing, July 3, 1991. Secret Service agents baited the President's hook with a Meppy spinner.

Gov. Bill Bulow had a three-mile section of Squaw Creek fenced off and stocked well with fish while President Coolidge was vacation in the Black Hills, 1927.

In 1991 anglers in South Dakota could possess up to 200 perch or catfish.

The largest tiger muskie caught in South Dakota weighed 26 pounds, 10 ounces, and was caught August 12, 1990, near the Oahe Dam (Pierre). The fish was 45.5 inches long and was caught on an eight-pound test line.

Persons fishing within South Dakota tribal waters need a tribal fishing license from the tribe and are subject to the restrictions imposed by the tribe.

Over 40% of the fishing in South Dakota is done on the 4 Missouri River reservoirs. A half million anglers catch over one million walleyes and 10,000 salmon each year there.

In 1989 anglers spent 600,000 hours to harvest over 220,000 walleye on Lake Francis Case.

Fish stocking in Lake Oahe started in 1983 and increased to one million walleye in 1990.

While living in South Dakota, W.H. Over discovered two unknown species of shells, one of which was named for the state and the other for Over. Seven years later he discovered another species of crab, also named for Over.

A Philadelphia publisher impressed with his fresh Black Hills trout, bought the lodge and nearby Sandy Creek that supplied the fish.

D.C. Booth Historic Fish Hatchery (Spearfish), established in 1896, is the oldest fish hatchery in the West.

South Dakota streams once held so many pickerel that settlers could fish with pitchforks.

SOME SOUTH DAKOTA ANGLERS:
• Teddy Roosevelt, in unstocked lake
• Calvin Coolidge, in lake stocked with hungry, liver-fed trout from Spearfish Hatchery
• Dwight Eisenhower used No. 2 Colorado spinner in unstocked French Creek
• George Bush, in stocked lake

Carl Grupp's Bet On It! Trivia Myths:

THE LAWRENCE WELK STORY

LITTLE LARRY WELK AT THE BLACKBOARD:
"AH-ONE AND AH-TWO EQUALS AH-THREE,
BOYCE AND GIRLCE.""

ART

COIN OF THE REALM

The buffalo nickel designed by James Fraser (Mitchell) is the only U.S. coin designed by a South Dakotan and the most reproduced item created by a South Dakotan. Three U.S. Mints minted 1,212,925,298 buffalo nickels. Fraser sketched the nickel in 1913 by employing three different Native American models, none of whom were South Dakotan. Fraser did not want to travel out to Custer to see buffalo that would wander all over the place, so he sketched a more confined buffalo, Black Diamond, found in a New York zoo. Fraser also designed a new Lincoln head penny, but the U.S. Mint later decided to not issue it.

The first appearance of South Dakota on a coin was as one of the 48 states on the reverse of a 1951 Washington Carver U.S. Commemorative coin. Over 2.5 million were minted, featuring 12 variations.

NOW, HOWE, HOW

Oscar Howe (Yankton), a Native American art instructor, painted striking works that profoundly affected the world of art and paved the way for more Native Americans to enter that discipline.

Howe painted the dome of the 1902 Carnegie Library (Mitchell) as a 1940 WPA project.

Talented — but out of work — Oscar Howe received 500 requests for his artwork, through a mailing sent out by a New Mexican school. Lacking money for paint and brushes, Howe stored the letters in a box until he could afford materials. His aunt unknowingly burned the box and letters, so Howe was never able to fulfill the requests.

Mobridge, S.D., officials obtained a two-week delay in 1942 from the draft board so that Oscar Howe could complete 10 murals in their new auditorium. Howe painted 20 hours a day, slept on the auditorium floor and had his meals delivered in an effort to get done before being drafted himself that June.

Winning first place in an Oklahoma art show afforded Oscar Howe the money to bring his German wife to America in 1947.

During one period in the life of Oscar Howe money was so scarce that he paid his bills with paintings.

In April 1960 Oscar Howe was featured as the special person on "This is Your Life," emceed by Ralph Edwards. During the program actor Vincent Price pointed out that Howe's paintings hung alongside work by Picasso, Van Gogh and Gauguin in major museums throughout the nation.

ALL DUNN

Young Harvey Dunn (Manchester) was always drawing locomotives, flowers and trees on the blackboard. To conserve her supply, the teacher hid her box of chalk.

When WWI broke out Harvey Dunn was immediately commissioned as a captain, given a portable sketch box and shipped off to Europe with orders to draw the war. His sketches later ended up in the Smithsonian Institution.

Harvey Dunn would paint only in a studio. If he wanted to paint a tree, he would go study it, sketch a rough copy, then return to the studio and capture the tree on canvas.

Harvey Dunn illustrated ads for Coca-Cola, Texas, Sinclair, John Hancock, plus, artwork for *McCalls, Cosmopolitan* and *The Saturday Evening Post.*

Harvey Dunn would use the steering wheel of his Mercury station wagon as an easel to sketch prairie scenes in South Dakota. Dunn would then return to his studio in New Jersey to transfer the sketches to canvas.

In his fireplace, Harvey Dunn burned paintings of his own that he disliked.

In 1950 Harvey Dunn was invited to display his paintings in the De Smet, S.D., high school gym. Dunn refused to show his work in any room filled with bleachers. The Masonic Temple was offered and accepted by Dunn. An exhibit that was to last a few days was so popular it stretched 14 weeks. Among the 5,000 spectators was the president of Dakota State College (Brookings), who offered their memorial building as a permanent site for the 52 paintings. Dunn took a sheet of paper, sat on a Temple chair, and immediately scribbled out ownership of all the paintings to "the people of South Dakota."

Harvey Dunn sketched endlessly but was reluctant to paint outside his studio. An exception was a portrait of his friend, which Dunn painted on a wall in DeSmet.

Twenty-four works of art by Harvey Dunn are displayed in the Smithsonian Institution.

Harvey Dunn's most celebrated mural, "The Prairie Is My Garden," features a farm wife holding scissors in her right hand, flowers in her left. Two girls are overshadowed by three cows and a dog.

A PALACE OF CORN

In the fall of 1892 the first Corn Palace was built in Mitchell. A larger structure was built in 1905, to accommodate the huge crowds.

Built in only 55 days, the new building was dubbed "Corn Palace." By 1937 an even larger palace was built.

Louis Beckwith and L.O. Gale built the first Corn Palace (Mitchell) in 1886, three years before statehood.

Woodrow Wilson was the first president to visit the Corn Palace, 1912.

Over 3,000 bushels of corn and grasses are used each September to decorate the Corn Palace. Only corn in its natural color is used to decorate the Corn Palace.

The Corn Palace uses at least 10 different colors of corn.

The murals of the Corn Palace were designed by Oscar Howe between 1948-1971. Six of Howe's murals are part of a permanent display there.

New designs decorate the Corn Palace every fall. Similar to a paint-by-number kit, local artists sketch designs on roofing material, indicating the color of corn to be used. Crews apply the corn to wooden panels. Instructions are printed on roofing paper. Natural corn colors include blue, green, red, maroon and yellow. After designs have been chosen, corncobs are cut lengthwise and nailed to panels. Edges are decorated with the state's native grasses and grains.

CAPITAL IDEAS

In order to save money, South Dakota used the basic design of Montana's state Capitol, for their own.

The 1905 law authorizing construction of a new state Capitol had no provision in it that said builders had to use South Dakota materials. As a result, a Sioux Falls granite company went all the way to the Supreme Court to stop Indiana granite from being used. Similar complaints held up construction for nearly two years.

The foundation for the current state Capitol's east wing is made of field boulders.

The 20 tons of copper forming the dome of the state Capitol were melted down in 1964, made into three-inch key chains and distributed by Gov. Nils Boe.

In 1978 a 100-ft. scaffolding was built under the Rotunda to clean the dome at the state Capitol. Despite an elderly age, Sen. Bill Grams (Sturgis) once hooked his cane to the scaffolding and climbed the entire 10 stories to check on the work.

All 18 railroad carloads of furniture for the original South Dakota Capitol were built in Red Wing, Minn.

The House section of the original South Dakota Capitol was made large so that it could serve as a dance hall when the legislature was not in session.

The state Capitol features Marquette sandstone and Indiana bedford limestone, and was built between 1907-1910.

The original Senate Chamber in the state Capitol featured theater seating in a horseshoe-shaped room, mahogany woodwork and green colors. The original House had tiered seating in a rectangular room and oak woodwork.

Dale Lamphere (Sturgis) completed four bronze statues for the rotunda in Pierre: wisdom, vision, courage and integrity.

"First Prayer of South Dakota" was the name of the mural painted on the ceiling of the House Chamber (Pierre) in 1910, by Charles Holloway. The controversial scene shows a clash between Arikara and whites near Mobridge in 1823.

"The Mercy and the Law" is the mural painted in the state Supreme Court (Pierre) by Charles Holloway.

A young Native American maiden is portrayed as an evil spirit in the mural entitled "The Spirit of the People," painted by Ed Blashfield in the state Capitol (Pierre) in 1910.

Paul War Cloud was the first South Dakota artist to paint a mural in the state Capitol. His 1971 "Unity Through the Great Spirit" shows harmony, through divine guidance.

An Iowa firm was hired to decorate the South Dakota Capitol in 1907. The first major art program undertaken by the state of South Dakota was commissioning a firm to paint the ceilings in the state Capitol.

SOUTH DAKOTA STATUES IN U.S. CAPITOL:
- •Gen. William Beadle, a six-foot, four-inch bronze by H. Daniel Webster, 1911
- • Educator Joseph Ward, a seven-foot, two-inch marble, by Bruno Beghe, 1963

ROYAL CHISELERS
Gutzon Borglum (Hermosa) has more statues in the U.S. Capitol than any other sculptor. Borglum also created a bronze bust of Gov. Peter Norbeck that was placed in the state Capitol (Pierre) March 1, 1951.

The only two bronze cast replicas of Michelangelo's David and Moses are in Sioux Falls. Augustana College has Moses. David is in a city park.

National Museum of Woodcarvers (Custer) features 36 life-size scenes. The museum features life work of an original animator of Disneyland, a Dr. Niblack. It took Niblack over 70,000 hours — more than 30 years — to create the display, some of which is composed of talking woodcarvings. Three scenes once appeared in the Smithsonian. The display at Custer has 36 scenes, some scenes composed of 1,100 carvings.

"Lasting Legacy" (Belle Fourche) is a bronze statue by Tony Chytka commemorating the cowboy.

Western Heritage Museum (Deadwood) has 70 costumed wax figures.

Rapid City, S.D., features a 50-foot environmental sculpture called TOTH, the Tower on the Hill. It sits atop Smelter Hill and symbolizes the role of gold mines.

Chapel in the Hills (Rapid City) is an exact copy of the 825-year-old, 12th-Century Borgund Stavkirke of Laerdal, Norway.

Parade of Presidents (Keystone) features all presidents, plus Winston Churchill, Betsy Ross and Mikhail Gorbachev.

Flintstones Bedrock City (Custer) serves Brontoburgers and Dino Dogs. The park is home to Mount Rockmore, Fred Flintstone's House, Barney Rubble's house; KROCK radio, Dr. Pulzit the dentist and Texrocko Gas station.

Native Americans left petroglyphs in Cave Hills.

Sen. Francis Case tried to get a "Christ on the Mountain" statue erected near Spearfish.

Centuries ago Native Americans used 104 boulders and rocks to create mosaics at Wessington Springs, including a 15-ft. long turtle, 13.5-ft. long man and eight-ft. long woman.

Korczak Ziolkowski (Crazy Horse) had no formal art training.

USA Today's Allen Neuharth (Eureka) dresses exclusively in gray, black and white.

A 21-inch diameter of the South Dakota State Seal is in the ceiling of the U.S. House in Washington, D.C.

South Dakota Bishop Martin Marty (Sioux Falls) presented a decorated buffalo robe to Pope Leo XIII. A Native American artist had decorated the fur with Native American history, including Custer's Last Stand. The pontiff also blessed a gold medallion.

PAINTING BY NUMBER
   In 1889 a New York society widow arrived in South Dakota to paint the formal portrait of Chief Sitting Bull. Artist Catherine Weldon also

cooked and cleaned for the chief, while she painted. The chief proposed marriage, even though he already had two wives. Weldon declined, and left, leaving the completed portrait behind. A few months later, when Sitting Bull was killed, a police officer slashed the painting, as if to kill the chief twice.

In 1843 James J. Audubon made a trip to South Dakota by steamboat to complete his drawings of four-legged North American animals, as well as birds.

The first white artist to do a painting in South Dakota was George Catlin, who spent a fast-paced 15 days doing artwork around a Dakota encampment near Fort Pierre in 1832.

Dahl Fine Arts Center (Rapid City) features a 200-foot mural by Bernard Thomas which depicts scenes from American history.

Berry Library (Spearfish) contains a collection of porcelain representations of U.S. First Ladies by Rowena Rachetts.

Termespherea were created by artist Dick Termes (Spearfish). The balls range from 10 inches to seven feet in diameter, the surfaces of which are painted with scenes.

The only example of Egyptian Revival architecture in South Dakota is the Masonic Temple (Mobridge), built in 1933.

Dahl Fine Arts Center (Rapid City) is home to a Bicentennial mural by Bernard Thomas. The cyclorama depicts the development of America, and is the largest mural in the western United States.

In 1974 Jim Langer (Spearfish) began creating Black Hills Silver Jewelry. Designs include the leaf, acorn, logs, flowers, fish, and animals.

EDUCATION

It costs South Dakota taxpayers more to house a murderer in prison than it would be to educate the person in the state's most expensive college, Augustana.

A high school prank pulled by Hubert Humphrey (Doland) was to hide several alarm clocks set to go off at two-minute intervals.

Emma Bradford instructed eight students in the first school built in South Dakota, near Bon Homme, in 1860. Three months later the school was disassembled, its logs used to build a fort.

In 1991 Watertown, S.D., parents circulated petitions banning "The Box," a closet-sized space used to house suspended high school students for three days at a time.

While in college sculptor Casimir Ziolkowski (Crazy Horse) collected the corners of $5 bills.

Because school had already let out for the year when President Nixon arrived in Sioux Falls during June 1969, "Hail to the Chief" was played by a Canadian band, on hand for a Lions Convention.

During WWII Sioux Falls trained over half of all radio operators and mechanics serving America in Europe. When the $12 million training school closed in 1945 the city turned the 200 empty classrooms into apartments, warehouses and businesses.

During the Great Depression Huron College accepted tuition in the form of merchandise to professors. Instructors got IOU's, which in turn could be exchanged at stores owned by parents of the students.

The most-requested author at the Sioux Falls Public Library is Danielle Steele.

With 270,000 books and documents, the Sioux Falls Public Library is the state's largest public library.

The University of South Dakota (Vermillion) has the state's largest library, with a half million books.

After Tom Fawick (Sioux Falls) quit eighth-grade, he went on to earn 200 patents and compose 3,000 musical works.

In 1990 South Dakota banned spanking in school.

In 1915, 56 percent of the 1,347 South Dakota teachers failed the licensure examination.

First Lady Linda Mickelson (Sioux Falls) taught high school English while her husband finished law school. She has since tutored English as a second language.

George S. Mickelson (Brookings) is the state's first governor to hold a doctorate degree, in law.

Educator Mentor Graham (Blunt) convinced student Abe Lincoln to study grammar and correct his speech. Graham stood near Lincoln at his 1861 Inauguration before returning to South Dakota to retire.

It was an invitation from fifth-grader Jamie Damon (Pierre), 9, that motivated President Kennedy to come to South Dakota and dedicate the Oahe Dam, August 17, 1962.

President Coolidge used the Rapid City High School as his Summer White House office in 1927. Coolidge would drive back to work every day from a state game lodge, where he stayed.

In 1905 the state legislature introduced legislation which suspended any high school boy who injured an opponent during a football game.

Joe Robbie (Sisseton) was the first person to be elected student body president of two different universities: Northern State University (Aberdeen) and University of South Dakota (Vermillion).

Sen. Jim Abdnor (Kennebec) holds a degree in Business Education.

Myron Floren (Roslyn) put himself through college by giving accordion lessons.

Sen. Karl Mundt (Madison) did his Master's Thesis on educational publicity.

After earning a Ph.D. in history, George McGovern was among the finalists for a position at the University of Iowa but was turned down. McGovern was then hired to teach in Mitchell, S.D.

McGovern addressed students at Oxford University as his opponent for the presidency, Richard Nixon, was sworn in, 1973.

Congressman Ben Reifel chose Parmalee, S.D., to complete sixth-grade, at age 15, because the town had a pool hall.

Ben Reifel (Sisseton) held a doctorate in public administration from Harvard. He later became the first Native American from South Dakota elected to Congress.

The state's largest campus is actually Kilian Community College, since the college without walls holds classes throughout the entire city of Sioux Falls.

Sen. Larry Pressler (Humboldt), a Rhodes Scholar, obtained a diploma — but not a degree — from Oxford University, because he had to quit to serve in the U.S. Army in Vietnam.

Paul Young (Vermillion) was the state's first Rhodes Scholar, 1904.

Lawrence Welk (Yankton) quit school in fourth-grade so he could go help in the fields.

Artist Harvey Dunn (Manchester) dropped out of school in the ninth-grade.

Dr. Frank Caulkins instructed students in the state's first school, at Fort Randall, 1857. South Dakota's first schoolhouse wasn't built until three years later, in Bon Homme.

Frank Edmunds (Yankton) was the state's first West Point graduate, 1871. Walter King was the state's first graduate from the U.S. Naval Academy, 1869.

South Dakota State University (Brookings) has one of America's five Animal Disease Research and Diagnostic Labs.

Kevin Falcon (Sioux Falls) joined Jerry Loomer (Rapid City) as the state's two finalists for the coveted Teacher-in-Space nomination ultimately won by S. Christa McAuliffe, who later died in the Challenger explosion.

Laura Ingalls Wilder (De Smet) taught school in order to raise money to send her sister to a school for the blind.

Russell Means (Pine Ridge) attended five colleges without earning a degree.

Brookings, S.D., college student Trever Sheldon was fined $3,000 and sentenced to six months in jail for tipping over a TV news car in 1991.

School bus driver Tyler Lehmann (Rapid City) was suspended for drunk driving, after asking if any high school students on his bus could drive for him, April 1991.

The University of South Dakota's first building was still under construction when students arrived for their first classes in 1882.

Until 1978 federal law prohibited Dakota from practicing many spiritual rites and Pine Ridge, S.D., students caught speaking the Lakota language at Catholic missions were punished.

America's first public/private single degree computer training program was announced in August 1991 by Dakota State University and Sioux Falls College.

The average SAT score in South Dakota during 1991 was 1047 points, down 14 points from the previous year.

The Oglala Sioux Tribal Court invalidated a March 1991 school board election because one poll closed early and reopened the next day.

Country western singer Sherwin Linton (Watertown) was nearly expelled from seventh-grade for singing a cowboy song that the principal thought was dirty. Linton was forced to write down the innocent lyrics, which satisfied the principal.

History 395 was the title of the University of North Dakota course Lawrence Welk (Yankton) taught to college students, about the impact of his band on popular culture.

The first students at the University of South Dakota did not begin attending classes until 20 years after the university was created. The first teacher was a former Jewish rabbi.

The Congregational Church (Yankton) started the state's first college, in 1881.

South Dakota sports 13 four-year colleges.

All Saints School (Sioux Falls) was built to educate the daughters of Episcopal missionaries. Its chapel contains signed Tiffany glass and the original 1884 organ.

Norwegians started a normal school in Sioux Falls in 1889 because they thought the public schools would not provide suitable teachers for their children. The normal school became Augustana College.

The first college in the state, Yankton College, first welcomed students on October 4, 1881.

In 1991 South Dakota had 83 one-room schoolhouses, each run by just one teacher.

South Dakota's first school for the blind was created when Gary residents offered the state their abandoned courthouse in 1895. Officials condemned the site, so Gary built a new one, in 1900. In 1959 the school was moved to Aberdeen where a new one-story School for the Visually Handicapped opened to students September 18, 1960. All 11 buildings are interconnected.

The University of Dakota began teaching its first 35 students in 1882 in the Clay County Courthouse in Vermillion.

The first publication about South Dakota ever published by the Smithsonian Institution was a Native American Grammar dictionary, by Dr. S.R. Riggs, in 1852.

Sarah Ward used her $100,000 inheritance, gained from selling cotton in New England, to keep Yankton College going.

Yankton College is the state's oldest college.

The South Dakota School for the Deaf is in Sioux Falls.

Calamity Jane (Deadwood) could neither read or write.

During WWII South Dakota still sported 3,229 one-room school-houses.

In 1913 South Dakota spent $15,000, fenced in 40 miles of former-school land near Custer, and created the Black Hills National Forest, which became the state's largest state park.

Religious and ethnic groups started many of the state's universities:

Augustana: Lutherans
Dakota Wesleyan: Methodists
Mt. Marty: Catholics
Presentation: Catholics
Sinte Gleska: Lakota
Sioux Falls College: Baptists

South Dakota State University (Brookings) offers students the most computers, 330.

Watertown High School (Watertown) was the world's first school to fingerprint its students, Oct. 19, 1936. The process started as an outgrowth of a talk by an FBI agent.

Mayor Ed McLaughlin (Rapid City), a former school superintendent, taught English to Air Force pilots, curriculum to college seniors and used to take students on environmental field trips deep within the Black Hills.

Emily Slaathaug (Summit) has been on the school board longer than any other South Dakotan, 1991.

The first written record of the visit of white men to South Dakota was a lead tablet buried March 30, 1743, by the Verendryes, near Fort Pierre. They claimed the area for France. The tablet was discovered Feb. 15, 1913, by school children.

COLLEGES, UNIVERSITIES:
- Augustana College (Sioux Falls)
- Black Hills State (Spearfish)
- Dakota State (Madison)
- Dakota Wesleyan (Mitchell)
- Huron (Huron)
- Kilian Community College (Sioux Falls)
- Mitchell Vocational Technical Institute (Mitchell)
- Mt. Marty College (Yankton)

- National College (Rapid City)
- Northern State University (Aberdeen)
- Oglala Lakota College (Kyle)
- Presentation College (Aberdeen)
- Sinte Gleska College (Rosebud)
- Sioux Falls College (Sioux Falls)
- Sisseton-Wahpeton Community College (Sisseton)
- South Dakota School of Mines (Rapid City)
- South Dakota State University (Brookings)
- Southeast Vocational Technical University (Sioux Falls)
- University of South Dakota (Vermillion)
- Western Dakota Vocational Technical Institute (Rapid City)

FARMING AND RANCHING

FEEDING THE WORLD

Milbank has the state's only remaining wind-powered flour mill, built in 1882.

Many South Dakota settlers started their sod houses at night, so they could square up with the North Star.

So few crops grew near Mitchell during the Great Depression that one year the Corn Palace was decorated with pine and spruce branches from the Black Hills.

In 1904 South Dakota held a lottery to distribute unallotted reservation land for homesteading. Thousands of applicants slept all night in lines. During the day business people rented out chairs and sold food. Some folks even sold their places in line.

In 1956 angry farmers threw eggs at Secretary of Agriculture Ezra Benson when he visited South Dakota.

Glenn Sloan suggested using mountain water from the Missouri River to develop irrigation in the James River Valley. Because of that suggestion, four dams were constructed in South Dakota.

During 1897 two-thirds of the world's wheat came from Eureka, S.D.

South Dakota has 44 million acres of farmland.

In 1946 South Dakota harvested so much wheat, 53 million bushels, that there were not enough railroad cars in the entire Midwest to haul it. Countless tons of valuable grain were simply dumped near railroad tracks for later shipment.

Nils Hansen (Brookings) endured choking dust in China in 1897 to bring to America its first crested wheat grass.

During the 1980s the number of farms in South Dakota decreased from 68,000 to 35,000.

The economic impact upon South Dakota during the Great Depression impressed Ted Schulz (Arlington) to the extent that his research eventually earned him the Nobel Prize in Economics.

The original goal of the Corn Palace, which now hosts 400,000 visitors each year, was to be proof that farming could be successful.

South Dakotans harvest $13 billion worth of crops each year.

Through his 1938 feature in *The Saturday Evening Post*, Robert Lusk (Huron) won national acclaim by chronicling the Dust Bowl plight of farmer Richard Haeder (Wolsey). Lusk's continued stories on irrigation helped create the state's Missouri River dams.

Fifty-four percent of South Dakotans live on farms or ranches.

Sen. Francis Case (Custer) introduced the first legislation regarding the sale of surplus farm produce to global countries.

The first flour mill in South Dakota was built in Bloomingdale, on the Vermillion River, in 1868.

Over 90 percent of South Dakota is farmland.

John Deere has had a booth at the South Dakota State Fair (Huron) since the first fair in 1885.

Over the half century following the Great Depression, South Dakota lost over half of its 83,000 farms.

The average South Dakota farm is 1,095 acres.

Seth Bullock (Belle Fourche) introduced alfalfa to South Dakota.

Peter Dorion (Yankton) was South Dakota's first white settler and farmer.

RANCHING
Seven of every $10 earned in South Dakota is derived from livestock.

A thousand bidders showed up at the March 19, 1991, auction of 31,500 acres owned by Ron and Don Jarrett. The Aberdeen land sale was double the amount Farm Credit Services sold in South Dakota during the entire previous year.

In 1911 a Badlands rancher dismantled his mower, hauled it up the side of Hay Butte, reassembled it, mowed a large, untapped hay crop and spilled the stacks down the sides.

A Belvidere rancher took his tractor, piece by piece, up a Badlands butte to plant 40 acres of corn.

A corridor of land six miles wide and 80 miles long was cut through the Standing Rock and Cheyenne River Reservations in the early 1900s to facilitate the shipment of cattle from West River towards the East. When ranchers brought cattle through "The Strip," they crossed the Missouri River on pontoon bridges. More railroad lines elsewhere caused "The Strip" to fade into history.

MONEY

PRICE TAGS

$519 million — South Dakota's budget, 1991

$435 million — Oahe Dam (Pierre)

$122.5 million — amount U.S. Supreme Court ordered government to pay Native Americans in South Dakota for land seized 103 years earlier, in 1877

$100 million — damages from the 1972 Rapid City flood

$100 million — budget of Sioux Falls, 1992

$60 million — budget of Rapid City, 1992

$40 million — donations sought for upkeep of Mount Rushmore, 1991

$21 million — McGovern's 1972 presidential campaign

$20 million — budget of Aberdeen, 1992

$20 million — disposal of the Pathfinder nuclear reactor (Sioux Falls)

$10 million — American Humane Society lawsuit against host Bob Barker (Mission), 1989

$8 million — state's largest ethanol plant (Brown County)

$7.2 million — DakotaDome (Vermillion)

$6.4 million — timber lost in Black Hills National Forest fire, 1988

$2 million — Lloyd's of London insurance policy on legs of Mary Hart (Sioux Falls)

$1,972,403.20 — price U.S. paid France for land that is now South Dakota

$1.7 million — KELO-Land's insurance policy in case storm blew over TV tower during critical 1958 Nielsen ratings

$1,246,857 — state Capitol (Pierre), twice over budget

$989,993.32 — cost to carve Mount Rushmore

$466,665 — U.S.S. South Dakota, as scrap metal

$70,000 — Homestake Mine (Lead), to George Hearst, 1877

$59,500 — average house in Sioux Falls, 1991

$35,000 — cost to decorate Corn Palace each September

$25,000 — state's first private college building (Yankton)

$25,000 — original state capitol, later sold for $1,000 to the Pierre School Board

$25,000 — one-day cost to hold a special session of the legislature to correct a redistricting mistake in Corson County, Nov. 26, 1991

$20,000 — Super 8 Motel (Aberdeen) franchise, plus royalties and advertising fees

$13,265 — one year at state's most expensive college, Augustana (Sioux Falls), 1991

$5,000 — reward by St. Mary's Hospital (Pierre) for a surgeon, 1991

$5,000 — reward for senate chandeliers stolen from state Capitol in 1946; reward expired in 1984

$2,000 — reward for escaped murderer George Sitts (Sioux Falls) 1947

$885 — one buffalo at Custer State Park, 1991

$719 — average sales and gas taxes paid by each South Dakotan, 1990

$280 — cost for Homestake Mine (Lead) to process single ounce of gold, 1991

$100 — daily cost to play cowboy at Dakota Ranch Vacations (Wall)

$50 — one minute ad on state's most expensive radio station, KGGG-FM (Rapid City), 1991

$25 — reward by Lawrence County for any Native American, dead or alive, 1876; offer rose to $250 year later

$20 — annual credit card fee, Citibank (Sioux Falls), 1992

$17.50 — only cash ever invested by Harvey Dunn in an art class

$15 — first accordion of Lawrence Welk (Yankton), bought at age 16

$13 — lowest value of an acre of South Dakota farmland, 1940

$12 — car fee to see Crazy Horse, 1992

$1.41 — coins resting in cornerstone of current state Capitol

5 cents — coffee at Wall Drug (Wall)

SOME FREE THINGS:
- Adams Museum, Mt. Moriah (Deadwood)
- Captain 11 T.V. Show (Sioux Falls)
- Condoms, University of South Dakota
- Corn Palace (Mitchell)
- Ice water at Wall Drug (Wall)
- Interstate highways 29, 90: no toll bridges
- Mount Rushmore
- Oahe Dam (Pierre)
- Petrified Park (Lemmon)
- Popcorn at Gurney's Seed & Nursery (Yankton)
- Storybook Land (Aberdeen)
- U.S.S. South Dakota Memorial (Sioux Falls)

STATEWIDE TAXES:
- Property
- Sales

STATE'S LEGAL GAMBLING:
- Poker, slot machines, blackjack (Deadwood)
- Pari-mutuel thoroughbred, quarter horse racing (Fort Pierre, Aberdeen)
- Greyhound racing (Rapid City, North Sioux City)
- Lottery tickets, video lottery, lotto (entire state)

INCOMES, SALARIES

$1.9 billion — annual livestock sales in South Dakota

$1 billion — annual farm receipts in South Dakota

$610 million — profit from Visa and MasterCards, Citibank (Sioux Falls), 1990

$379 million — taxes collected in South Dakota, 1989

$235 million — bet in South Dakota, 1987-1991: state's share was $58 million

$160 million — earnings on *Dances With Wolves*, filmed in South Dakota, as of August 1991

$25 million — worth of Lawrence Welk (Yankton), 1983

$18 million — seven-year NBC contract signed by Tom Brokaw (Yankton), 1982

$12.47 million — winning lottery ticket purchased by Ionia Klein (Dallas), 1991

$4 million — donations raised by Korczak Ziolkowski (Crazy Horse)

$2,998,065 — career winnings of jockey Earl Sande (Groton)

$2 million — average sales at state fair (Huron)

$2 million — awarded Deeann Hackett (Sioux Falls), first in state to get federal compensation from a national vaccine injury act, 1991

$950,000 — career earnings for Pro rodeo champ Paul Tierney (Piedmont)

$350,000 — entire state treasury embezzled by treasurer W.W. Taylor, 1895

$250,000 — lifetime bets by Poker Alice (Sturgis)

$190,000 — Nobel prizes won by Ernest Lawrence (Canton); Ted Schulz (Arlington)

$170,000 — Gutzon Borglum's salary to carve Mount Rushmore

$135,608 — Sen. Tom Daschle, as of June 1991

$128,658 — Sen. Larry Pressler, as of June 1991

$101,308 — Rep. Tim Johnson, as of June 1991

$67,288 — salary of South Dakota Supreme Court justices, 1991

$63,232 — Gov. George S. Mickelson, 1991

$57,000 — loot stolen by George "Baby Face" Nelson in Sioux Falls bank robbery, 1934

$50,000 — paid by *Saturday Evening Post* for exclusive rights to the Fischer Quints (Aberdeen), 1963

$47,000 — Mayor Ed McLaughlin (Rapid City), 1992

$42,000 — Mayor Jackson White (Sioux Falls), 1992

$23,800 — Doris Leader Change (Parmalee), for translating *Dances With Wolves*, and role in film

$22,363 — average teacher salary in state, 1989

$16,132 — salary of state's first efficiency expert; told government to reorganize bureaus, 1921

$15,000 — Mayor Tim Rich (Aberdeen), 1992

$8,219 — Lt. Gov. Walt Miller, 1991

$2,600 — Dakota Territorial governor, 1879

$1,000 — promised each American by presidential candidate George McGovern (Mitchell), 1972

$600 — reward to children for discovering the Verendrye plate (Fort Pierre), 1913

$500 — state's first check for Vietnam War fatality, to parents of Edgar Flowers (Sioux Falls), 1969

$200 — Jack McCall, to kill Wild Bill Hickok (Deadwood), 1876

$70 — donations received by surrogate grandmother Arlette Schweitzer (Aberdeen)

$55 — 250 movie extras, for each day in state, on *Dances With Wolves*

$50 — Chief Sitting Bull, each week with Wild West Show

$1.50 — Lincoln Borglum, hourly wage as teen helping carve Mount Rushmore

$1 — Al Neuharth (Eureka), each week as a butcher boy

$0 — Sacajawea, for guiding Lewis and Clark through state; her husband got $500

FOLKS WHO DIED PENNILESS:

- Horatio Ross, discoverer of gold in the Black Hills
- Gutzon Borglum, carved Mount Rushmore
- Gov. Andrew Mellette
- Wild Bill Hickok
- Calamity Jane

IT DOESN'T GROW ON TREES

Nineteen percent of all checks used to purchase lottery tickets in South Dakota, bounce.

A washtub containing $1 million in gold is still missing near Newton, S.D.

Sculptor Korczak Ziolkowski twice turned down $10 million from the government.

When Native Americans turned down a $6 million offer for the Black Hills in 1875, the government simply took the land.

After the Republican National Committee refused to give Larry Pressler (Humboldt) $35,000 when he sought his first seat in Congress in 1974, Pressler raised his own money, and won.

The children who found the historical Verendrye plate near Pierre were going to sell it for a nickel, for scrap metal.

The first hearing to determine whether Ionia Klein (Dallas) had legally won a $12.4 million lottery ticket, was held in Winner, S.D., 1991.

Potato Creek Johnny (Deadwood) discovered a gold nugget bigger than a chicken's egg.

Some 30,000 miners filled the Black Hills during America's final gold rush August 1875-80. Prospector James B. Pearson (Yankton) told newspapers Deadwood was yielding $10,000 a day and would soon yield $100,000 a day.

In June 1877 Homestake Mine (Lead) was sold to George Hearst for $70,000 and thus began the Homestake Mining Co., the longest continuously operated gold mine in the world. Homestake produces over 350,000 ounces of gold each year.

The wealthiest woman from South Dakota is Joan Kroc (Rapid City). Kroc's $950 million came from the estate of her husband, Ray, originator of McDonald's hamburgers. Kroc banned booze from her San Diego Padres clubhouse, has donated over $35 million to charity, and lives in California.

Mark Parmer opened the first bank in South Dakota in Yankton during September 1869.

Sam Elrod was the first governor to leave office with South Dakota debt-free.

As late as 1939 some Black Hills residents still paid for groceries with gold nuggets.

Gov. Andrew Lee used his own money to outfit South Dakota troops for the Spanish-American War.

Despite promises of $1.4 billion projected over a half century for South Dakota, a proposal to sell South Dakota's water dried up, during the 1980s.

The greatest placer mine in the Black Hills was Wheeler Brothers #2, where 30 miners extracted $1,000 in gold from the water every 24 hours. One half million dollars worth of gold was taken out, until Sept. 8, 1876, when the claim was sold for $3,000.

During the Great Depression South Dakota farmland was worth $17 an acre.

In August 1940 $100 in cash was left in Faith by a mysterious woman who said the town was named for her, and that she had a long-felt desire to visit the town. Many residents believed it was an East Coast heiress named Faith Rockefeller.

Super 8 (Aberdeen) has made more millionaires in South Dakota than any company doing business in the state.

South Dakota gets a minimum of 25 percent of video lottery profits.

BUSINESS & INDUSTRY

BIG SALES

Two cases of Scotch whiskey arrived at the Rapid City Grocery Company a half century after the order was placed. Records show that the store was one of the original customers of a 21,000-base shipment lost at sea aboard the S.S.Politician during WWII, and recovered in 1990.

Aberdeen's 3M plant made most of the millions of air masks used by Washington State residents, who needed them to battle the tons of volcanic dust spilling out of Mt. St. Helen's in 1980.

When W.O. Wells joined M.B. Lamont in opening the world's first Wells-Lamont Glove Company, in Aberdeen, their primary product was buggy whips.

Sioux Falls is the biggest retail center between the Twin Cities and Denver, Colo. Some 2,000 stores employ one-fifth of the city's labor force.

South Dakota's biggest gun collection is owned by Curt Carter (Kones Korner), who has a thousand on hand, and sells some 2,000 guns each year.

The first Lewis Drug opened in Sioux Falls in 1942 and was started by John Griffin.

Tom Brown joined Eugene Saenger in establishing their printing business in Sioux Falls May 1, 1889.

Since 1925 South Dakota has been the only state to own a cement plant.

From 1960-1982 60 Minnesota businesses, and 10,000 jobs, moved to South Dakota, including Control Data, OK Hardware, 3M and Litton Industries.

South Dakota has a four percent sales tax.

In 1974 Tom Brokaw bought KTOQ in Rapid City.

The state's first flour mill, Portland, was started in 1867 near Sioux Falls on the Big Sioux River.

The first labor strike in the state was in 1909, by miners at Homestake Mine.

Early workers to the pink Sioux Falls granite (Rowena) were from England and Scotland.

It is estimated that only eight percent of the 5,000 gold miners around Deadwood in 1876 were experienced.

During Prohibition the beer brewery in Sioux Falls was converted into a creamery, while the one in Yankton became an egg
storehouse.

The first trading post in South Dakota was established by Joe La
Framboise (Fort Pierre), 1817.

**The first business established in Custer was a saloon, August
1875.**

Betty and Bob Campbell joined sons Chad and Scott in creating
the Dakota Style potato chip, the world's first "Industrial Strength
Potato Chip" in Clark in 1986. A bar in Henry, S.D., served the first
bag of Dakota Style potato chips in 1986.

I'LL BET

More people buy lottery tickets in South Dakota than vote.

**In 1991 Deadwood sported 1,909 slot machines, 84 gaming
halls, 83 black jack tables and 27 poker tables.**

Deadwood's 84 gaming halls include the town's only laundromat
and gas station.

**Deadwood, now the gambling center of the Midwest, did not
allow gambling until 1989.**

Deadwood's successful gambling campaign was lead by a former-
Catholic priest.

**In 1989 a clothing store in downtown Deadwood sold for
$54,000. A few months later, after gambling was legalized, the
same place went for a cool million dollars!**

The first lottery in South Dakota was held in January 1876 when a
two-mile area near Deadwood was divided up into 300-foot lots, and
distributed, by lottery, to anxious gold miners.

EUREKA TODAY

Once when executives at *USA Today* had exceeded their budget,
founder Allen Neuharth (Eureka) invited them to dinner. Neuharth
showed up dressed as Jesus Christ, wearing a crown of thorns, carrying a cross and hosting a "Last Supper," to deliver a message: shape
up, or this is the paper's last supper.

**Allen Neuharth quit studying law in Aberdeen, S.D., during
WWII, and joined the army.**

While Al Neuharth was chairman of the biggest U.S. newspaper
chain, Gannett, the company's annual revenues increased from $200

million to $3.1 billion. The company enjoyed 21 years of uninterrupted earnings gains.

When Al Neuharth retired in 1989, at 65, Gannett Co. gave him stock worth $5.1 million and $300,000 a year, guaranteed for life. Upon retirement Neuharth became chairman of the Gannett Foundation, and had the name changed to Freedom Forum of Arlington, Va. In April 1991 Neuharth bought the foundation's holdings for $670 million and agreed to rename the foundation.

During the 19 years that Allen Neuharth was CEO of Gannett he spent nearly $1.5 billion buying 69 newspapers, 29 radio stations and 16 TV stations.

Financial World has named Allen Neuharth boss of the year more than any other South Dakotan.

BIG BUCKS
In 1981 Citibank moved their administrative credit card headquarters from New York to South Dakota to get around New York's usury laws, which used to limit interest to 12 percent. In 1992 Citibank charged 19.8 percent.

Citicorp's 30 million Visa and MasterCards realized a profit of $610 million in 1990.

In 1992 the Citibank Visa card was accepted at 8.3 million businesses and 91,000 Automated Teller Machines, worldwide.

Citibank is the largest employer in Sioux Falls, with 2,500 workers. The company has expanded operations to Yankton and Rapid City, adding 800 more jobs.

Citibank (Sioux Falls) processes 13 million Visa and MasterCard accounts each year.

Telephones were installed in Deadwood, S.D., two years before Boston got them. When the elegant Evans Hotel opened in Hot Springs in 1892, diners were fed by a Chicago chef, served by black waiters and ate in Victorian elegance. An orchestra and roulette wheels provided atmosphere.

In 1980 Deadwood closed its three oldest businesses: Pam's, Dixie's and the White Door brothels.

As late as 1980 Deadwood's largest employers were five brothers who ran a brothel employing 40 women — and more, during deer-hunting season.

When a $20 million uranium plant went into operation in Edgemont, S.D., June 24, 1955, its original goal was to process 200 tons a day. It never made it.

The Pathfinder nuclear reactor (Sioux Falls) produced electricity for only 13 months during the 1960s, and was buried in the state of Washington in 1991.

In 1944 Congress authorized a program for harnessing and storing fall water of the Missouri River and converting its weight and movement into electric energy in South Dakota and the Midwest.

Fort Randall Dam has eight turbine generators that can produce up to 320 megawatts of electric energy.

For years East Coast insurance companies refused to issue policies to ranchers living west of the 100 meridian because early maps labeled it the "Great American Desert," which covered most of South Dakota.

Sioux Falls is Deadwood's largest market.

Aberdeen had the world's second dial phone system, installed November 6, 1905.

Gov. Janklow had to cut the state's budget only once during his eight-year term.

In 1973 South Dakota was one vote away from having an income tax, but Lt. Gov. Bill Dougherty cast the deciding no vote.

Frank Ziebach published the first newspaper in South Dakota, *The Dakotian*, in Yankton, June 6, 1861.

In 1982 the 1890s scrapbook and diary of a notorious Deadwood madam, Black Nell, was discovered but the owner would not allow it to be shown to the public because it was feared residents would recognize names of their grandfathers.

Aberdeen's first newspaper, *The Aberdeen Pioneer*, was published in 1881 on white muslin, because the paper supply had failed to arrive by rail.

Nobel prize winner Theodore W. Schulz (Arlington) was considered among the foremost experts in agricultural economics and social development. Schulz was a critic of large-scale industrialization and the neglect of agriculture.

The first bank opened in South Dakota in Yankton in 1872.

The first bank in Ipswich was a board laid across two barrels. When the banker went to lunch he placed the cash in a satchel, and held a gun in the other, taking the deposits with him.

In 1885 25-year-old Joe Bailey (Sioux Falls) was the youngest bank president in America.

In 1870 Yankton was the first South Dakota town connected by telegraph to the outside world.

In 1990 South Dakota had 135 banks. In 1924 175 banks failed in South Dakota.

BE OUR GUEST
Super 8 Motels (Aberdeen) could have one-sixth of all South Dakotans as their guests on any given day.

Since 1974 the economy lodging chain has grown to 53,623 rooms in 870 inns in 48 states and Canada. Attorney Dennis Brown (Aberdeen) opened the world's first Super 8 Motel October 1, 1974, in Aberdeen, S.D.

Banker Ronal Rivett helped bankroll the motel that features the pineapple of friendliness.

The first four Super 8s in Mexico are scheduled to open during 1992.

The largest Super 8 is in Las Vegas, Nev.

Toothbrushes are the most common item left behind by Super 8 guests.

Super 8 founder Dennis Brown (Aberdeen) made his first million by the age of 34.

The Victorian Waldorf Hotel (Andover) opened in 1903, and was once considered the finest hotel between Aberdeen and the Twin Cities. Men needed a coat to eat in the dining room. Every Sunday an orchestra made a weekly trip from Minneapolis, to play for dinner.

The Historic Franklin Hotel (Deadwood) was once considered the finest hotel between Chicago and California. The Franklin Hotel had Teddy Roosevelt sleep there. So did William Taft, Buffalo Bill, Babe Ruth, John Wayne and Kevin Costner.

South Dakota's largest inn is Holiday Inn/City Centre (Sioux Falls), 306 rooms.

In 1991 the most expensive inn in South Dakota was Alex Johnson, (Rapid City) at $250 per suite.

Carl Grupp's Bet On It! Trivia Myths:

PREOCCUPATIONS

ROGER BUSGALIA MEDITATING ON WHETHER HIS
MARIGOLDS WILL BE KNEE-HIGH BY THE FOURTH OF JULY.

JOBS

YOU'RE FIRED!
Norm Van Brocklin (Parade) was fired from both pro football teams
he coached. The Minnesota Vikings canned Van Brocklin following a
public feud with player Fran Tarkenton. The Atlanta Falcons dismissed Van Brocklin after the team lost three times as many games as
they had won. Van Brocklin ended his football career by serving as an
assistant coach at a southern college.

**Wild Bill Hickok (Deadwood) was once fired as marshal for acci-
dentally shooting his own deputy.**

Tom Brokaw (Yankton) was kicked out of his senior class play.

**Gutzon Borglum was fired from the Stone Mountain project in
Georgia because of his temperamental outbursts. As a result of
his unemployment, he was free to accept the offer to carve Mount
Rushmore.**

While carving Mount Rushmore, sculptor Gutzon Borglum personally fired a worker for punching his son, Lincoln Borglum, in the jaw.
That worker was Korczak Ziolkowski, who moved 14 miles down the
road and began carving Crazy Horse.

**Over a three-year period Lawrence Welk (Yankton) was fired
from running a hotel, a restaurant, and a music store.**

Lawrence Welk was 68 years old when he learned from reporters in
March 1971 that ABC had cancelled the bandleader's show, even
though he had the only musical show to be on the air every week for
16 consecutive years. The cancellation resulted in ABC receiving over
one million letters from upset and angry viewers.

**Gov. Gilbert Pierce was forced to resign his office in 1887
because of a feud with President Cleveland.**

In an effort to help meet expenses, quint mother Mary Ann Fischer
(Aberdeen) decorated wedding cakes and worked at a day care center,
from which she was later dismissed after a disagreement in policy.

**When a Wild West Show employed Calamity Jane (Deadwood) to
shoot a gun while looking in a mirror, Jane would often miss,
would ad lib with profanity, and was soon fired.**

After Lt. Gov. Bill Dougherty (Sioux Falls) challenged incumbent
Gov. Kneip, who was running for an unprecedented third term in
1974, Kneip replaced Dougherty with Harvey Wollman.

**When Gov. Newton Edmunds accused Congressman Walt
Burleigh of taking funds, Burleigh got even by convincing President Johnson to fire Edmunds and replace him with Burleigh's
father-in-law, Andrew Faulk.**

Doug Lund (Sioux Falls) was announcing for KSOO when new owners axed him in order to bring in their own team. As a fortunate
result, Lund landed a position with KELO-Land in 1974.

ON THE JOB

Native American activist Russell Means (Pine Ridge) has worked as
a ballroom dance instructor in San Franciso, as an employment
agency executive, as a movie actor, and as a circus roustabout.

**Cheryl Ladd (Huron) worked as a carhop at The Barn restaurant
(Wolsey). Her first appearance on TV was as the cartoon voice of a
cat.**

Mary Hart taught for three years at Washington High School (Sioux
Falls), before doing a local cable TV show that helped launch her
entertainment career.

**Steve Hemmingsen (Sioux Falls) worked as an assistant under-
taker.**

Clint Roberts dropped his role as South Dakota Secretary of Agriculture for two days in 1979 to play a barber in *Orphan Train*, filmed
in Hill City. Roberts had convinced the owner of the 1880 Train to
make the property available to Hollywood. Clint Roberts also did cowboy and cigarette commercials.

**Dennis Brown was both a former Internal Revenue agent and a
tornado alarm maker, before creating the world's first Super 8
Motel (Aberdeen) during October 1974.**

Gov. Joe Foss (Sioux Falls) was a boxer. Foss was also commissioner of the American Football League (1959-1966) and the first
South Dakotan to head the National Boy Scouts (1954).

**As a teenager in Yankton, S.D., Tom Brokaw worked as a dam
guide, writing his own tour script. Brokaw worked his way
through college by doing sports reports for Yankton stations.**

Andy Fischer (Aberdeen) was earning $76 a week as a shipping
clerk when his wife gave birth to healthy quintuplets in 1963.

**Mary Ann Fischer (Aberdeen) became a cook for senior citizens,
once her quints graduated from high school.**

At age 78, Rose Wilder Lane (De Smet) was the oldest war corre-
spondent covering the Vietnam War.

**Sally Campbell (Deadwood) was Gen. Custer's black cook in
1874. She settled in the Black Hills and did not travel with the
general to Little Bighorn.**

Mayor Jackson White (Sioux Falls) sold popcorn during band con-
certs.

Mayor Tim Rich (Aberdeen) was a baker.

Gov. Richard Kneip (Salem) sold milking equipment.

Sen. George McGovern (Mitchell) was America's first Food for Peace director.

After Gladys Pyle served as the nation's first woman U.S. Senator she moved back to Huron, S.D., and sold life insurance.

Composer John Cacavas (Aberdeen) was a machine gun instructor before going into the U.S. Army band.

Sen. Francis Case (Custer) served as editor of a Methodist newspaper in order to get money to work on his doctorate.

Wild Bill Hickok (Deadwood) was a professional magician. As a youth, Wild Bill Hickok joined his parents in helping fugitive slaves escape to freedom with the Underground Railroad. Hickok twice lost two elections for police chief and sheriff before voters finally elected him sheriff. Hickok originally arrived in Deadwood, S.D., by leading a wagon train of women to camps full of eager miners.

Deadwood's first two madams were Madam Mustachio and Madam Dirty Em, 1876.

By the age of 14 Joe Robbie (Sisseton) was a newspaper reporter. Later on Robbie was a price stabilization manager, lawyer and owned professional hockey and football teams.

Because ushers weren't supposed to watch the movies, usher Joe Floyd (Sioux Falls) wore mirrored glasses which worked like a periscope. Floyd once managed a traveling strip-tease act and had a brief stint as the stage manager who handed humorist Will Rogers the most current newspaper as he walked on stage.

Dave Dedrick (Sioux Falls) was an ex-Marine who was running a theater when Joe Floyd hired him to come to KELO-Land. Dedrick later became Captain 11.

In 1886 one-sixth of Deadwood's 3,000 residents were prostitutes.

Mary Houston Atkinson, the first white child born in South Dakota, became a nun.

Herbert Schell was the state's first professionally trained historian.

So many homesteaders flooded Stanley County in 1907 that Dr. N.H. Wyckoff assumed the position as postmaster and distributed mail by leaving letters on rocks and tree stumps in his front yard.

Mount Rushmore carver Gutzon Borglum held a degree in aerodynamic engineering.

Commander Maxine Wilcox (Sioux Falls) is the first woman admiral of the Texas navy.

Keith Funston (Ramona) was president of the New York Stock Exchange.

Dr. Arthur Larson (Sioux Falls) was Eisenhower's speech writer.

In less than five years, Jerome Luhr (Clark) started growing grapes in California, and became a national wine distributor.

Garney Henley (Hayti) became a big pro-football star with the Canadian Football League.

Scientist Charles Linquist (Webster) built America's first satellite, Explorer I.

Felix Mansager (Cotton) headed the Hoover vacuum cleaner company.

Roswell Rogers (Sioux Falls) is a Hollywood scriptwriter.

An engineer who builds his own cannon, Lyle Scott (Esteline) holds 32 patents on oil drilling equipment.

Scotty Philip arrived in the Black Hills with 100 pounds of flour, and planned to mine for gold until the flour ran out. When it did run out, he moved east a couple hundred miles and became a buffalo rancher.

The South Dakota House killed a 1931 bill banning women from teaching when it was discovered that it would have created a vacancy in 40 percent of the state's classrooms.

San Diego Padres owner Joan Kroc (Rapid City) was an organist and TV music director.

Country western singer Sherwin Linton (Watertown) was a hotel bellhop.

John Pennington, namesake of the county, was a Confederate newspaper publisher serving in the Alabama legislature at the time President Grant appointed him Governor of Dakota Territory.

The first job of actress Mamie Van Doren (Rowena) was carrying water to her grandfather as he farmed in the fields near Sioux Falls. Van Doren was a secretary when discovered by Hollywood.

Truman's Secretary of Agriculture, Clinton Anderson, is the sole South Dakotan who served as a member of any Presidential Cabinet.

Vice President Hubert Humphrey (Huron) was a pharmacist.

Charles Rushmore, the namesake of Mount Rushmore, was a New York attorney.

Sen. Karl Mundt (Madison) ran a poetry society and was a speech teacher.

Gov. Frank Farrar (Britton) was a banker.

Author Ole Rolvaag (Sioux Falls) was a college professor.

Gov. Sam Elrod (Clark) was a janitor.

Bill Howard was both governor of Dakota Territory and a congressman from Michigan.

Madam Vestal (Deadwood) ran a gambling house and led a gang that robbed stage coaches. Vestal picked up gold tips from customers, then passed them along to her gang.

The first white woman to enter Black Hills, Annie Tallent (Sioux Falls), was a news reporter.

Two workers are employed nine months of the year sprucing up the 3,000 Wall Drug (Wall) billboards throughout the Midwest.

Sheriff Seth Bullock (Deadwood) made a lot of money selling chamber pots.

Mayor Bruce Oberlander (Deadwood) married his 30th couple May 31, 1991. The mayor can marry couples within city limits.

The jobs of the Chinese in Deadwood during the 1880s included mining, laundry and timber cutting. They ironed by filling their mouths with water and blowing the water over the garments as they ironed. They also ran opium dens under their homes. The Chinese in Deadwood also had a world champion fire hose team for 1888. The team included 6 men who raced 300 yards pulling a fire wagon and squirting water on a fire.

Sen. James Abourezk (Wood) was the son of a Lebanese peddler.

Gov. Gilbert Pierce was editor of the Minneapolis *Tribune* and authored a dictionary.

Among the 360 workers on Mount Rushmore was a full-time blacksmith whose sole duty was fixing all drilling equipment, including 19 air-compressors.

After directing the Hollywood movie *Dacotah*, Richard Lowe (Madison) served as governor of Guam, then Samoa. Lowe also authored handbooks for the U.S. Navy.

Korczak Ziolkowski (Crazy Horse) worked in a steel factory.

USA Today Publisher Allen Neuharth (Eureka) was a butcher boy. Neuharth later transformed the giant Gannett media corporation into the newspaper business having the best record of hiring women and minorities. Under Neuharth at *USA Today*, 52 percent of the jobs were held by women, 24 percent by minorities.

Gov. Tom Berry (Belvidere) wrote a column for United Features, replacing Will Rogers. Berry also raised buffalo and racing greyhounds.

Gov. Carl Gunderson (Mitchell) was a civil engineer.

J. Craig (Wessington Springs) was the state's youngest newspaper publisher, at age 28.

The muralistic talents of Oscar Howe (Joe Creek) were used by the U.S. Army during WWII to paint camouflage on tanks and jeeps in North Africa.

Allen Neuharth, the founder of America's largest national newspaper, *USA Today*, once worked for South Dakota's smallest newspaper, the Alpena Journal.

Muriel Humphrey Brown (Doland) was a turkey plucker.

STATE SYMBOLS

- ANIMAL: Coyote, also known as prairie wolf. Nickname arose during a horse race at a fort.
- BIRD: Chinese Ringneck pheasant was introduced into state in 1898.
- CAPITOL: completed in 1910 in Pierre; most fully-restored capitol in U.S.
- COLORS: Blue and gold.
- DRINK: Milk.
- FISH: walleye; Glacial Lakes are the "Walleye Capital of America".
- FLAG: Shows seal surrounded by a flaming sun of blue, blue background. Golden letters reading "South Dakota The Sunshine State" encircle the sun.
- FLOWER: Pasque is also called "May Day" flower. It is a five-petaled, lavender flower; member of buttercup family; grows 16 inches high; has gold center; blooms throughout state during April and May.
- FOSSIL: triceratops, a horned dinosaur of the late Cretaceous period (68 million years ago); was a vegetation-eating dinosaur and used its horns for defense. Discovered in Harding County, S.D., in 1927, the skeleton is now on display in Museum of Geology in Rapid City, S.D.
- GEMSTONE: Fairburn agate first discovered near Fairburn, S.D.
- INSECT: Honey bee; state leads in honey production; bee is (Apis Mellifera L.); state's mild, clear clover honey is often blended with darker honey.
- JEWELRY: Black Hills gold. Each design incorporates the traditional motif of grapes and leaves in tri-color combinations of green, rose and yellow gold.
- MINERAL: Rose quartz was discovered near Custer, S.D., in the late 1800s.
- MOTTO: "Under God the people rule."
- NICKNAMES: Mt. Rushmore, Coyote, Sunshine State.
- SEAL: Shows a smelter, hills, horse-drawn plow, cattle and a steamboat.
- SONG: "Hail, South Dakota." composed by DeCort Hammitt; marching song.
- TREE: Black Hills spruce; member of evergreen family, pyramid-shaped is characterized by dense foilage of short, blue-green needles and slender cones.

STAMPS

- LOUISIANA PURCHASE (features South Dakota), first issued April 30, 1904: 10 cents.
- U.S. AIRMAIL (features South Dakota), first issued during 1926: 10 cents.
- SOUTH DAKOTA STATEHOOD ANNIVERSARY, first issued Nov. 2, 1939: 3 cents.
- MOUNT RUSHMORE, first issued Aug. 11, 1952: 3 cents.
- LEWIS AND CLARK EXPEDITION, first issued July 28, 1954: 3 cents.
- GREAT RIVER ROAD SYSTEM (features South Dakota), first issued Oct. 21, 1966: 5 cents.
- MOUNT RUSHMORE, first issued Jan. 2, 1974: 26 cents.
- SOUTH DAKOTA STATE FLAG, first issued Feb. 23, 1976: 13 cents.
- CRAZY HORSE, first issued Oct. 31, 1980: 13 cents.
- SOUTH DAKOTA PHEASANT, first issued April 14, 1982: 20 cents.
- MOUNT RUSHMORE, first issued March 29, 1991: 29 cents.
- HUBERT H. HUMPHREY (Doland), first issued June 3, 1991: 52 cents

Mount Rushmore is the most popular South Dakota item featured on U.S. Postage Stamps.

The first Mount Rushmore stamp was inspired by a photograph taken by Robert Frankenfield (Vermillion) of his wife and son, Phyllis and Donald, in 1952. When Nila Berry, the daughter of Congressman E.Y. Berry, saw the photo, she added "Black Hills, South Dakota" to it, and submitted it to the U.S. Post Office. One hundred million stamps were printed.

PLANTS

WHITE HOUSE CHRISTMAS TREES FROM SOUTH DAKOTA:

- Mamie and Dwight Eisenhower received a 65-ft. Black Hills spruce in 1955. The president, recovering from a heart attack, turned the lights on from his home in Pennsylvania.
- Pat and Richard Nixon received a 78-ft. Black Hills spruce in 1970. After Christmas Nixon's tree was cut into 2,000 pieces and sold as $1 souvenir blocks, to pay transportation costs from the Black Hills.

AS LOVELY AS A TREE

The oldest tree in the Black Hills was the "Giant of Herbert Draw," a 122-foot tall ponderosa pine that died from infestations of the Mountain Pine Beetle, in 1972. The tree started growing in the year 1575.

The U.S. Geological Survey believes that a 250-ton petrified tree uncovered near Cash, S.D., was a Sequoia. The 95-ft. high tree had a nine-ft. diameter base.

Petrified cypress trees from the dinosaur age have been discovered in the Black Hills.

Native Americans used the Council Oak (Hermosa) as a council site for nearly 400 years.

The Lone Tree (Egan) was planted as a cottonwood seedling in a hole left by pulling out the original stake in 1880. Mrs. George Cameron planted the seedling in 1881. The tree became controversial years later when a highway was planned through the tree. The highway, which was paved around the tree, eventually killed the tree's roots.

The oldest known apple orchard in South Dakota is Ridpaths, near the ghost town of Carbonite.

The Mellette Tree was an ash planted by the state Capitol by Gov. Art Mellette on May 1, 1890, the first Arbor Day celebrated after statehood.

Three cottonwood trees planted by Charles Ingalls still stand in DeSmet.

Badger Clark had his house built around a large Ponderosa Pine at Custer State Park. Clark hated electricity and carried water from a spring.

South Dakota is home to the world's first ponderosa pine trees. Cycads, an ancestral tree of palms and ferns, once grew in south-

western South Dakota. Cycads have now fossilized, and are under protection of the federal government.

The first timber sale in the U.S. on public lands took place in 1898 in the Black Hills, when Homestake bought timber for its mines. This was also the first time trained foresters were used to cut the trees.

GURNEY

Col. George Gurney, a Civil War veteran, sold his first seeds from Yankton in 1872.

Gurney's Seed & Nursery Co. (Yankton) stores eight million trees in a refrigerated and humidified environment. The company also farms over a thousand acres.

Gurney's prints 10 million seed labels for the one million orders received each year.

Gurney Seed started radio station WNAX in 1927 in order to promote catalog sales. Radio announcer Chad Gurney (Yankton) worked for his family's station, and turned the name recognition he earned by announcing state basketball tournaments into a seat on the U.S. Senate.

Chad Gurney was the first announcer to have Lawrence Welk play his accordion on the air.

Every year over nine million Americans receive catalogs from Gurney Seed and Nursery.

Over one-third of American households recognize the name of Gurney Seed and Nursery (Yankton).

By 1992 Gurney's had been helping gardeners for 126 years.

Gurney's features 1,400 items in their annual catalog, from Ajuga to zinnias.

ITEMS IN GURNEY'S 1992 SPRING CATALOG:
- Blue roses
- Vegetable spaghetti
- Strawberry popcorn
- Mold that grows cucumbers into faces
- Pumpkins bred especially for carving
- Children's seed packets for a penny
- Pruning video
- Rat trap that catches 10 at a time
- Hybrid worms, 500 in a box
- Buffalo grass
- Apple tree with five varieties on it
- Nut Picker-Upper
- 200-pound watermelons

PLANT EXPLORER

Professor Niels Hansen (Brookings) was America's first plant explorer. Hansen traveled through China, Soviet Union, Europe, Japan and Turkey to find crops that could flourish in the cold climate of the Great Plains, and resist drought.

After Prof. Hansen was accused by the Soviets of being a spy, he talked his way out of it and thereafter traveled with three interpreters.

Hansen introduced the first crested wheat grass to the U.S.

Hansen developed the Anoka apple, South Dakota Plum, Hansen hybrid plum, Siberian Pea Shrub, sand cherries, hedge roses and the Manchu apricot.

Hansen built the first greenhouse in America that conducted research on plant varieties.

Hansen spent a half century traveling around the world, yet never learned to drive a car.

GREEN THUMBS

While strawberries are native to South Dakota, dandelions are not.

When Gen. Custer and his troops neared Belle Fourche in 1876 so luxurious was the growth of plants that soldiers plucked thousands of flowers without dismounting. Soldiers made floral wreaths for their horses. The area was then named Floral Valley.

Ten orchids are native to South Dakota.

The first sunflower in the state of South Dakota was planted in Groton, which has since become the Sunflower Capital of the World.

During the Great Depression Aberdeen briefly was known as "Rose City" because florist Ben Siebrecht was able to supply the Midwest with large quantities of that particular flower. Siebrecht and his staff gathered some 20,000 roses on any given day, for shipping as far away as Canada, Chicago and Ohio.

A world-record 14-leaf clover was discovered by Randy Farland (Sioux Falls) June 16, 1975. The white clover was known as Trifolium repens.

The South Dakota state flower is the pasque.

The Black Hills gold motif of grapes and vines was designed as appreciation for the cool waters and green vineyards of California.

Edgar McFadden (Webster) created the world's first rust-resistant bread wheat.

McCrory Gardens (Brookings) have 1,000 varieties of roses, 10,000 flowering plants and 2,000 perennials.

During the 1890s the large wheat crops of Eureka, S.D., kept 36 grain elevators running nearly 24 hours a day.

Fossil Cycad National Monument (Badlands) contains the largest deposit known of fernlike plants of the Mesozoic period. The prehistoric cycad produced a pineapple fruit favored by dinosaurs.

SCIENCE

NOBEL PRIZE WINNERS
- Ernest Lawrence (Canton), in Physics, 1939
- Ted Schulz (Arlington), in Economics, 1979

PETRIFIED STIFF
There are 22 acres of Petrified Forest (Piedmont), the state's sole petrified forest.

The Catholic Church (Kennel) features an altar built of petrified wood.

Over 100 unusual items are featured in Petrified Park (Lemmon), an odyssey conceived by Ole S. Quammen, who wanted to further study petrified wood and give work to jobless people during the Great Depression. All the petrified wood used was gathered within 25 miles of Lemmon.

MINERALS AND MINES
At one time Native Americans heard distant rumblings in the Black Hills. The thunder sounds, which stopped in 1830, were later discovered to have been made by coal deposits.

Minerals from the Black Hills were used to produce the atom bomb in Tennessee.

The first diamond discovered in the state was found in Hutchinson County in 1871.

The Black Hills embraces 250 different minerals.

Half a million dollars worth of silver is mined each year from Homestake Gold mine.

The Silver King Uranium Mine (Edgemont) was in operation until 1989. A single cafe sold $25,000 worth of geiger counters the 12 months after a uranium mine was discovered near Edgemont.

A 90-ton spodumene crystal was discovered near Keystone, S.D.

Belle Fourche, S.D., is the center for a large bentonite mine. Bentonite is called the clay of a thousand uses, from cosmetics to steel.

The Fort (Custer) displays a 13,000-pound rose quartz boulder.

Quarries in the state provide folks with granite, crushed stone, sand and gravel.

Six granite quarries near Milbank provide one-third of the deep red granite used in monuments throughout America.

Salt works were established in the Black Hills in 1877, to supply the railroads.

Sioux Quartzite, deposited over a billion years ago, is the oldest exposed rock in the state. The grains of the quart were deposited and rounded by wave action on the floor of an ancient sea. The Big Sioux Rivers has been flowing over it for about 10,000 years. Settlers used the rock as the principal building and paving material in the area.

South Dakota is home to one of the world's largest manganese deposits, discovered near Onamia in 1927.

Since being opened in 1889 the unique Etta Mine (Hill City) has been a major supplier of 60 different minerals, including arsenic, spodumene and tin.

UP, UP AND AWAY
Three world-record balloon flights have launched from Rapid City, S.D.

• **EXPLORER I**, July 28, 1934. World's largest balloon created by gluing 2.5 acres of cotton cloth together. Balloon weighed 2.5 tons. Cemented seams were stronger than the fabric. Wife of Gov. Tom Berry christened balloon with flask of South Dakota air. Reached altitude of 12 miles before balloon tore. Three-man crew parachuted to safety. The $60,000 balloon, insured by Lloyd's of London, torn to shreds by souvenir hunters.

• **EXPLORER II**, November 11, 1935. Reached world record height of 13.8 miles, a record that endured over 21 years. Balloon made of rubberized cotton and weighed 2.5 tons. Diameter was 192 feet. Flight demonstrated that life could be sustained in the stratosphere. Photos taken while aboard were first to show lateral curvature of horizon, first of planet from 13 miles above and first showing clear division between atmosphere and stratosphere. The perfect eight-hour flight included talks with a seaplane in the Pacific and an editor in London. Not until the Apollo moon shots, 1969-72, would so much scientific data be gathered on a single space flight. Cosmic ray counts recorded during flight allowed development of atomic bomb. Landed intact.

• **STRATOS-LAB**, November 8, 1956. Set new world record of 14.3 miles. Balloon made of polyethylene plastic 1/500th of an inch thick, and weighed a scant 595 pounds. Diameter was 128 feet. Flight demonstrated that a light balloon could penetrate stratosphere. Gondola built, but never used, 10 years earlier. General Mills built the world's first ultra-wide lens for use on the flight. Balloon launched from same moorings used by Explorer II. Instead of shoes, pilots wrapped feet in plastic. Inside gondola was racist poster featuring Native American with arrows in his head, saying "Keep Smiling, Have Faith, Good Luck." Landed intact.

Balloons from around the world may be viewed at the Soukup and Thomas Balloon Museum (Mitchell).

A Sioux Falls-made helium balloon breezed entirely across America in the first non-stop balloon flight. Raven Industries made the 250,000-cubic-ft. balloon named Super Chicken III. The 10-story balloon sailed 2,515 miles in 55 hours, 25 minutes, before safely landing in Georgia on October 12, 1981. Other Super Chickens named for their egg-shaped gondolas, failed earlier flights on September 22 and December 5, 1980.

Nicholas Piantanida reached a world-record altitude of 23.4 miles in a balloon launched from Sioux Falls on Feb. 1, 1966. He was killed when the craft crashed in a cornfield.

Raven Industries (Sioux Falls) made a balloon carrying monkeys, beetles and hamsters in a 51-hour odyssey over Canada, at an altitude of 25 miles, in 1962.

In 1976 Ed Yost (Tea) set a world's record for the longest solo aircraft flight over the Atlantic. Yost and his balloon floated for 107 hours, 37 minutes.

Maxine Anderson and Don Ida launched their balloon from Rapid City Nov. 7, 1982, in an attempt to encircle the globe. A tear caused a premature landing in Ohio.

The Soukup & Thomas Balloon Museum (Mitchell) is the world's largest privately owned fleet of balloons. The museum features the first balloon to fly over the Soviet Union, a WWI observation basket and special shape balloons.

LAWRENCE, NOT OF ARABIA
The 103rd element, lawrencium, was named for Dr. Ernest O. Lawrence (Canton).

Dr. Lawrence was the first South Dakotan awarded the Nobel Prize, in 1939, for his invention of the cyclotron which, in turn, made possible the atomic bomb. Lawrence had perfected the nuclear warhead used on Hiroshima and Nagasaki.

Dr. Lawrence built his first cyclotron by using an 80-ton electromagnet donated by a telegraph company who abandoned plans to ship it to China.

Right after the bombing of Pearl Harbor, Nobel Prize Winner Dr. Ernest Lawrence (Canton) was one of three American scientists secretly picked to work on a uranium-fission bomb.

Dr. Lawrence built his own TV in 1925.

In 1951 Paramount Studios bought a "talking tube" invented by Dr. Lawrence in his garage, to answer his children's homework questions.

Dr. Lawrence invented television's color tube, the Chromatron, in 1954.

Dr. Lawrence became an active proponent of the peaceful use of atomic energy.

The year before Lawrence won the Nobel Prize, a California promoter wanted to display Lawrence's cyclotron. When Lawrence humorously mentioned that loose neutrons could spill out and sterilize spectators, the promoter withdrew his offer.

EROS

South Dakota's highest concentration of scientists, computer scientists, mathematicians, geographers, hydrologists and foresters is found at EROS (Sioux Falls), where over 300 are employed.

EROS houses six million frames on satellite and aircraft photography.

EROS holds more than five million photographs of the U.S. and two million images of Earth, acquired by satellites.

EROS mails 270,000 photographs and tapes to answer an average of 60,000 letters each year.

EROS Data Center (Sioux Falls) is the world's largest lab for processing photos of Earth. EROS opened its 110,000-ft. facility Aug. 7, 1973, with only 70 employees.

EROS collects information from orbiting satellites.

MORE HIGH TECH

The Great San Francisco Earthquake of 1906 was felt in South Dakota.

Gen. George Custer brought the largest assembled expedition of scientists in the Northwest, through South Dakota in 1874.

The first telegraph line in South Dakota was strung November 11, 1870, near Iowa.

Merle Tuve (Canton) developed the first "radio proximity fuse" used during WWII.

A time capsule planted July 25, 1964, on the parade grounds of Fort Sisseton is scheduled to be opened July 25, 2064.

The first artesian well was drilled during August 1881, in Yankton. A Chicago contractor charged $4-per-foot to drill the 460-foot deep well. During the next century over 15,000 wells were drilled throughout South Dakota.

The first commercial oil well in South Dakota was drilled in Harding County in 1953.

The artesian well in front of the state Capitol (Pierre) never freezes.

In 1870 Yankton became the first South Dakota town connected by telegraph to the outside world.

South Dakota has both a sea shell and a crab named for it. Historian W.H.Over discovered two unknown species of shells in South Dakota, one of which was named for the state, Anodonta dakota, and the other for himself, Pisidium overi. Over discovered another species of crab, also named for the state and him, Dakotacaner overana.

Art Dickerson (Huron) holds numerous 3M patents for high-speed machines.

DakotaDome (Vermillion), South Dakota's largest air-supported structure, has a fiberglass roof made by Owens-Corning.

A controversy occurred in 1991 when the state cement plant (Rapid City) considered using hazardous waste in plant kilns.

A grandmother Jeanne Chord stopped a bulldozer from digging up uranium on her Edgemont property.

Since 1965 scientists deep within Homestake Gold Mine (Lead) have been monitoring the neutrons transmitted from the sun. A 105,000-gallon tank 4,850 deep is used for detecting the neutrons.

Pierre Chouteau (Pierre) discovered a 100-pound meteor near Fort Pierre. Pieces are now displayed in German museums.

A French geographer drew the first accurate map of South Dakota in 1702, over a century before Lewis and Clark explored the area.

In 1981 South Dakota officials eyed a billion dollar proposal that quickly dried up. The idea called for mixing South Dakota water with crushed Wyoming coal, and flushing the solution 1,400 miles through a pipeline to Arkansas, where the water would be removed and used and the coal, burned for fuel.

Helen Van Zante (Bruce) conducted research which pioneered microwave use for the kitchen.

Big Stone is the state's largest power plant.

Most of South Dakota's electricity is provided by the earthen dam at Lake Oahe.

Carl Grupp's Bet On It! Trivia Myths:

WINTER 1968

A SNOW-BLOWER DUEL BETWEEN NEIGHTBORS ENDED
ABRUPTLY WHEN OLE OLSON'S MACHINE PITCHED
A FROZEN DOG TURD 280 FEET AND THROUGH SOLVEIG
JOHNSON'S PICTURE WINDOW.

TRANSPORTATION

SKY KINGS
Accordionist Myron Floren turned down a plane ride over Webster, S.D., because he couldn't afford the $2 ticket. Nine months later the pilot, Charles Lindbergh, flew across the Atlantic, and into the history books.

Joe Foss was the first American pilot to destroy as many enemy planes during WWII, as did Eddie Rickenbacher in WWI.

Joe Foss shot down 26 Japanese planes, Lt. Cecil Harris (Cresbard) destroyed 24 enemy aircraft and Dr. Harry Armstrong (De Smet) was Eddie Rickenbacker's flight surgeon during WWI.

George McGovern (Mitchell) broke a WWII bombing record, by going on 35 bombing missions. McGovern flew 51,465 miles through 64 cities campaigning as the 1972 Democratic Presidential nominee.

South Dakota's only Air & Space Museum (Rapid City) features Eisenhower's personal Mitchell B-25 bomber.

Nellie Willhite, South Dakota's first female pilot, died in 1991 at the age of 98. Her first plane was a silver and blue Eagle Rock biplane.

ELLSWORTH
Since 1962 Ellsworth Air Force Base (Rapid City) has been the most complete center of potential nuclear destruction in the U.S. The base has included three Titan launching sites, 150 Minuteman missiles, and a center for B52s.

The Pentagon selected Rapid City as a site for an air force base because it was inland, on flat land, had open skies and was known for good flying weather.

Initially opened as a training base for B-17 bombers, Ellsworth AFB began operations September 28,1942. During WWII Ellsworth trained thousands of bombing crews. Area ranchers plowed stars and circles into pastures to make practice targets for pilots.

In 1947 Ellsworth was developed as a Strategic Air Command (SAC) base and soon became home to B-29 bombers, each equipped to carry nuclear bombs. Forty years later Ellsworth AFB received 35 B-1B bombers, the Lancer.

The first nuclear missile was positioned near Wall, S.D., in April 1963. Today 150 missile sites are spread over 13,500-sq.-miles of western South Dakota.

Thirty years of B-52s at Ellsworth came to an end as the last B-52 was flown out in 1986.

NUCLEAR MISSILES IN BADLANDS
- Nine Titan I, 1962-1965
- 150 Minuteman I, 1963-1971
- 150 Minuteman II, 1971-present

FLYING SAUCERS, AND MORE
South Dakotans report an average of 80 UFO sightings each year.

South Dakota is a part of one of three "flap areas," a triangular section of the country known for rich UFO sightings.

Electric trolleys, instead of locomotives, provided passenger service between Lead and Deadwood in the late 1800s.

The only gas engine company in South Dakota was a short-lived one in Canton. In 1904 a blacksmith Jeff Knowlton conceived the "open jacket" design for gas engines. Knowlton showed his concept to an Iowa company to have some castings made. The Waterloo Gas Engine Company agreed to cast Knowlton's designs if they could use his ideas. A bargain was struck. By 1913 Knowlton was offering gas engines between 1.5 hp and 12 hp, with prices as high as $283. Two years later his company went bankrupt, but Waterloo's continued, using his original ideas.

Rushmore Aerial Tramway (Keystone) offers a 1,600-ft. ride a mile high.

The average tourist spends 3.5 hours in the Badlands.

SHIP AHOY
The USS South Dakota was scheduled to receive the official surrender of Japan in Tokyo Bay, until Missourian President Truman sent the USS Missouri, at the last minute, Sept. 2, 1945.

Forty ships have been honored with South Dakota names.

The USS South Dakota spent WWI quietly patrolling near Brazil. Afterwards her name was changed to Huron.

The Yankton, a schooner that saw action during the Spanish-American War, was seized in the shadow of the State of Liberty, with her holds full of illegal rum.

The John C. Waldron was named after a Fort Pierre pilot shot down in the battle of Midway. The Ernest L. Hilbert was named after a Quinn lad lost in the same battle.

The Arthur L. Gustafson was named after a Watertown sailor, and sold to Holland following WWII.

Navy tank landing ships have been named Grant, Lake, Lawrence, Lincoln, Lyman, Potter and Walworth.

Navy transport ships have been named Butte, Clay, Custer, Brule, Brookings, Mellette, Deuel, Hyde, Codington, Jerauld, Kingsbury and Sunborn.

The U.S.S. Oglala, a mine layer, was sunk by the Japanese in Pearl Harbor on December 7, 1941.

Two Navy ships have been named Mount Rushmore.

The U.S.S. General Sam Sturgis was named for a major assigned to the Black Hills in the 1880s.

In 1969 125.5 links and a 26,194-pound anchor from the U.S.S. South Dakota were laid out in a park in Sioux Falls.

South Dakota has never had a navy, but she has had a 'navy yard.' Near Fort Pierre in the 1830s was the 'navy yard,' a spot where carpenters built and launched keelboats and pirogues.

The first steamboat in South Dakota was the Yellow Stone, which reached Fort Pierre in June 1831.

Pierre Chouteau, Jr., namesake of the state's capital, owned the Yellow Stone. Chouteau wanted a steamboat, instead of a keel boat, because both ship and crew would be easier to handle. Worried about mechanical breakdown in South Dakota, Chouteau brought along spare parts and a blacksmith.

Jean Valle, sailing with the Lewis and Clark exploration, was the first black to visit the state.

The Yellow Stone's career began by bringing the first white artist to South Dakota, and ended by carrying the body of Stephen Austin to his resting place in Texas.

During the six and one-half years the state's first steamboat, Yellow Stone, operated, its furnace consumed some 40,000 trees.

The South Dakota Armored Cruiser was launched in San Francisco, Calif., July 30, 1904, at a cost of $3.5 million. The state of South Dakota provided a full silver service, at a cost of $5,000, with each piece bearing the image of Hunkpapa Chief Gall. After fighting during WWI, the ship was renamed "Huron."

The first ferry in South Dakota was run by Captain P.T. Turnley, across the Big Sioux River, near Sioux Falls, 1855.

The first bridges across the Missouri River in South Dakota were built for railroads, in 1907. The first cars were ferried across, until 1924.

The U.S.S. South Dakota earned more battle stars (13) in the Pacific than any other ship.

The first steamboat to sink in South Dakota was the "Kate Swinney," between Vermillion and Elk Point, August 1, 1855.

It took Lewis and Clark 54 days to travel through South Dakota going out to the Pacific, but only two weeks coming back through two years later.

Lewis and Clark first sighted South Dakota on August 21, 1804, but camped that night on the Nebraska side of the Missouri River. The next day they entered South Dakota, near Elk Point.

Riverboat captains would bulletproof their pilot houses with sheet iron while navigating the Missouri River through South Dakota, and barricade the decks with cargo, because they were fearful of raids by Native Americans.

The first bridge to span the Missouri River was in Pierre, 1907.

While paddling through South Dakota Lewis and Clark passed out silver medals of Jefferson to Native Americans who they believed important, and white medals of Washington to those who weren't.

Gov. McMaster dedicated the first bridge across the Missouri River at Mobridge by unlocking a chain barrier with a golden key, and tossing the key in the river.

The U.S.S. South Dakota was launched in 1941, served five years and was scrapped in 1962. It had 100 five-inch guns.

The first steamboat arrived in Columbia, S.D., by being hauled over land by several wagons.

Chamberlain was the last steamboat town in South Dakota.

BIKES AND HIKES

The state's first safety code for motorcycles was sponsored by state Representative Gladys Pyle (Huron), who had never been on one.

Sturgis hosts the world's largest motorcycle event each August.

Nine bikers, driving seven Indian models, and two Harley Davidsons, drove in the first Black Hills Motorcycle Classic, 1938.

Two Yamaha motorcycles are the only vehicles to ever make it to the top of Bear Butte (Sturgis). On May 10, 1963, Jack Hoel and Bill Erickson drove — and pushed — their cycles to the top of the 4,422-ft. high butte that overlooks five states. The site has since been designated a National Monument, and no traffic is allowed.

Retreads (Sturgis) are cyclists over the age of 40.

Through the energies of Pappy Hoel (Sturgis) the Jackpine Gypsy Motorcycle Club was formed, followed by the Black Hills Motor Classic.

In 1982 the White Plate Flat Trackers Association (Sturgis) was formed, and built a six-sided monument to famous motorcyclists.

ORIGINATORS OF CYCLE CLASSIC (STURGIS), 1938:
• Bruce Barnes
• Pappy Hoel
• Clyde Sinclair
• Katherine Soldat

Reporter Annie Tallent (Sioux Falls) wore out seven pairs of shoes walking through the state to become the first white woman to enter the Black Hills, arriving December 23, 1874. When shoes were unavailable, Tallent wrapped her feet in gunnysacks.

In 1823 an injured Hugh Glass crawled 200 miles through western South Dakota only at night, when he could get his bearings by watching the North Star.

Calamity Jane wore rubber-soled shoes when she became the first woman to climb Calamity Peak (Black Hills).

WAGON WHEELS
Legendary Harvey Fellows holds the world's record for driving a stagecoach, some 500,000 miles over a half century. Fellows learned to control up to six horses in hilly and muddy conditions. Fellows operated a stagecoach (seven miles-per hour) between Deadwood and Spearfish until 1913.

Black Hills stagecoach drivers saved their best teams for the last relay into towns so that drivers could arrive with a galloping team, making a grand entrance.

Teamster Fred T. Evans singledhandedly hauled over seven million pounds of freight from Pierre to Deadwood in 1880 by bull train.

South Dakota stage coach drivers were given authority to use only necessary violence to get passengers to pay for their tickets.

Gold miners brought the first wagons to Deadwood by lowering them into a nearby gulch by ropes, pulleys and chains.

August 29, 1989, two wagon trains — one originating from Philip in the west, and the other, from Elk Point in the east — met at the fairgrounds (Huron) to commemorate the state's centennial.

In order to hide their Black Hills' destination in 1874, the first group of white settlers to illegally enter the lands traveled aboard six ox-drawn wagons lettered "O'Neill's Colony."

Custer's Main Street was originally wide enough to enable an eight-yoke bull train to make a complete U-turn.

South Dakota's "last pioneer" was Charlotte Clark (Deadwood), who died at the age of 102 in 1978. Charlotte was three when she arrived in the Black Hills, by stagecoach, and was 90 when she had her first plane ride.

Surveyor Art Mitchell, namesake of the town, measured thousands of acres of land in eastern South Dakota by counting the revolutions of his wagon wheel spokes.

The average stage coach through South Dakota traveled eight mph.

Wyatt Earp rode shotgun on the richest load of gold ever shipped out of the Black Hills by stagecoach, $200,000.

CHROME WHEELS

Montgomery Ward provided the first car in South Dakota, a Haynes Electric, driven at the state fair in Yankton in 1897.

When the antique car carrying actor Jimmy Stewart broke down during a Fourth of July parade in Rapid City in 1991, scores of appreciative fans pushed the vehicle the rest of the route.

E.S. Callilhan introduced a three-wheel, steam-driven "Autocycle" in Woonsocket in 1884. The auto frightened horses and startled people a dozen years before Henry Ford introduced his first car in Detroit.

America's first four-door car was invented by 19-year-old Tom Fawick (Sioux Falls). President Roosevelt rode in the auto when he visited the state. Fawick went on to collect 200 patents, including one for a revolutionary design adapted by Ford, for tractors. Fawick also composed 3,000 songs.

In the 1890s Harry Adams and Louis Greenough (Pierre) attached a two-cylinder gas engine on wagon and created a car that carried eight passengers. The duo tried to give rides at the state's county fairs but officials wouldn't let them in.

Pioneer Auto and Antique Museum (Murdo) has 250 cars, and Elvis Presley's motorcycle. It is America's largest private collection of autos.

Three cowboys used their horses and lariats to pull the first car into the Black Hills, in April 1905. Sen. Peter Norbeck's Cadillac needed help to cross the Cheyenne River.

When a Rapid City station raised the price of a gallon of gas to the unheard of 29 cents in 1923, Gov. Bill McMaster had the state buy gasoline in Chicago, shipped by tank cars to the Black Hills, and resold for 16 cents a gallon. The public was glad, while oil companies were angry. The U.S. Supreme Court eventually ruled that state government could not sell gas.

Gov. George Mickelson drives a pickup truck to work at the Capitol in Pierre.

Deadwood, S.D., has the state's only English Double Decker Bus.

On any given day fifty-eight percent of the license plates on vehicles at Wall Drug are out-of-state.

Trucks transport over half of all the products sold in South Dakota.

Black Hills Corvette Classic (Spearfish) features an annual July parade with over 600 Corvettes.

In August 1991 the Big Stone Power Plant (Milbank) announced they would begin using shredded tires from Florida because the tires were good fuel, cost less and burned cheaply.

Sioux Falls officials banned tire dumping in 1991 because commissioners were worried about an onslaught of tire dumping before fees went up.

HIGHWAYS AND BYWAYS
Pierre is among the three capitals not on an interstate system. The others are in Hawaii and Alaska.

Dallas, S.D., is the only town in the U.S. with a water tower on a federal highway.

The first national trail through South Dakota was the "Black and Yellow Trail," a gravel auto trail.

With 65 curves within 24 miles near Philip, Highway 14 is the state's windiest road.

The Washington Channel Bridge in the nation's capital is named after Sen. Francis Case.

Sioux Falls is the smallest city in America to enjoy an interstate bypass, I-229.

Sen. Francis Case (Custer) originated the U.S. Interstate Highway System.

Senators Hubert Humphrey and Francis Case each wanted Interstate 29 to extend north from Sioux Falls to Fargo, N.D. Humphrey wanted it to go through Minnesota. Case, who wanted it to go through South Dakota, took a highway map, penciled in a line from Sioux Falls to Fargo and showed it to the head of the Public Works committee. It worked. With help from an Oklahoma

senator, South Dakota and Oklahoma, were beneficiaries of
another thousand miles of interstate. Case was accused of steal-
ing the interstate from Minnesota, but he didn't mind. Later Case
worked on getting I-90 to run a branch north from Vivian to
Pierre, but he died before those plans could be completed.

It took 16 years, 1944-1960, to build Interstates 29 and 90 across
South Dakota. It took only 14 years to carve Mount Rushmore.

**South Dakota had mud highways until 1921, when gravel was
added, with concrete on the way two years later.**

South Dakota's busiest intersection is where Interstates 29 and 90
intersect in Sioux Falls.

**Army colonel Bill Nobels built the first major highway through
South Dakota, using boulders, in 1857. Gov. Sam Medary helped
engineer the road. The 254-mile long path was nicknamed
"Nobels' Trail" and "The Hole." The Hole, which stretched from
Minnesota westward to the Missouri River, was originally
intended to reach the Pacific, but never made it. The trail was
graded in bad spots, with streams paved with boulders.**

Joe Parmley (Ipswich) founded the Yellowstone Trail in 1912. Start-
ing in South Dakota, the highway eventually spanned from Plymouth
Rock to Puget Sound. Parmley's Yellowstone Trail had a wide-reputa-
tion as the best route from Chicago to Yellowstone, even though it was
a dirt road.

South Dakota has 679 miles of interstate highways.

The highway between Doland and Redfield, S.D., was built entirely
by the state's first all-black road crew, 1922-23.

**Through South Dakota is the world's longest Interstate High-
way. I-90 stretches 3,087.65 miles from Boston to Seattle.**

South Dakota has two drag-race tracks: Belle Fourche, Marion.

**Needles Highway Scenic Drive (Black Hills) has three tunnels
within 14 miles.**

South Dakota has 80,000 miles of highways, of which only 80% are
surfaced.

CHOO-CHOOS

America's crookedest railroad was the 30-mile line between Mystic
and Rapid City. Nearly every rail was curved to fit Rapid Canyon. A
portion of every train was always over a bridge, some four to each
mile. In 1907 a flood took out all but five of the 110 bridges.

**The Chicago and Northwestern Depot (Brookings) was built
with separate waiting rooms for men and women. When trains**

arrived, a waiter would step onto the sidewalk in front of the depot and ring a dinner bell. The train always waited until all passengers had finished eating.

The Chapel Car Emmanuel (Madison) was designed as a portable church, for use in remote areas of the Midwest. Emmanuel contains pews, a brass lectern, an organ, book shelves for Bibles in different languages and living quarters for the preacher. Emmanuel was given free passage by the railroads and offered services every two hours when pulled behind passenger trains. Emmanuel is the only chapel car left in America.

South Dakota's first railroads laid its ties and tracks directly on the prairie sod in the interests of speedy construction.

During the harsh winter of 1881 a locomotive between Pierre and Elk Point ended up burning 50 bushels of corn when coal supplies ran out.

The first railroad line into South Dakota was laid in 1871 from Minnesota, to Gary.

The Crouch Line railroad (Rapid City) had a record 10 different names over its half-century existence.

Dozens of railroad tracks crisscrossing through Aberdeen, S.D., gave it the nickname of "Hub City," since the pattern of the tracks made it look like the hub, or spokes, of a giant wheel.

During 1991 only six railroads operated on 2,000 miles of South Dakota tracks. Passenger trains no longer cross South Dakota.

South Dakota's first train locomotive was named "Judge Brookings," after attorney W.W. Brookings, who supported railroad construction within the state.

The first train through the Black Hills was the Black Hills & Fort Pierre, built in 1881. The first engine was "George Hearst," named after one of Homestake's founding directors.

The Black Hills Central railroad, still in operation, was originally built in 1870 to carry prospectors to gold mines.

The1880 Train (Hill City) takes riders on an 18-mile trip up Oblivion Hill. Passengers purchase tickets in the original CB & Q Station. Engine 104 was built originally for an Oregon timber company. The 104 is a 2-6-2 saddle tank engine well suited to mountains. Locomotive No. 7 was built in 1919 for the Prescott and Northwestern Railroad Co. The train has appeared in *Gunsmoke*, *Orphan Train*, and *Scandalous John*.

Even though its tracks were washed away, the 1880 train (Hill City) survived the 1972 Rapid City flood.

Homestake Mine (Lead) has 60 miles of railroad track.

Aberdeen was founded as a railroad town because a natural slough could provide water for the steam engines.

Six railroads use 3,000 miles of tracks in the state.

Seventeen wealthy Aberdonians wanted their three-block area in the exclusive end of North Main opened to traffic. When railroad employees ignored a court order and refused to open a crossing, angry homeowners anchored a locomotive to the tracks and doused railroad employees with a firehose. The railroad gave in and laid a crossing to North Main.

The Minneapolis and St. Louis Depot opened in Aberdeen in 1900 but waited eight years to welcome its first passenger train.

The Chicago, Milwaukee and St. Paul Depot (Aberdeen) is the largest depot in South Dakota.

At one time Lead, S.D., had three sets of tracks stacked one atop the other. Tracks on the ground carried the Deadwood Central. A bridge carried the Fremont Elkhorn & Missouri Valley. The highest elevated set of tracks was used by Homestake Gold Mine.

Aberdeen was born at the junction of four railroads.

In the 1890s Charles D. Crouch started a railroad near Rapid City, with promises his line would span all the way to the Pacific. It only made it 110 miles, to Mystic.

Sioux Falls was home to the most extensive street railway system in the state. Four companies operated horse-drawn and electric street cars, from the 1880s to 1929.

TEMPERATURES

HOT TIMES

3,300 F — Torch used on surface of Crazy Horse sculpture; flame travels three times speed of sound

275 F — Furnace of U.S.S. South Dakota

134 F — Gold and rock mined 8,000 feet below surface by Homestake Mine

120 F — Hottest spot in state, Seymour, July 1936

93 F — Black Hills, when forest fire broke out, Sept. 8, 1959

87 F — World's largest natural warm water indoor pool (Hot Springs)

50 F — Free water served at Wall Drug (Wall)

47 F — Wind Cave (Rapid City)

45 F — Spearfish, S.D., after a freakish rise of 49 degrees, Jan. 22, 1943

Minus 20 F — Blizzard of Jan. 12, 1888; 100 people frozen in state

Minus 58 F — Coldest spot in state, McIntosh, 1936

THRILLS AND CHILLS

Frank Baum, author of *The Wizard of Oz*, picked up his knowledge about tornadoes while living in Aberdeen, S.D., even though the book is set in Kansas.

The nation's first photograph of a tornado was taken as one passed near Huron in 1883.

The driest spot in South Dakota is the 382-sq. miles of Badlands National Monument, which receives only 15 inches of rain each year.

When an unexpected blizzard hit Yankton in April 1873 Elizabeth Custer not only cared for her feverish husband but used her new rugs to wrap some dozen frozen soldiers who stumbled into her unheated quarters.

South Dakota began cloud seeding in 1972. Officials claim that was not a factor in the infamous Rapid City flood of 1972.

South Dakota has been the "Sunshine State" since 1909. The state has more clear, sunny days than Florida.

The first thermometer in South Dakota was made by a physician traveling with Lewis and Clark. Dr. Saugrain scraped silver from his wife's mirror, melted the glass and shaped it into a tube. Lewis and Clark originally misplaced it among their belongings, but discovered it at Onamia and thereafter kept a daily record of temperature, 1804.

Carl Grupp's Bet On It! Trivia Myths:

SOUTH DAKOTA HUNTERS' QUIZ
WHICH ONE DO YOU SHOOT? (CIRCLE ONE)
A.   B.   C.   D.
CORRECT ANSWER BELOW

A.

D.

B.

C.

A. NO! THIS IS A COW,
NOT A PHEASANT.
C. ALTHOUGH OFTEN MIS-
TAKEN FOR A
PHEASANT, THIS IS
A RURAL STOP SIGN.
D. TWICE MISTAKEN FOR A
PHEASANT, THIS IS
IN ACTUALITY
LLOYD MENARD.
B. IF YOU PICKED B, CON-
GRATULATIONS AND
HAPPY HUNTING!

SPORTS

LACROSSE

The oldest known organized team sport in South Dakota is lacrosse. As early as the 1700s, Native Americans played with long sticks, with male players all wearing the same outfits: nothing.

Playing courses sometimes stretched miles across the Great Plains, and the scarcity of rules made the sport rough and tumble, and fun.

Each South Dakota tribe always selected an "athlete of the year," for lacrosse.

OWNERS OF PRO TEAMS
- Joan Kroc (Rapid City), the San Diego Padres
- Joe Robbie (Sisseton), the Miami Dolphins

RECORD BUFFALO CHIP TOSSES (PIERRE)
- Men's Team, 542 feet, 1982
- Women's Team, 253, 1982
- Men's, 206 feet, 1977
- Children's, 165 feet, 1974
- Women's, 133 feet, 1980

FITNESS RULES OF CHERYL LADD (HURON)
- Get doctor's advice
- Stop it when you feel pain
- Breath normally
- Use weights carefully

STADIUMS
- **Hubert Humphrey** (Huron), Humphrey Metrodome, Minneapolis
- **Joe Robbie** (Sisseton), Robbie Stadium, Miami

In 1991 Dan Wollman (Aberdeen) sold the backyard recreational court to President Bush for his vacation home in Kennebunkport, Me. Wollman, a biochemist, is an executive with Sport Court, the largest athletic floor company in the world. Wollman sold the president a court that is plastic with rubber additives that snap together like a puzzle.

The largest athletic facility in South Dakota is the Dakota-Dome (Vermillion) built in 1979. The multi-purpose structure features an air-supported roof made of Teflon-coated fiberglass.

The original design of the DakotaDome called for an inclined, metal roof, instead of an inflatable one.

The scoreboard in Australia's National Athletic Stadium was built with hardware from Daktronics Inc. (Brookings).

GOLF

South Dakota built a special golf course in the Black Hills in 1927 for President Coolidge. All the greens were slanted towards the holes.

Golf was first played in South Dakota during September 1895 in Yankton by three Scots and a Briton.

Phil Campbell (Sioux Falls) golfed on his one hundredth birthday in 1967.

All five sons of Hall of famer Everett Comstock (Aberdeen) are pro golfers.

Pro golfers Alice and Marlene Bauer are sisters raised in Aberdeen.

BASEBALL

When Babe Ruth played baseball in Deadwood in 1922, every ball Ruth hit out of the park landed foul.

Homestake Gold Mine (Lead) spent $50,000 to have a peak sliced off in order for a baseball diamond to be built.

As of 1991 there are 82 athletes honored in the South Dakota Amateur Baseball Hall of Fame (Lake Norden).

Lawrence Welk (Yankton) credits his first successful dance to a rained out Fourth of July baseball game in Aberdeen. Wet crowds happened to seek shelter in the otherwise empty pavilion Welk and his band had just set up in.

Cleveland Indian Tito Francona (Aberdeen) was the most-traded professional baseball player from South Dakota: nine times in 15 years. Francona also had a record 81 career pinch hits.

Minnesota Twin Tony Oliva was the groom at the first wedding he ever attended, marrying Gordette Du Bois (Hitchcock) in 1968.

Hubert Humphrey (Huron) threw out the first ball at the 1965 World Series, in Minnesota. His wife, Muriel (Doland) threw out the first ball at the 1991 American League playoffs, in Minneapolis.

The world's only amateur Baseball Hall of Fame is in Lake Norden, S.D.

Floyd Bannister (Pierre) is a pitcher who led the American League in strikeouts with the 1982 Seattle Mariners. Bannister posted a 13-1 second-half record while leading the Chicago White Sox to the American League West title in 1973.

Amanda Clement (Hudson) was baseball's first woman umpire. The 83-year-old is enshrined in four separate Halls of Fame.

Dave Collins (Rapid City) stole 79 bases with the 1980 Cincinnati Reds and 60 bases with the 1984 Toronto Blue Jays.

Terry Forster (Sioux Falls) led the American League with 24 saves in 1974. Forster also pitched a record 614 career games, in 16 years.

Aberdeen was once home to a baseball farm club of the Baltimore Orioles.

Although Milbank is the birthplace of American Legion baseball, the idea came from attorney Frank Sieh (Aberdeen), April 17, 1925. It was Sieh who pushed a national project of developing a program for the youth of America.

ANDERSON
Sparky Anderson (Bridgewater) was the first South Dakotan to play in a World Series.

Anderson is the only manager to win a World Series title with teams in both leagues. He did it with Cincinnati, National League, in 1975 and 1976 and Detroit, American League, in 1984.

At age 35 Sparky Anderson became the youngest major league manager in America when he took over the Cincinnati Reds during October 1969.

Anderson led the Cincinnati Reds to two World Series, four pennants, and five division titles in nine years. Anderson led the Detroit Tigers to two division titles and the 1984 World Series.

WORLD SERIES, SPARKY ANDERSON (BRIDGEWATER)
- Oct. 15, 1970: Sparky's Cincinnati Reds lost to Baltimore, 4-1
- Oct. 22, 1972: Sparky's Reds lost to Oakland, 4-3
- Oct. 22, 1975: Led Reds to victory over Boston, 4-3
- Oct. 21, 1976: Led Reds to victory over the Yankees, 4-0
- Oct. 14, 1984: Led Detroit Tigers to victory over San Diego, 4-1

BASEBALL CARD VALUES, 1992
75 cents, Detroit Tiger Sparky Anderson (Bridgewater), Twin Jerry Crider (Sioux Falls)
50 cents, John Strohmayer (Belle Fourche)
15 cents, Twin Kevin Stanfield (Huron)
12 cents California Angel Terry Forrester (Sioux Falls)
5 cents, Houston Astro Floyd Bannister (Pierre)
4 cents, Detroit Tiger Dave Collins (Rapid City)

SKI LIFTS, TERRY PEAK (LEAD)
- Blue: 4,400 feet long
- Blue 3,470 feet

- Red 3,315 feet
- Yellow 3,210 feet
- Green 1,315 feet
- Orange 300 feet

BOXING
In 1923 the state legislature legalized boxing, stipulating that all South Dakota boxers must weigh at least 140 pounds.

Gov. Joe Foss (Sioux Falls) was a boxer.

South Dakotan Oscar "Battling" Nelson won the 1908 World Lightweight Title by knocking out Joe Gaus in the 17th round in California. Nelson's career included 300 fights.

FOOTBALL HELMETS
- Worn by two scientists as crash helmets in world-record flight launched from Rapid City, 1935
- Worn by murderer George Sitts to hold soggy sponge against his shaved head, when he got the electric chair in Sioux Falls, 1947

FOOTBALL
Notre Dame football coach Frank Leahy (Winner) compiled a 107-13-9 career record, including five national championships. Leahy's .864 percentage is second only to that of Knute Rockne.

Norm Van Brocklin (Parade) is the first South Dakotan named to the Football Hall of Fame.

Van Brocklin held the record for passing completion, in 1958, with 198.

Van Brocklin quarterbacked the Los Angeles Rams and Philadelphia Eagles to National Championships, and coached the Minnesota Vikings and Atlanta Falcons.

Van Brocklin led the football league in passing, three times, and in punting, twice.

Van Brocklin was the only quarterback to beat Lombardi's Green Bay Packers in a title game.

Van Brocklin quarterbacked the Los Angeles Rams to its only NFL championship, 1951.

The first football game played in the DakotaDome (Yankton) saw Vermillion pitted against Yankton, August 31, 1979.

ROBBIE
Miami Dolphins owner Joe Robbie (Sisseton) founded the Florida football team in 1965. The state-of-the-art stadium was America's first

stadium built with private funds. The team's name was selected in a contest.

In 1973 Joe Robbie's Miami Dolphins became the first NFL team to go through a complete season with all wins.

Joe Robbie stadium measures 410 ft. to center for baseball. It is America's southernmost professional football stadium.

Joe Robbie lost races for governor of South Dakota and for congress, from Minnesota.

Using a small pocket calculator, Joe Robbie figured out the financing for Joe Robbie Stadium, even putting up his Miami Dolphins as collateral. Even before ground was broken on Joe Robbie Stadium in 1985, the 1989 Super Bowl was awarded to Miami. Robbie got it built in time. Super Bowl XXIII was played at Robbie Stadium on January 22, 1989, in the most modern facility ever to host that game.

Joe Robbie was owner of professional football's only undefeated team. Under Robbie's ownership, the Dolphins won nine division titles.

Joe Robbie owned a professional hockey team, the Florida Strikers.

SUPER BOWLS, ROBBIE'S DOLPHINS
- **Super Bowl VI, Jan. 16, 1972.** Miami lost to Dallas, 24-3. For the next three years a ticket cost $15.
- **Super Bowl VII, Jan. 14, 1973.** Miami beat the Washington Redskins, 14-7. A crowd of 90,182 fans saw the game in Los Angeles, while 75 million viewers watched on TV.
- **Super Bowl VIII, Jan. 13, 1974.** Miami beat the Minnesota Vikings, 24-7. A crowd of 68,142 fans saw the game in Houston, while 60 million viewers watched on TV. TV commercials sold for $40,000 a minute.
- **Super Bowl XVII, Jan. 30, 1983.** Washington Redskins beat Miami, 27-17 in California. A ticket cost $40.
- **Super Bowl XIX, Jan. 20, 1985.** The 49ers beat Miami 38-16 in California.

BASKETBALL
Bruce Crevier (Elkton) set a new world's record in the number of basketballs juggled and spun at the same time, 15, on April 7, 1991.

Yankton High School lost the national basketball title to Colorado in the 1920s.

Basketball was first played by high schools in South Dakota in 1901.

Dan Moran (Viborg) has a basketball career coaching record of 406-168 in 25 seasons at five schools.

Thirteen years passed between when professional basketball games were played in South Dakota, with none of the four teams from the state. In 1976 the Houston Rockets defeated Kansas City in Sioux Falls. In 1989 the neighboring Minnesota Timberwolves raised $54,000 for the American Cancer Society, as they lost to the Phoenix Suns, also in Sioux Falls.

South Dakota is home to two Continental Basketball Association teams: Rapid City Thrillers and Sioux Falls Skyforce.

The Thrillers (Rapid City) moved from Tampa, Fla., in 1986. Thrillers have enjoyed three coaches: Keith Fowler, Jim Calvin and Eric Musselman.

Thrillers won the 1987 CBA championship.

Thriller Stephen Thompson (Rapid City) was named 1990-91 CBA Rookie of the Year.

Bill Musselman coached Tampa Thrillers in Florida. In 1986 the team moved to Rapid City, S.D., where, four coaches later, son Eric Musselman took over guiding the team.

The Thrillers (Rapid City) beat Albany, N.Y., 120-111, in their first CBA basketball game, December 6, 1986.

Eric Musselman, 26, became the CBA's youngest coach when hired to coach the Rapid City Thrillers, 1991.

The first coach of Skyforce (Sioux Falls), a Continental Basketball Association team, was Ron Ekker, named in 1989.

Skyforce coach Kevin McKenna played on four NBA teams: Bullets, Lakers, Nets and Pacers.

Skyforce won its first televised game on Jan. 13, 1992, in Oklahoma.

Skyforce holds the franchise record by winning six games in a row in Sioux Falls, 1991. Skyforce also holds a franchise record of losing eight games in a row, away from home.

A record 134 points were earned by Skyforce Nov. 21, 1991, against Columbus Horizons. The team's lowest score has been 89.

The 1990-91 season finale ended with Skyforce (Sioux Falls) beating Thrillers, 124-122.

ORIGINAL SKYFORCE, 1989
- Chris Cheeks
- Laurent Crawford

- Leonard Harris
- Willie Hayes
- Bryon Heron
- Terrence Rayford
- Kennard Winchester

HORSES

Jockey Earle Sande (Groton) won five Belmont Stakes, three Kentucky Derbys, one Preakness. Sande went to the post 3,673 times, coming in first 968 times.

During a single day jockey Earle Sande (Groton) rode in 23 races at the age of 18.

Sande won horseracing's Triple Crown on Gallant Fox in 1930. Sande won 968 races in 70 years riding such famous horses as Man O'War.

Polo was once played by soldiers at Fort Meade. In 1924 the state's first polo tournament was held in the state.

Since 1922 a polo club in Pierre has taken top honors in the U.S., Canada and Africa. The club was started by a retired army colonel, with the first equipment coming from India.

RUNNINGS OF THE KENTUCKY DERBY WON BY EARLE SANDE (GROTON)

- **May 5, 1923**, riding Zev in 2 minutes, 5 1/5 seconds
- **May 2, 1925**, riding Flying Ebony in 2 minutes, 7 3/5 seconds
- **May 3, 1930**, riding Gallant Fox in 2 minutes, 7 3/5 seconds

RODEOS

Since rodeo champ Paul Tierney (Piedmont) got on his first horse at the age of two, he went on to compete in 2,000 rodeos in 20 states and three countries.

ALL-AROUND PRO RODEO CHAMPS

1929 Earl Hode (West River)
1951 Casey Tibbs (Fort Pierre)
1958 Casey Tibbs (Fort Pierre)
1980 Paul Tierney (Rapid City)

TRACK AND FIELD:

Oct. 14, 1964, Billy Mills (Pine Ridge) became the first American to win the Gold Medal in the 10,000-meter run. Mills record time was 28 minutes, 24.4 seconds. Mills finished only 12 feet ahead of Tunisia's Mohammed Gamoudi at the 18th Olympia, in Tokyo, Japan.

Hirohito welcomed Billy Mills, who wore No. 722.

The odds were a thousand to one against Billy Mills winning the race. Mills was involved in an elbow skirmish near the end of the race. Such was the disbelief that an unknown runner such as Mills could win the race that officials delayed the results for 35 minutes in order to confirm everything.

South Dakotan Buddy Edelen (Sioux Falls) also ran in the 1964 Olympics.

Don Jorgenson, a TV anchor at KELO-TV in Sioux Falls, S.D., drove to Minneapolis in April 1991 to try out for "American Gladiators." Jorgenson, a former college football player who said he passed up a professional tryout camp because he didn't have air fare to Chicago, did 19 pull-ups in 30 seconds. His shot fell short.

Four colleges organized the first inter-collegiate sports in South Dakota in 1889 in Sioux Falls.

The first sport played by college students in South Dakota was track, 1889.

Mayor Ed McLaughlin (Rapid City) held the state track and field record in hurdles.

Tom Brokaw (Yankton) lettered in track, basketball and football.

In 1991 Nick Johannson (Miller) tied a state record high jump of seven feet, two inches, set earlier by Scott Benson (Rapid City).

COLLEGE MASCOTS:
- Augustana **Vikings** (Sioux Falls)
- Black Hills State **Yellowjackets** (Spearfish)
- Dakota State **Trojans** (Madison)
- Dakota Wesleyan **Tigers** (Mitchell)
- Huron **Tigers** (Huron)
- Mt. Marty **Lancers** (Yankton)
- Northern State **Wolves** (Aberdeen)
- Sioux Falls **Cougars** (Sioux Falls)
- South Dakota School of Mines **Hardrockers** (Rapid City)
- South Dakota State University **Jackrabbits** (Brookings)
- University of South Dakota **Coyotes** (Vermillion)

BIBLIOGRAPHY

AHA Guide to the Health Care Field. Chicago: American Hospital Association, 1990.

Artz, Don. *The Town in the Frog Pond.* Aberdeen, S.D.: Memories, Inc., 1991.

Aurandt, Paul. *Destiny.* New York: William Morrow and Company, Inc., 1983.

Baden, Michael M. *Unnatural History.* New York: Ivy Books, 1989.

Barnard, Edward S. *Story of the Great American West.* Pleasantville, N.Y.: The Reader's Digest Association, Inc., 1977.

Baum, L. Frank. *The Wizard of Oz.* New York: Grosset & Dunlop, 1900.

Beebe, Lucius, and Clegg, Charles. *The American West.* New York: E.P. Dutton & Co., Inc., 1955.

Biographical Directory of the South Dakota Legislature 1889-1989. Pierre, S.D.: South Dakota Legislative Research Council, 1989.

Birds of South Dakota. Aberdeen, S.D.: Northern State University Press, 1991.

Blake, Michael. *Dances With Wolves.* New York: Fawcett Gold Medal, 1988.

Boone, C.F. *The Rapid City Flood.* Lubbock, Tex.: C.F. Boone, Publisher, 1972.

Brooks, Tim and Marsh, Earle. *The Complete Directory to Prime Time Network Shows 1946-Present.* New York: Ballantine Books, 19481.

Brown, Dee. *Bury My Heart at Wounded Knee.* New York: Holt, Rinehart & Winston, Inc., 1970.

College Handbook 1992. New York: College Board Publications, 1991.

Conn, Herb and Jan. *The Jewel Cave Adventure.* Teaneck, N.J.: Zephyrus Press, Inc., 1977.

David, Lester and David, Irene. *Bobby Kennedy, the Making of a Folk Hero.* New York: Dodd, Mead & Company, 1986.

DeWald, Robb. *Crazy Horse and Korczak.* Crazy Horse, S.D.: Korczak's Heritage, Inc., 1982.

_____. *The Saga of Sitting Bull's Bones.* Crazy Horse, S.D.: Korczak's Heritage, Inc., 1984.

Early History of Brown County. Aberdeen, S.D.: Western Printing Co., 1965.

Engelmayer, Sheldon and Wagman, Robert. *Hubert Humphrey.* New York: Methuen, 1978.

Facts on File. New York: Facts on File, Inc., 1977.

Feldman, Michael. *Whad'Ya Know?* New York: William Morrow and Company, 1991.

Fielder, Mildred. *The Treasure of Homestake Gold.* Aberdeen, S.D.: North Plains Press, 1970.

Fisher, Henry. *They Said It Couldn't Be Done!* Sioux Falls, S.D.: Missouri Basin Municipal Power Agency, 1990.

Fite, Gilbert C. *Mount Rushmore.* Norman, Okla.: University of Oklahoma Press, 1952.

Floren, Myron. *Accordian Man.* Brattleboro, Vt.: The Stephen Greene Press, 1981.

Goldberg, Robert, and Goldberg, Gerald Jay. *Anchors.* New York: Birch Lane Press, 1990.

Gurney's Seed & Nursery 1992 Spring Catalog. Yankton, S.D.: Gurney's Seed & Nursery, 1991.

Hafnor, John. *Black Hills Believables.* Billings, Mont.: Falcon Press Publishing Co., 1983.

Hallock, Morris. *First Half Century.* Philip, S.D.: Pioneer Publishing Co., 1957.

Hart, Gary. *Right from the Start.* New York: Quadrangle, 1973.

Hatch, Jane M. *The American Book of Days.* New York: H.W. Wilson Company, 1978.

Historic Sites of South Dakota. Sioux Falls, S.D.: Modern Press, 1980.

Hoel, J.C. *Life's Bits & Pieces.* Sturgis, S.D.: Allison Publishing, 1982.

Hoffman, Mark S. *The World Almanac.* New York: Scripps Howard Company, 1989.

Hoover, Herbert T., and Zimmerman, Larry J. *South Dakota Leaders.* Vermillion, S.D.: University of South Dakota Press, 1989.

Humphrey, Hubert H. *The Education of a Public Man.* Garden City, N.Y.: Doubleday & Company, Inc., 1976.

Jackson, Donald. *Voyages of the Steamboat Yellow Stone.* New York: Ticknor & Fields, 1985.

Jennings, Dana. *Free Ice Water.* Aberdeen, S.D.: North Plains Press, 1969.

Judge, Clark S. *The Book of American Rankings.* New York: Facts on File, 1979.

Kant, Juanita. *A History of the South Dakota Century Farm.* Dallas: Taylor Publishing Co., 1945.

Karolevitz, Robert F. *Challenge, The South Dakota Story.* Sioux Falls, S.D.: Brevet Press, Inc., 1975.

_____. *Joe Floyd, A Helluva Salesman.* Mission Hill, S.D.: Dakota Homestead Publishers, 1990.

Kiernan, John, and Daley, Arthur. *The Story of the Olympic Games.* Philadelphia: J.B. Lippincott Co., 1969.

Kellar, Ken. *Seth Bullock.* Aberdeen, S.D.: North Plains Press, 1972.

Koek, Karin E. and Winklepleck, Julie. *Gale Directory of Publications and Broadcast Media.* Detroit: Gale Research Inc., 1991.

Kolbe, Robert. *Minnehaha County.* Sioux Falls: Minnehaha County Historical Society, 1988.

Kovats, Nancy Niethammer. *Annie Tallent.* Hermosa, S.D.: Lame Johnny Press, 1983.

Lepthien, Emilie. *South Dakota.* Chicago: Children's Press, 1991.

Maltin, Leonard. *TV Movies and Video Guide.* New York: New American Library, 1987.

Manfred, Frederick. *Lord Grizzly.* New York: McGraw-Hill Book Co., Inc., 1954.

Matthiessen, Peter. *In the Spirit of Crazy Horse.* New York: Viking Press, 1980.

McGovern, Eleanor. *Uphill.* Boston: Houghton Mifflin Company, 1974.

Meadowcraft, Enid. *Crazy Horse: Sioux Warrior.* Champaign, Ill.: Garrard Publishing Company, 1965.

Million Dollar Directory. Parsippany, N.J.: Dun's Marketing Service, 1990.

Morehead, Albert H. *Official Rules of Card Games.* Cincinnati: The U.S. Playing Card Card Co., 1968.

Moskowitz, Milton, Levering, Robert and Katz, Michael. *Everybody's Business.* New York: Doubleday Currency, 1990.

Neft, David S. and Cohen, Richard M. *The Football Encyclopedia.* New York: St. Martin's Press, 1991.

Olson, Virginia F. *Dear Friend.* Aberdeen, S.D.: North Plains Press, 1981.

O'Neal, Bill. *Encyclopedia of Western Gunfighters.* Norman, Okla.: University of Oklahoma, 1979.

Rezatto, Helen. *Mount Moriah.* Aberdeen, S.D.: North Plains Press, 1980.

_____. *Tales of the Black Hills.* Aberdeen, S.D.: North Plains Press, 1983.

Rivera, Geraldo. *Exposing Myself.* New York: Bantam, 1991.

Robinson, Doane. *Encyclopedia of South Dakota.* Sioux Falls, S.D.: Will A. Beach Printing Co., 1925.

Rolvaag, Ole. *Giants in the Earth.* New York: Harper & Row, 1927.

Ross, Dana Fuller. *DAKOTA!* New York: Bantam Books, 1983.

Schlesinger, Arthur J. *Robert Kennedy & His Times.* Boston: Houghton Mifflin, 1978.

Schroeder, Allen. *Architectural History of Vermillion, South Dakota.* Vermillion, S.D.: Educational Media Center, 1980.

Schuler, Harold. *The South Dakota Capitol in Pierre.* Pierre, S.D.: State Publishing Co., 1985.

Schuttler, Linfred. *South Dakota Territorial and Statehood Post Offices 1860-1983.* Spearfish, S.D.: Unknown, 1983.

Scott, Lawrence. *1989 Standard Postage Stamp Catalogue.* Sidney, Ohio: Scott Publishing Company, 1988.

Sifakis, Carl. *Official Guide to UFO Sightings.* New York: Sterling Publishing Co., 1979.

Sneve, Virginia Driving Hawk. *South Dakota Geographical Names.* Sioux Falls: Brevet Press, 1973.

Solomon, Abbot. *Baseball Records Illustrated.* Secaucus, N.J.: Chartwell Books, 1988.

South Dakota 99. Sioux Falls: Ex Machina Publishing Co., 1989.

Spoto, Donald. *The Dark Side of Genius.* Boston: Little, Brown & Co., 1983.

Steinberg, Cobbett. *TV Facts.* New York: Facts on File, 1985.

Stuart, Joseph. *Art of South Dakota.* Brookings, S.D.: South Dakota State University Press, 1974.

Super 8 Motels International Directory. Aberdeen, S.D.: Super 8 Motels, Inc., 1991.

Van Doren, Mamie. *Playing the Field.* New York: Berkley Books, 1987.

Variety's Complete Home Video Directory. New York: R.R. Bowker, 1989.

Walker, Leo. *The Wonderful Era of the Great Dance Bands.* Garden City, N.Y.: Doubleday & Co., Inc., 1964.

Wallace, Mike and Paul, Gary. *Close Encounters.* New York: William Morrow & Co., 1984.

Watson, Parker. *Deadwood, The Golden Years.* Lincoln, Neb.: University of Nebraska Press, 1981.

Welk, Lawrence. *Ah-One, Ah-Two!* Englewood Cliffs, N.J.: Prentice-Hall, 1974.

_____. *My America Your America.* Englewood Cliffs, N.J.: Prentice-Hall, Inc., 1976.

_____. *This I Believe.* Englewood Cliffs, N.J.: Prentice-Hall, Inc., 1979.

_____. *Wunnerful, Wunnerful!* Englewood Cliffs, N.J.: Prentice-Hall, Inc., 1971.

_____. *You're Never Too Young.* Englewood Cliffs, N.J.: Prentice-Hall, Inc., 1981.

Wendel, C.H. *American Gasoline Engines Since 1872.* Sarasota, Fla.: Crestline Publishing, 1983.

White, Theodore H. *The Making of the President 1964.* New York: Atheneum Publishers, 1964.

_____. *The Making of the President 1968.* New York: Atheneum Publishers, 1969.

_____. *The Making of the President 1972.* New York: Atheneum Publishers, 1973.

Wicker, Tom. *One of Us.* New York: Random House, 1991.

Wilder, Laura Ingalls. *By the Shores of Silver Lake.* New York: Harper & Row, 1939.

Wiley, Mason and Bona, Damien. *Inside Oscar.* New York: Ballantine Books, 1987.

Worth, Fred L. *The Trivia Encyclopedia.* New York: Bell Publishing Company, 1974.

Yeoman, R.S. *A Guide Book of U.S. Coins,* Racine, Wis.: Western Publishing Co., Inc., 1977.

Zip Code Finder. Chicago: Rand McNally & Co., 1987.

Sparky Anderson, Detroit Tigers
Clifford Bakken, Albany, Wis.
Lincoln Borglum
Citibank, Sioux Falls
Bob Clayton, NBC
Bruce Crevier, Elkton
Harry Creve, Miami Dolphins
Sen. Tom Daschle
Dave Dedrick, KELO-Land TV
James Dertien, Sioux Falls Public Library
Billie Dougherty, Sioux Falls
William J. Dougherty, Sioux Falls
Ellsworth Air Force Base
Mary Lynn Elsberry, *Quick 'n Easy Country Cookin'*
EROS
Sen. James Exon
Mary Ann Fischer, Aberdeen
Sandra Fisk, Governor's Office
Sue Fox, United Hospital
Bill Gould, Aberdeen
Great Plains Zoo
Steve Hemmingsen, KELO-Land TV
Pearl Hoel, Black Hills Motor Classic
Ted Hustead, Wall Drug
Willie O Jans, KJLY Radio
Lemmon Chamber of Commerce
Congressman Tim Johnson
Nancy Kneip, Sioux Falls
Josh Lesnik, SKYFORCE
Sherwin Linton, Minneapolis
Doug Lund, KELO-Land TV
Joe Maierhauser, Reptile Gardens
Mayor Ed McLaughlin (Rapid City)
Linda Mickelson, Pierre
Billy Mills
Dr. Mary Mock, Vermillion
Mount Rushmore
Pat O'Brien, CBS Sports
Mavis Olstad, Miss South Dakota Pageant
Jack Pacak, Super 8 Motels, Inc.
Leonard Peltier, Leavenworth Federal Correctional Facility
Becky Pope, Soukup & Thomas Balloon Museum
Mayor Tim Rich, Aberdeen
Barry Schloss, KRRO, Sioux Falls
Jannel Schumaker, *Dances With Wolves* hair stylist
Arlette Schweitzer, Aberdeen
Sioux Falls Public Library

Barry Schloss, KRRO, Sioux Falls
Jannel Schumaker, *Dances With Wolves* hair stylist
Arlette Schweitzer, Aberdeen
Sioux Falls Public Library
South Dakota State Historical Society
State Capitol
Red "Blondie" Stangland, Norse Press
Storybook Land, Aberdeen
Rancher Jim Sutton
Rodeo champ Paul Tierney (Piedmont)
U.S.S. South Dakota Memorial
Linda Vickers, *USA Today*
J.Craig Wenzel, Alpena Journal
Betty and Lloyd West, Black Hills Gold
Mayor Jackson White, Sioux Falls
Casimir Ziolkowski, Crazy Horse
Monique Ziolkowski, Crazy Horse
Ruth Ziolkowski, Crazy Horse

MEDIA
Aberdeen American News
Black Hills, Badlands and Lakes
BUFFALO! Magazine
Current Biographies
Dances With Wolves
Good Housekeeping
How the West was Won
McCalls
Mermaids
Millennium
Minneapolis Star Tribune
National Geographic
The New York Times
North by Northwest
One and Only, Genuine, Original Family Band
Pump Up the Volume
People Magazine
Reader's Digest
Saturday Evening Post
Sioux Falls *Argus Leader*
Sixty Minutes
South Dakota Magazine
Sports Illustrated
USA Today

Cotton King, used by permission, Wayne Carson Thompson, Earl Barton Music, copyright 1966.